D1595339

The Medieval Marriage Scene
Prudence, Passion, Policy

Medieval and Renaissance Texts and Studies

Volume 299

Penn State Medieval Studies
Number 1

The Medieval Marriage Scene: Prudence, Passion, Policy

Edited by

Sherry Roush and Cristelle L. Baskins

Arizona Center for Medieval and Renaissance Studies
Tempe, Arizona
2005

Library of Congress Cataloging-in-Publication Data

The medieval marriage scene : prudence, passion, policy / edited by Sherry Roush and Cristelle L. Baskins.
p. cm. -- (Medieval and Renaissance texts and studies ; v 299)
Conference papers.
Summary: "Discusses the latest research on medieval marriage, family, and related topics from the perspectives of literature, history, art history, law, religious studies, and economics, in multiple contexts from London to Valencia to the Levant"--Provided by publisher.
Includes bibliographical references and index.
ISBN-13: 978-0-86698-343-3 (alk. paper)
ISBN-10: 0-86698-343-0 (alk. paper)
1. Marriage--Europe--History. 2. Social history--Medieval, 500-1500. I. Roush, Sherry. II. Baskins, Cristelle Louise. III. Medieval & Renaissance Texts & Studies (Series) ; 299.
HQ611.M43 2005
306.81094'0902--dc22

2005027784

∞

This book is made to last.
It is set in Adobe Caslon Pro,
smyth-sewn and printed on acid-free paper
to library specifications.
Printed in the United States of America

Contents

Policy: Property, Propriety, and Legislation

List of Illustrations

About the Cover

Art by Ken Hull

Layout and design by Todd Halvorsen of ACMRS

Introduction

Few generalizations can accurately define the variety and complexity of both the institution and the quotidian experience of marriage in the European Middle Ages. Marriage, either to a secular spouse or in a mystical union, was the norm. Singles, from the never-married to widows of all ages, presented special challenges to their societies. Yet the very strangeness of medieval expectations for marriage, as well as the questions that surround the roles of the unmarried, continue to attract scholarly attention from a wide variety of academic disciplines. This volume brings together some of the latest research on medieval marriage from the perspectives of literature, history, art history, law, religious studies, and economics, in very different contexts, from London to Valencia to the Levant, building on a wealth of scholarship on marriage, family, and related topics.

There has been a tremendous amount of scholarship on medieval marriage produced over the past thirty years, and it should not seem surprising that the rising interest in the topic coincided with the introduction of feminist theory and gender studies into the academy. Georges Duby's groundbreaking work *The Knight, the Lady, and the Priest* (1981) demonstrates the way in which marriage changed as an institution during the eleventh and twelfth centuries in accordance with increasing concerns over personal wealth within an evolving feudal economy. The conflicts between secular and ecclesiastical authorities over who had the power to recognize, sanction, and dissolve marriages participated in a larger discourse surrounding the roles of the Church and the state (as represented by the aristocracy) in regulating social order. Having examined mainly ecclesiastical records, the writings of bishops, monks, priests, and other religious figures, Duby concludes his book by asking what the study of marriage practices might reveal about women in the Middle Ages, offering a call for further inquiry that has not gone unheeded.

Marriage and the Family in the Middle Ages by Frances and Joseph Gies (1987) and *The Medieval Idea of Marriage* by Christopher Brooke (1989) provide general overviews of the practice and representation of marriage throughout the Middle Ages. The Gieses situate medieval marriage within a broad historical context, explaining the origins of matrimonial practices in Roman law and examining the Catholic Church's efforts to regulate marriage as an institution. They utilize a variety of sources, including art, literature, legal records, and ecclesiastical writings in discussing the development of marriage practices and familial structures at all levels of society. Brooke also offers a wide-ranging study in terms of both chronology and methodology. His book includes chapters on the cult of celibacy, the letters of Abelard and Heloise, ecclesiastical and secular law, and literary representations of marriage in French and English literature.

Recent studies of marriage and canon law owe a great deal to the work of Michael Sheehan and James A. Brundage. Sheehan's essays, collected in *Marriage, Family, and Law in Medieval Europe* (1996), have profoundly influenced a generation of scholars studying not only the formation and practice of Christian marriage but also, as Joel Rosenthal points out in the introduction to the collection, women's history in the medieval period (xxvi–xxvii). Brundage's study *Law, Sex, and Christian Society in Medieval Europe* (1987) provides a valuable analysis of the foundation, evolution, and effects of medieval laws concerning sex and marriage. The book surveys preceding historical scholarship on early Christian doctrines and medieval attitudes toward sexuality before moving toward an important and insightful investigation into medieval canon law that looks at a vast number of primary sources, including canonical texts, commentaries, papal letters, and, most significantly, Gratian's *Decretum*. Brundage's expansive work discusses formulations of the institution of marriage as well as ecclesiastical and secular legal efforts to regulate marital and extra-marital sexuality, divorce, and concubinage.

Building on Sheehan and Brundage's scholarship on the formation of medieval canon law, Frederik Pedersen's *Marriage Disputes in Medieval England* (2000) focuses on cases from the ecclesiastical court in York in the fourteenth century in order to investigate the ways in which the laity understood and utilized the legal system with regard to marriage. Using court documents, Pedersen investigates "how the people who appeared before ecclesiastical courts applied the canon law of marriage to their own lives" (62). Although limited in geographic and historical scope, the book offers valuable insight into how individuals in the laity viewed the conditions of marriage and interpreted the legal recourse available to them through church courts. Pedersen's work uses the documents of the ecclesiastical court, primarily the depositions of litigants, in order to illustrate how both men and women responded to newly formulated laws governing matrimony.

The work of David Herlihy has significantly contributed to modern understandings and methodological approaches to family structures in the Middle Ages. His important study written with Christiane Klapisch-Zuber, *Tuscans and Their Families*, first published in Italian in 1978 and then in English in 1985, analyzes the 1427 Catasto, a fiscal survey of Florentine households, in order to provide a social history of Italian family structures and marriage practices in the fifteenth century. *Medieval Households* (1985) offers a broader examination of the evolution of marriage and the family on the Continent throughout the Middle Ages. Herlihy finds that the family as a unit became much more commensurate across the social hierarchy beginning in the seventh and eighth centuries and that the eleventh century marks the emergence of a familial patrilineage, which came to dominate, though it continued to stand in tension with, the bilineal system of descent that "ran indifferently through males and females" (vi). His work has provided the foundation for economic considerations of medieval marriage and familial relations, such as Anthony Molho's *Marriage Alliance in Late Medieval Florence* (1994).

Although many of the primary sources available for studying medieval marriage present a male voice, important developments in theory and methodology have allowed medieval women to begin to be heard. Feminist theorists like Judith Butler have offered new ways of thinking about gender and discourse, which has led to a reevaluation of the idea that a woman in the Middle Ages was restricted to the distinct role of wife, widow, nun, or prostitute. Barbara Hanawalt and Judith Bennett have both studied working women and their place within a patriarchal society and masculine discourse. Hanawalt's essay "Peasant Women's Contribution to the Home Economy in Late Medieval England" in *Women and Work in Preindustrial Europe* (ed. Barbara A. Hanawalt, 1986) demonstrates that "the peasant family economy . . . was based on the partnership of husband and wife, each contributing their separate skills and their separate domains of labor" (17). In *Ale, Beer, and Brewsters in England: Women's Work in a Changing World, 1300–1600* (1996), Bennett discusses the predominance of women brewers in the Middle Ages, the involvement of married women, and the discourse and conditions that led to a masculinization of the industry in the fifteenth and sixteenth centuries.

As scholars continue to explore the legal, economic, and political ramifications of the institution of marriage, it becomes increasingly important to investigate those members of medieval society who exist outside of marriage or seek alternatives to what was increasingly becoming a societal norm. Kim Phillips examines the role of young, unmarried women in *Medieval Maidens: Young Women and Gender in England, 1270–1540* (2003) and finds that "[m]aidenhood was an age of intense socialization in preferred forms of femininity, and was also itself, with its characteristic combination of sexuality and virginity, considered an ideal of womanhood" (17). Prostitutes, concubines, and homosexuals represented a threat to the social order that marriage seemed to maintain, thereby necessitating governmental regulation of extramarital sexuality, as Guido Ruggiero argues in *The Boundaries of Eros: Sex Crime and Sexuality in Renaissance Venice* (1985). The essays in the recent *Handbook of Medieval Sexuality* (1996) provide useful overviews of a variety of topics dealing with sexual practices in religious thought (Christian, Jewish, and Muslim), secular literature, and the social sphere.

New considerations of medieval marriage and sexuality reflect contemporary concerns about the definition and place of marriage in modern American society. With a steadily rising divorce rate, the increasingly prominent debate over the legalization of same-sex unions, and important shifts in men's and women's familial roles over the past thirty years, it is not surprising that scholars have looked to the foundations of the institution of marriage in the Middle Ages. In his preface to *Law, Sex, and Christian Society in Medieval Europe*, Brundage notes that his work is directed to not only an audience of medieval historians but also, among others, to "sexologists and practicing therapists who may be interested in the origins and development of law and public policy relating to sexual behavior" (xxi). Georges Duby recognizes his inability to objectively separate his scholarship from his own experiences: "The men I am studying are my ancestors, and the models of behavior I am tracing have survived into my own lifetime. The marriage I speak of is my own marriage, and I am not sure if I can free myself from the ideological system I am trying to analyze, demystify. I am involved; can I really be impartial?" (21). As scholars investigate the complexity of medieval marriage and continue to recognize alternative models to what has been accepted as the traditional paradigm, they also question the foundations for their inquiries.

This volume comprises three sections corresponding to the work's subtitle: Prudence, Passion, and Policy. In the first part, all four authors seek to define marriage and widowhood by emphasizing different aspects of the providential nature of the married state. Investigations of *prudentia* focus on the ways in which marriage seeks to provide for the financial stability or personal satisfaction of those who enter into it and on those people or entities that control the institution of marriage. **Judith R. Baskin** in her essay portrays a complex picture of Jewish marriage based on the examination of rabbinic legal and mystical writings and considerations of common practices. She is particularly interested in changes in female agency in marital arrangements over time. Baskin argues that Muslim and Christian traditions influence Jewish views of marriage, including the adoption of monogamy. Moreover, these influences complicate Jewish notions of both actual and metaphoric marital roles, especially in the way in which husbands and the male-coded community of Israel begin to view their wives or women in general as hindrances to a mystical union with God.

Konrad Eisenbichler's essay is concerned preeminently with the sociological and economic status of women, particularly in the case of widowed women in late-quattrocento Italy. He focuses on Florence, a city whose societal norms both encouraged the care of widowed women, but also perpetuated the widowed state. He cites statistics from the catasto, examples of widows from history (such as Alessandra Macinghi Strozzi) and literature (from Giovanni Boccaccio's *Decameron*), and presents a fresh reading of Dominican preacher Girolamo Savonarola's treatise on widows.

In "Lollardy and the Integrity of the Family," **Dyan Elliott** brings into focus the rhetorical ploys that England's heretical movement used to denounce what it perceived to be the Church's undermining of marriage and the family unit. Through a careful reading of Lollard positions in *The Office of Curates, On the*

Seven Deadly Sins, and *The Lanterne of Light*, among others, Elliott argues that Lollardy represented a systematic attack on female agency and a hardening of the most conservative traditional gender roles.

In "Germanic Marriage: The Case of Medieval Iceland" **Jenny Jochens** presents her research concerning the institution of marriage from the relatively scarce documents of the Anglo-Saxon and Germanic Continental communities. Through a comparison of these documents with Icelandic sources, Jochens concludes that the Germanic world as a whole shared key tenets of pagan marriage.

The second section of the volume presents different facets of marital passion — sex and love, but above all, passion's discontents. **John W. Baldwin** offers a six-stage description of Philip Augustus's love life. He suggests that the sex scandals that plagued the French ruler may indicate how lay French society viewed sexuality at the turn of the thirteenth century.

In "Scenes from a Marriage: Hospitality and Commerce in Boccaccio's Tale of *Saladin and Torello*," **Cristelle L. Baskins** argues that fifteenth-century painted panels depicting scenes from the *Decameron* present a window onto Florentine views of marriage. More specifically, marriage in quattrocento Florence is not the seal of love between two individuals, nor a representation of a mystical union with the Divine, nor even merely a familial financial contract. Instead, Baskins asserts that Florentine marriage functions "as a microcosm of the State." The painted *cassone*, a hope chest given as a marriage gift, portrays in pictorial form the Florentine ideal of subjugation and domestication of foreign rivals.

Priscilla Bawcutt's contribution compares and contrasts the Scottish and German views of marriage as presented by William Dunbar and Hans Sachs respectively. While acknowledging that the sources she examines are literary artifacts, Bawcutt deftly argues for an understanding of underlying truths about marriage held by the authors' contemporary readers.

Elizabeth W. Poe in "The Old and the Feckless: Fabliau Husbands" studies adultery in the French fabliaux. She finds that while these racy narratives poke fun at courtly love models, the fabliaux are ultimately not subversive. They do not exalt extramarital affairs as noble and refined, Poe writes, but make their participants appear exaggeratedly silly. Just as contemporary moralists tried to teach through didactic modes, fabliaux avert their readers' minds from adulterous "ridiculousness," but do so in an entertaining mode.

Considerations of marital policy — especially in terms of legal status and litigation — link the four essays in the final section of this anthology. **Barbara A. Hanawalt** in "The Dilemma of the Widow of Property for Late Medieval London" examines the role of wealthy London widows as market commodities. Hanawalt's study of legal wills and marriage contracts leads her to conclude that the transfer of property upon remarriage reinforced guild and economic class identifications at the same time that it encouraged the growth of a group of mercantile socio-economic climbers to whom the new wives transferred their previous inheritance.

In his essay **Frederik Pedersen** shifts the focus of marriage law to fourteenth-century York, examining in detail eight court cases and in some instances their pre-court tribunals, bringing to light how the various parties coordinated their legal strategies and how lay tribunals differed from ecclesiastical courts at the time.

Susan Mosher Stuard in "Marriage Gifts and Fashion Mischief" details Italian wedding transactions, including the Lombard "male dowry," and the Roman bride's fiscal gift to her husband. She links the increasing pressure from husbands to receive liquid assets, rather than clothes, jewelry, linens, or domestic furnishings, to the advent of sumptuary laws in "the first age of European fashion."

Finally, **Ronald E. Surtz**'s essay examines the ecclesiastical condemnation of Tecla Servent in Valencia in the late 1400s. He argues that, before her punishment by Church officials, Tecla Servent, likely inspired by her namesake Saint Thecla, managed to escape an abusive marriage to embrace Christ as her divine husband. The visions that Tecla had during this period, Surtz asserts, permit the enterprising single mother to sustain herself and her dependent child.

All of these essays challenge preconceived notions of the marital state in the Middle Ages. The reader takes away from these studies a nuanced sense of both the radical difference in expectations and practices of marriage that medieval men and women had, as opposed to the expectations that people have of marriage today, but also of their sometimes surprising similarities to our ideals and predicaments of marriage. Medieval singles sought the same emotional and financial stability from a match that many do today, and medieval society struggled, as ours does, with the effects of ended marriages across geographic, economic, and religious lines, including inheritance issues and the status of widows and stepchildren.

Sherry Roush and Timothy D. Arner
The Pennsylvania State University, University Park

Bibliography

Bennett, Judith M. *Ale, Beer, and Brewsters in England: Women's Work in a Changing World, 1300–1600*. Oxford: Oxford University Press, 1996.

Brooke, Christopher N. L. *The Medieval Idea of Marriage*. Oxford: Oxford University Press, 1989.

Brundage, James A. *Law, Sex, and Christian Society in Medieval Europe*. Chicago: University of Chicago Press, 1987.

Bullough, Vern L. and James A. Brundage. *Handbook of Medieval Sexuality*. New York: Garland, 1996.

Butler, Judith. *Gender Trouble: Feminism and the Subversion of Identity*. New York: Routledge, 1990.

Duby, Georges. *The Knight, the Lady, and the Priest: The Making of Modern Marriage in Medieval France,* trans. Barbara Bray. New York: Pantheon Books, 1983.

Gies, Frances and Joseph. *Marriage and the Family in the Middle Ages*. New York: Harper and Row, 1987.

Hanawalt, Barbara. "Peasant Women's Contribution to the Home Economy in Late Medieval England." In *Women and Work in Preindustrial Europe*, ed. Barbara Hanawalt, 3–19. Bloomington: Indiana University Press, 1986.

Herlihy, David. *Medieval Households*. Cambridge, MA: Harvard University Press, 1985.

———, and Christiane Klapisch-Zuber. *Tuscans and Their Families: A Study of the Florentine Catasto of 1427*. New Haven: Yale University Press, 1985.

Klapisch-Zuber, Christiane. *Women, Family, and Ritual in Renaissance Italy*. Chicago: Chicago University Press, 1985.

Molho, Anthony. *Marriage Alliance in Late Medieval Florence*. Cambridge, MA: Harvard University Press, 1994.

Pedersen, Frederik. *Marriage Disputes in Medieval England*. London: Hambledon Press, 2000.

Phillips, Kim M. *Medieval Maidens: Young Women and Gender in England, 1270–1540*. Manchester: Manchester University Press, 2003.

Ruggiero, Guido. *The Boundaries of Eros: Sex Crime and Sexuality in Renaissance Venice*. Oxford: Oxford University Press, 1985.

Sheehan, Michael M. *Marriage, Family, and Law in Medieval Europe: Collected Studies*, ed. James K. Farge. Toronto: University of Toronto Press, 1996.

Acknowledgments

The editors of this volume wish to thank the individuals and organizations that made possible the conference and the publication of this volume of essays. We are grateful to Vickie L. Ziegler, Professor of German and Director of the Center for Medieval Studies at Penn State University, whose tireless commitment to organizing the 2001 medieval conference — as well as a dozen other such conferences on the University Park campus on different topics in Medieval Studies over the years, has helped to revolutionize the way scholars understand Medieval Studies today by reaching out to disciplines and audiences beyond those of literature, history, and art history. Special thanks go to the conference planning committee and to conference manager Alan Jalowitz. The conference was organized by the Center for Medieval Studies and sponsored by the Office of Intercollegiate Research Programs and the Institute for the Arts and Humanistic Studies with the support of the departments of comparative literature, English, French, history, and Germanic and Slavic languages.

Norris Lacy spearheaded the volume's publication, providing much appreciated guidance and support. Adam Miyashiro prepared the manuscript as camera-ready copy. Jana Byars contributed to the introduction.

We thank all the 2001 conference participants, including the many members of the audience and teachers' program, who took such active roles in the event's success. Six of the contributors to this volume presented much shorter versions of their studies at the conference (Baldwin, Bawcutt, Hanawalt, Jochens, Pedersen, and Poe). The other six contributors (Baskin, Baskins, Eisenbichler, Elliott, Stuard, and Surtz) submitted essays specifically commissioned for the anthology. We warmly acknowledge all of the volume's contributors for their excellent research, clarity, patience, and unparalleled promptness.

Medieval Jewish Models of Marriage

Judith R. Baskin

Medieval Jewish attitudes and customs regarding marriage are based on legal guidelines and communal norms established during the rabbinic period (first to sixth centuries of the Common Era) and codified in the Babylonian Talmud, the voluminous compendium of Jewish law and lore completed in Iraq in the mid-sixth century C. E. However, practices in the Muslim and Christian societies in which Jews lived also had a significant impact on medieval Jewish models of this most intimate of human relationships. This essay examines a number of aspects of Jewish marriage in the Middles Ages in both Muslim and Christian milieus, including the interplay between the rabbinic legal tradition and the larger social context, Jewish ethical and mystical attitudes towards human sexuality and the marital bond, documentary sources about an actual marriage, evidence about marital relationships between Jews and non-Jews, and medieval innovations in the Jewish marriage ceremony.

The Legalities of Marriage in Rabbinic Judaism

Rabbinic Judaism considered marriage as foreordained and essential for all adults.[1] Within the marital union, procreation, a legal obligation for men, could take place and the lineage of children, a significant concern in rabbinic culture, could best be assured. Marriage not only served as a licit channel for sexual energies for both women and men but also provided the sustaining societal mortar and gender-based division of labor on which rabbinic society depended. Marital roles were strictly defined for women and men since the framers of rabbininic Judaism discouraged a female presence in the communal realms of worship, study, and governance. Rather, rabbinic social policy directed women's energies to domestic activities to provide for their husband's and children's needs; women are praised

[1] On constructions of women and marriage in rabbinic Judaism, see Judith R. Baskin, *Midrashic Women: Formations of the Feminine in Rabbinic Literature* (Hanover, NH: Brandeis University Press, 2002), 88–118. Rabbinic literature is voluminous; among its central documents are the Mishnah, a law code of sixty-three tractates divided into six divisions, completed in the Land of Israel in the third century C. E. (cited here as M., followed by tractate and location), and the Babylonian Talmud, the comprehensive elucidation and expansion of the Mishnah, completed in Western Asia in the sixth century C. E. (cited here as B., followed by tractate and location).

for modest and self-sacrificing behavior that enables their husbands and sons to achieve success in the public domain. The extent to which Jewish women's lives in late antiquity actually conformed to rabbinic strictures, however, is uncertain since the vision of society represented in rabbinic literature seems more idealized than real in many of its aspects. Nevertheless, in the course of the Middle Ages, the prescribed patterns recorded in rabbinic writings by a small group of sages became increasingly normative for Jewish life in general.

According to the Mishnah, the third-century C. E. law code that became the foundation document of rabbinic legal tradition, marriage could be effected in any of three ways: by money, by contract, or by intercourse (M. Qiddushin 1:1). Over time, the formal mechanisms of marriage became more complex. Elaborating on the mishnaic framework, the Babylonian Talmud (B. Ketubbot 57a) presents an ordered progression of steps comprising engagement (*shiddukhin*), betrothal (*'erusin / qiddushin*), and consummation (*nissu'in*). Betrothal, which constituted a legally binding marriage, was achieved by the reading of the marriage contract *(ketubbah)*, a statement of the groom's obligations, financial and otherwise, toward the bride, and the presentation of an object of value by the groom to the bride in the presence of two witnesses. The marriage was finalized through *nissu'in* (literally "elevation"), also known as *huppah*, when the bride was escorted to her husband's home and benedictions were recited. *Nissu'in* often did not take place until a year after the betrothal in order to enable both families to make the necessary preparations for the young couple's married life. This standardization and formalization of the marital process indicates how the social dynamics of marriage changed in the course of late antiquity during the transition from biblical to rabbinic times, generally in directions with positive consequences for women and their status.[2]

The most significant aspect of these modifications was the ratification of marriage through a written contract. This *ketubbah* (B. Qiddushin 2a) imposed rights and obligations on both sides, transforming a wife from an acquired object into a subject in a shared enterprise who received specific benefits in return for her domestic and sexual services. As Judith Hauptman has written of the importance of this innovation, "The patriarchal construction of marriage, although certainly not dismantled with the development of the *ketubbah*, was significantly altered. Marriage became a relationship into which two people entered."[3] While the Mishnah assumed that betrothal and marriage resulted from negotiations

---

[2] For the evolution of Jewish marriage practices from biblical through rabbinic times in the context of surrounding cultures, see Michael Satlow, *Jewish Marriage in Antiquity* (Princeton: Princeton University Press, 2001).

[3] Judith Hauptman, *Rereading the Rabbis: A Woman's Voice* (Boulder: Westview, 1998), 68.

between a would-be groom and a prospective bride's male relatives, later rabbinic sources, including the Babylonian Talmud, imply that a woman must agree to her betrothal and in some cases might even negotiate her own marriage.[4]

The rabbinic *ketubbah* enumerated ten obligations of the husband towards the wife. These included a husband's providing his wife with food, appropriate clothing (M. Ketubbot 5:8), and conjugal rights.[5] He is to ransom her, provide for her support after his death, and guarantee that her property will pass from him to her heirs, an important concern in a polygynous society. The husband also pledged to his wife sufficient money to cover her minor expenses; if he did not, then she could keep the proceeds of her work in wool, which normally belonged to her husband (M. Ketubbot 5:9). Should a man take more than one wife, as he was permitted to do, he was required to fulfill his obligations to each wife in an equitable way. Even if no written *ketubbah* existed, these responsibilities incumbent upon the husband became widely accepted and would be enforced by a Jewish court.[6] The most important provision of the *ketubbah* was the arrangement for a wife's financial protection should the marriage end. This *ketubbah* payment, the only economic benefit the wife would receive from her husband's estate, consisted not only of any dowry she brought into the marriage but also a stipulated amount from the husband's resources, set aside at the time of the marriage and payable in case of divorce or the husband's death.[7]

---

[4] On consent to marriage, see Hauptman, *Rereading the Rabbis*, who argues, 73–74, that such innovations represent a progression over time from women being married off by their fathers, to women having the right of consent, to women negotiating their own marriages. It seems more likely that different situations are represented. From ancient to early modern times young girls almost always entered into marriages contracted for them by parents or guardians. On the other hand, a financially independent adult woman, whether widowed, divorced, or previously unmarried, could usually negotiate her own marriage.

[5] These obligations are discussed by Judith Romney Wegner, *Chattel or Person?: The Status of Women in the Mishnah* (New York: Oxford University Press, 1988), 71–75. Isaiah Gafni, "The Institution of Marriage in Rabbinic Times," in *The Jewish Family: Metaphor and Memory*, ed. David Kraemer (New York: Oxford University Press, 1989), 15–17, notes there was always room for individual flexibility in negotiating these provisions. The wife's right to conjugal attentions is based on Exodus 21:10, "If he marries another, he must not withhold from this one her food, her clothing, or her conjugal rights."

[6] See "Husbands and Wives," *Encyclopedia Judaica* 8:1120–28, for the full particulars of spousal rights and duties, both as laid out in rabbinic literature and as interpreted and modified in the rabbinic Judaisms of the medieval and early modern periods. A written *ketubbah* for all marriages became the norm by medieval times.

[7] In rabbinic *halakhah* (legal tradition) women did not inherit property from their husbands; this is why *ketubbah* support was so important.

In the marriage agreement entered into by both parties, a wife still kept certain degrees of independence, particularly in the financial sphere. She retained title to property she brought into her marriage, although her husband was entitled to any profit it yielded. She also had the power to sell the property and her husband could not sell it against her will (M. Gittin 5:6) From these and other similar provisions, it is clear that the wife was expected to play a significant role in the economic life of the family, contributing not only investment revenues but also her earnings from the making of cloth and needlework. Her commercial transactions were ordinarily considered activities belonging to the household, the domestic/private realm in which women ideally functioned. In certain situations, in fact, a wife might undertake to support her husband financially or to take full financial responsibility for her household in her husband's absence.

The duties incumbent upon the wife were not enumerated in the *ketubbah* since they were assumed by her agreement to enter into marriage. They are listed in M. Ketubbot 5:5:

> The following are the kinds of work which a woman must perform for her husband: grinding corn, baking bread, washing clothes, cooking, suckling her child, making ready his bed, and working in wool. If she brought him one bondwoman she need not do any grinding or baking or washing. If she brought two bondwomen, she need not even cook or suckle her child. If three, she need neither make ready his bed nor work in wool. If four, she may lounge in an easy chair.

The Mishnah goes on to note, however, that a rabbinic sage, R. Eliezer, objected to this easy life for the wealthy woman, insisting that, "Even if she brought him a hundred bondwomen he may compel her to work in wool since idleness leads to unchastity. And she should nevertheless fill her husband's cup, make ready his bed and wash his face, hands and feet." Rabban Simeon b. Gamaliel concurred, adding that idleness leads to boredom (M. Ketubbot 5:5). In its explication of this passage at B. Ketubbot 61a–b, the Babylonian Talmud states that the law is in agreement with R. Eliezer: No matter the extent of her wealth, a woman must engage in worthwhile activities and must fulfill her husband's personal needs. One might note here, as well, the rabbinic conviction of fundamental female unreliability in the face of sexual temptation and the consequent need to keep women occupied in useful ways.

Although in some situations, such as infertility, spousal abuse, desertion, or pronounced incompatibility, a wife could petition the court to compel her husband to divorce her (M. Ketubbot 7:1–5, 10), she had no power to end her marriage unilaterally. This was the right of the husband alone; the sources make clear that he could divorce his wife for any reason (M. Gittin 9:10), however, provided that he returned the monetary settlement specified by her *ketubbah*. Indeed, this requirement of financial restitution, from his means as well as hers, offered women a degree of protection. Raising the funds needed to pay the contracted *ketubbah* amount could constitute a strong financial disincentive to a rash husband who might then reconsider ending his marriage. When divorce did occur, the payment of the *ketubbah* provided a crucial economic base on which a second marriage or the possibility of an independent livelihood might be built for a cast-off wife.[8] In this way, the institution of the *ketubbah* not only enhanced women's rights and status but also played a positive part in rabbinic and medieval social policy, both by preventing rash divorces and by limiting the numbers of indigent widows and divorcées dependent on community support.

Another aspect of marriage that is central to rabbinic Judaism and its medieval manifestations is the system of legal ordinances requiring marital separation when women are in states of ritual impurity.[9] Biblical canons in Leviticus 12, 15, and 18 designate menstruating or postpartum women as ritually unclean and forbid husbands to have carnal relations with them. Talmudic strictures developed these prohibitions into a complicated system of rules for avoiding not only sexual intercourse but any physical contact between husband and wife during the wife's menses and for an additional seven days following the cessation of flow. On the eighth "white" day, the wife was to observe the rules of immersion in the *mikveh*, or ritual bath, after which marital relations could resume.[10]

Jewish Marriage in the Muslim World

During the Middle Ages most Jews lived outside the land of Israel, with significant populations in the Muslim worlds of Egypt, North Africa, the Middle East, and Spain; far smaller numbers of Jews lived in Christian Europe. In both environments Jewish communities were granted almost total autonomy over their own lives and internal affairs, as long as taxes to the political authorities were paid.

[8] On divorce and its consequences in rabbinic *halakhah*, see Wegner, *Chattel or Person*, 80–84; Rachel Biale, *Women and Jewish Law: An Exploration of Women's Issues in Halakhic Sources* (New York: Schocken, 1984), 70–101, especially 84–89; and "Divorce," *Encyclopedia Judaica* 6:122–35.

[9] On biblical and rabbinic strictures concerning the *niddah*, the menstruating woman, see Baskin, *Midrashic Women*, 22–29; Charlotte Elisheva Fonrobert, *Menstrual Purity: Rabbinic and Christian Reconstructions of Biblical Gender* (Stanford: Stanford University Press, 2000); and the essays collected in *Women and Water: Menstruation in Jewish Life and Law*, ed. Rahel Wasserfall (Hanover, NH: Brandeis University Press, 1999).

[10] On this topic, see also Shaye J. D. Cohen, "Menstruants and the Sacred in Judaism and Christianity," in *Women's History and Ancient History*, ed. Sarah B. Pomeroy (Chapel Hill: University of North Carolina Press, 1991), 273–99.

Jewish self-government, across geographical and political boundaries, was based on the dictates of the Babylonian Talmud, providing a uniform pattern for Jewish family, business, community, and religious life.[11]

The discovery of the Cairo Genizah has provided an abundance of information about medieval Jewish society and institutions in the medieval Muslim world, particularly between the ninth to twelfth centuries. This capacious storeroom, used for centuries to store unusable sacred texts and preserve them from desecration, was discovered when the ancient Ben Ezra synagogue to which it was attached was being renovated, shortly before 1890. Its voluminous contents also included discarded secular writings such as official, business, learned and private correspondence, court proceedings, contracts, and other legal writings.[12] A number of these documents shed light on the status of Jewish women and Jewish marriage practices and also reveal the ways in which Jewish social life was strongly influenced by Islamic norms. While Jewish women of prosperous families, for example, were not literally isolated in women's quarters as were Muslim women of comparable social status, religious and community ideals dictated that women should remain at home as much as possible. In reality, however, Jewish women usually insisted on freedom of movement, and many Genizah records of marital squabbles make this an explicit right for the wife if reconciliation is to be achieved.[13]

Genizah documents indicate that a young woman was generally married at the age of thirteen or fourteen, usually to a considerably older man. The first preference for a spouse was a first cousin or other suitable relative; a marriage within the extended family conserved family resources while also allowing a young wife to remain within a known and supportive setting. However, marriages could also

[11] Overviews of medieval Jewish history include Mark R. Cohen, *Under Crescent and Cross: The Jews in the Middle Ages* (Princeton: Princeton University Press, 1994); and Kenneth R. Stow, *Alienated Minority: The Jews of Medieval Latin Europe* (Cambridge, MA: Harvard University Press, 1992). Thérèse and Mendel Metzger, *Jewish Life in the Middle Ages* (New York: Alpine Fine Arts Collection, 1982), is copiously illustrated with representations of everyday scenes from a variety of medieval illuminated manuscripts. On medieval Jewish women and families, see Judith R. Baskin, "Jewish Women in the Middle Ages," in *Jewish Women in Historical Perspective*, ed. eadem, 2nd Ed. (Detroit: Wayne State University Press, 1998), 101–27; Avraham Grossman, *Pious and Rebellious: Jewish Women in Europe in the Middle Ages* [Hebrew] (Jerusalem: The Zalman Shazar Center for Jewish History, 2001); and Kenneth R. Stow, "The Jewish Family in the Rhineland in the High Middle Ages: Form and Function," *American Historical Review* 92 (1987): 1085–1110.

[12] On the Cairo Genizah, see S. D. Goitein, *A Mediterranean Society*, 5 vols. (Berkeley: University of California Press, 1967–1988); and "Cairo Genizah," *Encyclopedia Judaica* 16:1333.

[13] Goitein, *Mediterranean Society* 3: 153–55.

be ways of extending business connections. The Genizah documents matches between young people in distant communities, from Spain, to North Africa, to Iran, to Syria, to Egypt, and even to the Byzantine Empire, to strengthen ties between two trading houses by establishing family alliances. Sometimes young businessmen from abroad would marry into a successful local family as a way of establishing themselves and eventually attaining a prominent position in the new country. Often girls from scholarly families were considered particularly desirable brides in the hope that their sons would show similar proclivities.[14]

Following biblical custom, the groom contributed a marriage gift (*mohar*), part of which was payable to the bride's father at the time of the wedding; a portion was also reserved for the bride in the event of a divorce or her husband's death. The bride, too, brought property into the marriage in the form of her dowry, also known by the term *ketubbah*, since its contents were specified in the marriage contract. This dowry, which would be returned to the wife in case of divorce or her husband's death, was generally far more valuable than the husband's marriage gift; a large dowry gave the bride's family "significant leverage in finding her a suitable match and insuring her proper treatment during marriage."[15] The value of the dowry, which often included items such as gold and silver jewelry, clothing, household goods such as bedding, copper, carpets, and hangings, as well as other possessions of the bride, such as real estate holdings, one or more maidservants, and occasionally books, was evaluated by professional assessors, and an itemized list was attached to the marriage contract.[16]

This marriage contract might also contain added protections for the wife; these were a way of effecting changes in Jewish laws and practices which were unfavorable to women, and they provided safeguards against many sources of marital friction. These supplements to a *ketubbah* could include guarantees that in case of separation a divorce document would be promptly produced by the husband; that the husband would not take a second wife or initiate a liaison with a concubine without his wife's permission; that the husband would not beat the wife; that he would not travel anywhere without her consent or separate the wife

---

[14] Goitein, *Mediterranean Society* 3: 53–58; and see Mordechai A. Friedman, "The Ethics of Medieval Jewish Marriage," in *Religion in a Religious Age*, ed. S. D. Goitein (Cambridge, MA: Harvard University Press, 1974), 83–102, esp. 87–95; idem, *Jewish Marriage in Palestine: A Cairo Genizah Study*, 2 vols. (Tel Aviv and New York: Tel Aviv University and The Jewish Theological Seminary of America, 1980); and idem, "Marriage as an Institution: Jewry under Islam," in *The Jewish Family*, ed. Kraemer, 31–45. It should be noted that conditions in prosperous Egypt, the main provenance for the Genizah documents, may have differed from some other places and times in the Muslim world.

[15] Friedman, "Ethics of Medieval Jewish Marriage," 33.

[16] Goitein, *Mediterranean Society*, 3:125.

from her parents against her will; and that before traveling he would prepare a conditional bill of divorce and deposit the delayed installment of his marriage gift so that his wife would be able to remarry if he perished on his journey.[17]

In addition to the unilateral *ketubbah* issued in the husband's name, which has generally been the norm in Jewish practice, the Geniza also preserves evidence of an alternate *ketubbah* form, written according to the custom of the land of Israel, which is based on a statement of mutual obligations by groom and bride. These documents define marriage as a *shutafot*, "partnership," and promise the wife the right to initiate divorce proceedings against her husband if she is unable to live with him.[18]

Polygyny was a feature not only of biblical and rabbinic social policy but also of Muslim life, and in this area there appears to have been considerable Jewish conformity to the majority culture. Genizah texts frequently contain agreements to grant equal rights to wives in a polygynous family, the husband generally undertaking to alternate nights with each spouse. Rabbinic sources from this era encouraged married men who had affairs with slave girls to marry them after they were emancipated.[19]

Divorce was by no means uncommon in this time and place of Jewish history. Not only did both Jewish tradition and Islamic social custom accept divorce, but arranged marriages, geographic mobility, and the raised expectations which accompany economic prosperity all led to marital unhappiness.[20] Divorcées who recovered the values of their dowry would generally remarry, but less fortunate women were often left in want, together with other indigent women, many of whom had been deserted by their husbands.

A series of legal inquiries to Moses Maimonides (1135–1204), the great Spanish-born philosopher, legal scholar, and physician who spent most of his life in Egypt, tell of one deserted wife who was able to make herself independent by running a school, assisted by her elder son. After some years her husband reappeared and demanded that she give up the school because it injured his dignity for his wife to be a teacher, and besides, he had no one to serve him. He insisted that she give up her teaching and stay with him; otherwise, he asked permission to take a second wife. The wife, in turn, argued that her husband had been repeatedly undependable in the past, that she had built up her student clientele over

[17] Goitein, *Mediterranean Society,* 3:114. According to *halakhah,* a woman whose husband disappeared with no evidence of his death could never remarry. She was designated an *agunah*, a "bound woman." The deposit of the conditional divorce document and delayed payment protected women from this potential tragedy in an age when travel was perilous.

[18] Friedman, "Marriage as an Institution," 34–35.

[19] Friedman, "Marriage as an Institution," 39.

[20] Goitein, *Mediterranean Society,* 3:263.

time, and that were she to give up her teaching she would not easily be able to resume her school should her husband again disappear. Maimonides's remedy is that the Jewish rabbinical court compel the husband to divorce his independent wife on the grounds that he had not fulfilled his legal obligation to support her. Moreover, he advises the wife to refuse all relations with her husband and to forfeit her marriage portion, since these actions, too, would constitute grounds for divorce. After that, Maimonides says, "She will have disposition over herself, she may teach what she likes, and do what she likes;" but he rules that "If she stays with her husband, he has the right to forbid her to teach."[21]

Jewish Marriage in the Christian World

Jewish girls in Ashkenaz, the place name by which medieval Jews referred to their communities in France and Germany, were betrothed very young, often at the age of eight or nine, despite talmudic prohibitions to the contrary. A young woman might be married at eleven or twelve, while her husband would be almost the same age. Since it was the custom, in both the Muslim and Christian spheres, for young couples to spend the first years of their marriage living with one or other of the in-laws, some of the obvious problems associated with child marriage, such as running a household, were not an issue. One thirteenth-century talmudic commentary explains child marriage as a response to the difficult conditions of Jewish life:

> The reason we nowadays are accustomed to betroth our daughters even while they are minors is that our life in the diaspora is becoming harder; consequently, if a person is now in a financial position to give his daughter an adequate dowry, he is apprehensive lest after the lapse of some years he will be in no position to do so and his daughter will remain unwed forever (*Tosaphot* to B. Kiddushin 41a).

Other motivations would be the religious desire to remove young people from sexual tensions and temptations, as well as the economic impetus to take advantage of favorable business conditions. Moreover, marriage could form an enduring and profitable partnership between two prosperous families. Early marriages also had a social aspect since settling a young daughter well proved her desirability and increased her family's prestige. Conversely, a broken engagement might give

---

[21] Moses Maimonides, *Responsa of R. Moses b. Maimon*, vol. 1 [Hebrew], ed. Yehoshua Blau (Jerusalem, 1958), no. 34, no. 45. For a translation and analysis of these documents, see Renée Levine Melammed, "He Said, She Said: The Case of a Woman Teacher in Maimonides's Twelfth-Century Cairo," *Association for Jewish Studies Review* 22 (1997): 19–36.

rise to rumors concerning the rejected bride and her relatives that could harm her own future marriage chances and those of other family members. Avraham Grossman has suggested that there was particular fear that an annulled betrothal might imply that a family was "tainted by the conversion of one of its members to Christianity."[22] Such anxieties no doubt contributed to an eleventh-century rabbinic ruling imposing a ban of excommunication against those who violated a betrothal agreement; in most cases the guilty parties were bridegrooms and their families.[23]

Like the Christian women among whom they lived, Jewish women had significantly more freedom of movement than women in the Muslim world. Active participants in the family economy, their status was higher than that of Jewish women in the Islamic milieu; this is indicated, in part, by their large dowries that might constitute ten percent of their parents' worth.[24] The custom of the groom's payment (*mohar*), common among Jews in Muslim countries, was not followed among Jews living in Christian communities. While the dowry of a deceased childless wife legally belonged to her husband, a twelfth-century enactment made all the dowry returnable to the father should his daughter die in the first year of marriage. This was to encourage fathers to endow their daughters generously; if a woman died in the second year of marriage without children, one half was to be returned.[25] Since the capital with which a young couple started life had its origin mainly in the bride's portion, parents also demanded strong guarantees in the marriage contract that the bride would be treated with respect, that her marriage would have some permanence, and that she would have financial security. Thus, the significant value of her dowry could assure a wife a prominent economic role in her household. As a tenth-century sage remarked in a rabbinic opinion addressing a family quarrel, "It is the custom of men to appoint their wives as masters over their possessions."[26]

One issue on which the Ashkenazic sages spoke out very strongly, and another indication of women's prominent social status, was the condemnation of

---

[22] Avraham Grossman, "The Status of Jewish Women in Germany (Tenth to Twelfth Centuries)," in *Zur Geschichte der jüdischen Frau in Deutschland*, ed. Julius Carlebach (Berlin: Metropol-Verlag, 1993), 23.

[23] On this ban see Grossman, "Status of Jewish Women," 21–23.

[24] Irving Agus, *The Heroic Age of Franco-German Jewry* (New York: Yeshiva University Press, 1969), 278; idem, "The Development of the Money Clause in the Ashkenazic Ketubah," *Jewish Quarterly Review* 42 (1951): 221–56.

[25] Louis M. Epstein, *The Jewish Marriage Contract: A Study in the Status of Women in Jewish Law* (New York: Jewish Theological Seminary of America, 1927), 138–41.

[26] Rabbi Meshullam b. Kalonymus (c. 910–985), in a *responsum* (a rabbinic legal query) printed in Louis Ginzberg, *Ginzei Shechter* (New York: Jewish Theological Seminary of America, 1928–1929; repr. New York:Hermon Press, 1969), 275, no. 6.

spousal abuse for any reason. Wife-beating was recognized as grounds for divorce and methods of compelling husbands to release their wives in such cases were taken far more seriously than in any other part of the Jewish world.[27] Grossman notes that "the gravity with which the sages of Germany viewed wife-beating surfaces not only in the *responsa* [legal rulings] but also in the punishments imposed on the offenders, especially in cases of those who repeatedly beat their wives."[28] A further recognition of the high status accorded to Jewish women in this milieu, as well as an indication of the influence of the prevailing mores of the Christian environment, is the eleventh-century *takkanah* (rabbinic ruling) forbidding polygyny for Jews in Christian countries.[29] This change in traditional Jewish law is attributed to Rabbi Gershom ben Judah (c. 960–1028), the first great rabbinic authority of Western European (Ashkenazic) Jewry, who is also credited with the even more significant pronouncement that no woman could be divorced against her will. In fact, divorce appears to have been less common among Jews in medieval Christian Europe than in the Muslim milieu, perhaps because it was not a sanctioned act within Christian society. Nevertheless, it was also the custom here for husbands to leave behind a conditional divorce document when they set out on journeys so that their wives would be free to remarry should they fail to return after a specified length of time.

The ban on polygyny attributed to Rabbi Gershom was never universally accepted among Jews in Christian Spain where well into the fourteenth century special royal permissions to take a second wife could be obtained for a fee. Although a man might take a second wife for numerous reasons, the most frequent was ten years of childlessness in the original marriage. This continuation of rabbinic practice indicates a lower status of women in the Iberian peninsula, as well as the continued influence of Muslim social mores even after Spain had once again come under Christian rule.[30]

---

[27] On this topic see Grossman, "Status of Jewish Women," 26–32; and idem, "Medieval Rabbinic Views on Wife-Beating, 800–1300," *Jewish History* 5 (1991): 53–62.

[28] Grossman, "Status of Jewish Women," 29–30.

[29] On the *takkanot* of R. Gershom, see Biale, *Women and Jewish Law*, 49–52; and Ze'ev W. Falk, *Jewish Matrimonial Law in the Middle Ages* (Oxford: Oxford University Press, 1966), 1–15. Falk points out (34) that "the early founders of the French/German communities acquired the monogamous structure of the Christian family and turned it into an integral element of their piety and way of life." Grossman, "Ordinances on Family Affairs," 14, stresses the high status of women in Ashkenazic society as a major motivation for this ruling, writing that women's position in this milieu "was better and more firmly based than in any other part of the contemporary Jewish world."

[30] Renée Levine Melammed, "Sephardi Women in the Middle Ages and Early Modern Period," in *Jewish Women in Historical Perspective*, ed. Baskin, 2nd ed., 113.

The Ethics of Medieval Jewish Sexuality and Marriage

Rabbinic Judaism taught that fulfilling his wife's sexual needs was among a husband's obligations within marriage, and medieval Jewish writers generally praised pleasurable sexual activity as an essential component of a harmonious union.[31] In his ethical will from the fourteenth century, Eleazar of Mainz wrote that the men of his family "must honor their wives more than themselves; they must not have sexual relations with them in a state of anger but are to wait until they consent willingly and disputes are resolved."[32] Such favorable attitudes about the value of marital sexual expression for its own sake apparently explain the willingness of various twelfth- and thirteenth-century rabbinic authorities to allow the use of the contraceptive *mokh*, a cervical sponge or cap, for marital intercourse without fear of pregnancy.[33]

These positive Jewish attitudes towards marriage and sexuality contrasted with medieval Christian traditions of celibacy for priests and monks, and Church mandates attempting to restrict licit sexual activity to procreation. It is not surprising that Christian preachers criticized Jewish sexual behavior, real and imagined, as lascivious and incestuous.[34] Influence from the Christian environment may account for the ambivalence towards sexuality characteristic of the twelfth-century German-Jewish pietists, the *Hasidei Ashkenaz*, who express not only an obsessive concern with the ubiquity of extramarital sexual temptations, but also a profound ambivalence about the joys of licensed sexual activities. While their writings strongly endorse happy marital relationships as lessening the likelihood of extramarital involvements, leaders of this movement also express concern that a man's love for his wife could distract him from full concentration on God, who should be the focus of his highest degree of devotion. Since all Jewish men were legally obligated to procreate, the Jewish mystic was enjoined to marital sexuality as a part of everyday life at the same time as he sought profound encounters with the divine. One unfortunate consequence of the dissonance occasioned by these contradictory mandates was the objectification of all women and their representation as vessels of sexuality and erotic distraction in certain influential medieval Jewish writings.[35]

---

[31] Stow, *Alienated Minority*, 207.

[32] Israel Abrahams, ed., *Hebrew Ethical Wills* (Philadelphia: Jewish Publication Society, 1926; rep. 1954), 207–18.

[33] Stow, *Alienated Minority*, 208.

[34] Stow, *Alienated Minority*, 208. Particular sources of Christian condemnation were the prevalence of first-cousin marriage in the Jewish community, a liaison that the Church considered incestuous; the option of divorce; and the remarriage of widows and widowers.

[35] On the *Hasidei Ashkenaz* and their ambivalence about marital sexuality, see Judith R. Baskin, "From Separation to Displacement: The Problem of Women in *Sefer Hasidim*," *Association for Jewish Studies Review* 19 (1994): 1–18.

The generally positive Jewish emphasis on marital sexuality was tempered by the need for spousal separation for as much as half of every month while the wife was in a state of ritual impurity. Rabbinic strictures around menstruating and post-partum women were intended to protect male ritual purity. Women were considered trustworthy to report accurately as to whether or not they were sexually available to their husbands and they were expected to visit the *mikveh* as soon as they were legally able to do so. Thus a significant theme in the education of medieval Jewish girls was the need for strict and prompt compliance with the laws connected applying to the *niddah*, the menstruating woman. Women were urged to be assiduous in protecting their husbands from pollution and as expeditious as possible in observing these regulations so that their husbands would not be deprived of marital relations any longer than necessary. These shared concerns are evident in this passage from the fourteenth-century ethical will of Eleazar of Mainz:

> The women of my family must be exceedingly careful to examine themselves throughout their monthly cycles and to stay apart from their husbands during their unclean days. They should have sexual relations with their husbands in modesty and sanctity, not with passion and not with frivolity but in reverence and silence. They must be as scrupulous as possible to undertake their ritual immersions with care, accompanied by trustworthy women lest anyone encounter them. They should cover their eyes while returning home so that they won't see anything unclean. They must honor their husbands as much as possible, and they should be agreeable to them night and day.[36]

Refusal to immerse in the *mikveh* could play a central role in domestic quarrels. There was always the suspicion that a woman might delay her immersion or report inaccurately on her state of ritual purity in order to achieve certain objectives in her marriage. Such possibilities are implied in these remarks from the thirteenth-century *Hasidei-Ashkenaz* compendium, *Sefer Hasidim* (Book of the Pious):

> A man who is about to give his daughter in marriage must instruct her never to delay the time of her immersion in the *mikveh*. She must never say to her husband, "I will not immerse unless you give me such and such a sum of money, or a certain object." If the two of them devote their thoughts to heaven when they are intimate, their sons will be good and righteous.

---

[36] *Hebrew Ethical Wills*, ed. Abrahams, 207–18; see also Judith R. Baskin, "Women and Ritual Immersion in Medieval Ashkenaz: The Sexual Politics of Piety," in *Judaism in Practice: From the Middle Ages through the Early Modern Period*, ed. Lawrence Fine (Princeton: Princeton University Press, 2001) 131–42.

An anecdote in the same work describes a devout woman who refused to visit the *mikveh* until her miserly husband agreed to contribute to charity and buy religious books. When her husband complained to a rabbi, he was told, "For this may she be blessed for she is trying to compel you to fulfill a commandment and she doesn't know any other way to do it." But the rabbi said to the wife, "If you can manage to convince him by words to act properly, that's good, but concerning your marital relations don't delay in fulfilling his desire. Otherwise, he will fantasize about illicit sexual activities, you will not become pregnant, and you will only increase his wrath."[37]

Some women used their refusals to immerse in the *mikveh* as a stratagem out of an unhappy marriage when their husbands would not agree to a divorce. A wife who refused sexual relations was considered a *moredet*, a rebel, and was subject to a daily monetary fine; when the value of her dowry had been exhausted, the husband was compelled to divorce her. Such an expedient might be acceptable to an unhappy wife who had the financial support of her relatives. In cases where rabbinic authorities determined that a woman had refused sexual relations or fled because her husband was repulsive to her, to escape blatant physical or emotional abuse, or due to a lack of economic support, her husband could be compelled to give her a divorce and return her dowry.[38]

The Role of Marriage in Jewish Mystical Writings

In the Hebrew Bible and throughout later Jewish literature, the relationship between a husband and wife was often understood metaphorically as signifying the intimate bonds between God and human beings. Traditional rabbinic interpretation of the Song of Songs, for example, assumed that the biblical book's love poetry was actually an allegory detailing the passion between God and the people of Israel. As Jacob Neusner has written of this common exegetical trope, "Implicit in this representation of the right relationship, of course, is the promise that the feminine Israel will evoke from the masculine God the response of commitment and intervention: God will intervene to save Israel, when Israel makes herself into the perfect wife of God."[39] However, such mystical yearnings could

[37] The excerpts cited here are my translations from the Bologna edition of *Sefer Hasidim*, ed. Reuven Margolit (Jerusalem: Mosad ha-Rav Kook, 1964); paragraphs 506 and 873.

[38] See Baskin, "Women and Ritual Immersion in Medieval Ashkenaz", 137.

[39] Jacob Neusner, "Judaism," in *Women and Families,* ed. idem (Cleveland: Pilgrim Press, 1999), 59–60; and see Neusner's *Androgynous Judaism: Masculine and Feminine in the Dual Torah* (Macon: Mercer University Press, 1993).

have damaging human ramifications since total devotion to the divine could have the effect of displacing a wife in her husband's affections and devaluing the human marital relationship. This dilemma of divided spiritual and mundane loyalties remained unresolved in medieval Judaism.

In Jewish theosophical mysticism the marital relationship took on a specifically redemptive function. Mystical writers maintained that each religiously inspired act of marital intercourse, particularly on the eve of Sabbath, secured among the Jewish people the indwelling presence of the Shekhinah, the nurturing aspect of God most accessible to human experience. Moreover, conjugal unions could play a crucial role in restoring cosmic harmony by simultaneously presaging and enacting the ultimate reunification of the masculine and feminine aspects of the divine, believed to be in exile from each other. The *Iggeret ha-Kodesh* (The Holy Letter), a thirteenth-century mystical text on matrimonial relations, is among the earliest Jewish medieval works to constitute connubial sexuality as a salvific activity.[40] As David Biale has pointed out, this treatise is part of a larger literary genre of marital guidance literature that had Christian and Muslim counterparts, as well, but it is also a book with a religious purpose.[41] The *Iggeret* provides guidance on making marital intercourse mutually pleasurable but it also fulfils a larger eugenic agenda by suggesting sexual techniques and strategies that are supposed to result in the births of scholarly sons. Moreover, its advice on how men may please their wives is directed to higher mystical purposes. As Biale writes,

> In kabbalistic terms intercourse is the uniting of the male and female aspects of God, rather than a mere physical act. . . . When a man understands the mystical meaning of intercourse, he transforms the act into communion with the divine: the physical becomes epistemological. In the act of reproducing, the Kabbalist also produces mystical knowledge.[42]

The *Iggeret* is profoundly concerned that marital sexuality be infused with appropriate intention: only if both participants in sexual intercourse direct their thoughts towards God will they beget worthy offspring and produce the appropriate theurgic effect in the divine realms:

---

[40] For a dual Hebrew/English edition of the *Iggeret HaKodesh* see Seymour J. Cohen, trans. and introduction, *The Holy Letter: A Study in Jewish Morality* (Northvale, NJ: Jason Aronson, 1993). There is no scholarly consensus on the identity of the author of this text.

[41] David Biale, *Eros and the Jews: From Biblical Israel to Contemporary America* (New York: Basic Books, 1992), 102.

[42] Biale, *Eros and the Jews*, 104.

> Therefore when you and your wife are engaged in sexual union, do not behave lightheartedly and regard this act as vain, idle, and improper. Certainly, be not lightheaded in the presence of your wife . . . . Therefore, when engaging in the sex act, you must begin by speaking to her in a manner that will draw her heart to you, calm her spirits, and make her happy. Thus your minds will be bound upon one another as one, and your intention will unite with hers. Speak to her so that your words will provoke desire, love, will, and passion, as well as words leading to reverence for God, piety, and modesty . . . . A man should never force himself upon his wife and never overpower her, for the Divine Spirit never rests upon one whose conjugal relations occur in the absence of desire, love, and free will. The Shekhinah does not rest there . . . . Therefore, examine the secret that is incorporated in these chapters and when you practice what I have taught you, I will pledge that you will merit a righteous and saintly son who hallows God's name.[43]

As Moshe Idel has written of this effort to draw down the brilliant light of the Shekhinah by means of the act of human sexual union, "The husband has to elevate his thought to its source, to achieve an *unio mystica*, which will following by the descent of supernal spiritual forces on the *semen virile*. Here *ascensio mentis*, *unio mystica*, and *reversio* are prerequisite stages of the ideal conception."[44] In this scenario, as opposed to the allegorical imagery connected with the Song of Songs, neither human partner represents the divine. Rather performance of intercourse with the proper intention and righteousness prompts the Shekhinah to establish her presence in the human realm, in effect as a second female partner in the marriage relationship. Ironically, the mystic achieves his spiritual goal through a physical means, yet his affection for the human wife to whom he must be tender is necessarily secondary to his yearning for divine companionship. As Idel writes, "This combination of corporeal marriage as a first step, with the spiritual one as the second step, seemingly points to a synthesis of the theosophical importance of the marriage with the emphasis that the ecstatic kabbalah puts on the spiritual nature of the relation between man and God."[45]

A Model Medieval Jewish Marriage

There are no extant medieval documents that reveal Jewish women's views of their marriages. However, some of the autobiographical writings of Rabbi Eleazar ben Judah of Worms (1165–1230) tell us a great deal about his relationship with his

[43] Cohen, ed., *The Holy Letter*, 170–86.

[44] Moshe Idel, "Sexual Metaphors and Praxis in the Kabbalah," in *The Jewish Family*, ed. Kraemer, 205.

[45] Idel, "Sexual Metaphors and Praxis," 207.

wife Dolce, as well as her range of activities. Dolce and her husband were members of a small circle of Jews distinguished for their piety, the *Hasidei Ashkenaz* or German-Jewish pietists, whose introspective and penitential religious outlook had a significant impact on the Jews of Germany and France in the unsettled atmosphere following the First Crusade of 1096. Among Eleazar ben Judah's many surviving papers are two accounts, one in prose and one in poetry, describing the lives and the deaths of his wife Dolce, and their daughters, Bellette and Hannah, who were murdered by intruders in 1196.

While the prose account concentrates on the events of the attack and its devastating aftermath, the poetic eulogy recounts the range of endeavors of "the saintly Mistress Dolce" and her daughters. Based in part on Proverbs 31, the biblical description of the "woman of valor," this document, which records numerous and poignant details of its subjects' daily lives, constitutes an important source for the activities of medieval Jewish women in general, as well as a moving tribute to Dolce and her daughters. The epithets Eleazar uses in describing his wife, "pious" or "saintly" (*hasidah*), three times in the prose account and again at the very outset of the poetic eulogy, as well as "righteous" (*tzadeket*), tell us a great deal about the qualities for which women in her culture were most esteemed. He also uses the Hebrew *ne'imah*, "pleasant," three times in the elegy, a play on the meaning of Dolce's name which derives from the Latin adjective *dulcis*, as in the following passage from the beginning of the elegy:

> *A woman of valor* (Proverbs 31:10): the crown of her husband, the daughter of community benefactors. A woman who feared God, she was renowned for her good deeds.
>
> *Her husband put his confidence in her* (31:11): She fed him and dressed him in honor to sit with *the elders of the land* (31:23) and involve himself in Torah study and good deeds.
>
> *She was good to him, never bad, all the days of* (31:12) his life with her. She made him books from her labor; her name [signifies] "Pleasant."
>
> *She looked for* white *wool* for fringes [for ritual garments]; *and set her hand to them with a will* (31:13). *She set her mind* (31: 16) to fulfill divine commandments and all who observed her praised her.[46]

---

[46] On Dolce of Worms and for translations of all the documents concerning her, see J. Baskin, "Dolce of Worms: The Lives and Deaths of an Exemplary Medieval Jewish Woman and her Daughters," in *Judaism in Practice*, ed. Fine, 429–37; and eadem, "Women Saints in Judaism: Dolce of Worms," in *Women Saints in World Religions*, ed. Arvind Sharma (Albany: State University of New York Press, 2000), 39–69. For a comparison of R. Eleazar's depiction of Dolce and the unmediated voice of Glikl bas Judah Leib of Hameln, a seventeenth-century Jewish woman who discusses her marital experiences in her memoirs, see J. Baskin, "Jewish Women's Piety and the Impact of Printing in Early Modern Europe," in *Culture and Change: Attending to Early Modern Women*, ed. Margaret Mikesell and Adele Seeff (Newark: University of Delaware Press, 2003), 221–40.

Dolce was a successful moneylender who supported her family with her earnings. However, financial matters were not the only focus of her marital responsibilities. Eleazar describes Dolce as managing an extensive household; in addition to caring for the needs of her husband and three or more children, her ménage also included her husband's students and at least one junior teacher. She also had full responsibility for the domestic and religious educations of her daughters to whom she taught needlework skills as well as prayers and songs.

As a rabbi's wife, Dolce undertook communal responsibilities as well. She is said to have sewed books together from thread she had herself spun and she is also credited with preparing gut thread and sewing together Torah scrolls (the handwritten scroll containing the first five books of the Hebrew Bible, which is used in synagogue worship and is symbolic of the revelation of the divine word to the people of Israel), and with making candles for religious use. As a member of the learned rabbinic class, Dolce had knowledge of the traditional Hebrew liturgy unusual for a woman, and she is said to have led other women in song and prayer. Yet it is significant that R. Eleazar's final words of praise for Dolce in his poetic eulogy are that she rejoiced to perform her husband's will and never angered him. More than anything, Dolce is revered for having facilitated in every way the spiritual activities of the men of her household, and this is why her husband has not the slightest doubt of her overwhelming merit. The reward that R. Eleazar invokes for his beloved wife in the final phrase of the poetic lament, to be "wrapped in the eternal life of Paradise," is a recognition of her deeds, upon which so many were utterly dependent. Although R. Eleazar survived his wife by more than thirty years, there is no evidence that he married again, an unusual decision in a Jewish culture that strongly encouraged remarriage, and a likely indication of his devotion to Dolce's memory.

Intermarriage

Before the modern period, there was no such thing as civil marriage; all marriages were religious acts in that they followed formalized rituals developed by specific religious communities. Thus a sanctioned marriage between a professing Jew and a Christian, or a Jew and a Muslim, would appear to have been a virtual impossibility. Moreover, during the Middle Ages such marriages were generally forbidden by religious and secular law in both Muslim and Christian realms. This is not to say that sexual liaisons between Jews and non-Jews did not exist; they were common and at many different levels of intensity. For a romance between a Jew and a non-Jew to progress to a recognized marriage, however, one of the parties to the relationship would have had to convert. Generally speaking it was the woman who did so. An eleventh-century letter found in the Cairo

Genizah, probably from Monieux in France, sought support for a proselyte who had left a noble, wealthy family to become a Jew. She married a Rabbi David Todros in Narbonne and they fled to Monieux to escape pursuit by her relatives. Six years later, her husband was killed in an attack on the community, her two older children were taken captive, and she was left bereft with an infant. It is not clear from the letter, however, if this woman's conversion was prompted by a prior relationship with the man who became her husband or if the marriage was subsequent to it.[47] *Sefer Hasidim* writes that the children of a female proselyte of good character, modesty, and piety ought to be preferred as marriage partners over those of a Jewish woman who does not possess the same qualities, although whether this discussion is theoretical or based on reality is open to question.[48] Most of the known male Christians who became converts to Judaism in the Middle Ages converted for spiritual reasons. Some of these individuals, who generally had to leave Christian Europe if they were to escape prosecution, later married Jewish women.

In both Muslim and Christian realms, Jews and gentiles entered into a variety of sexual interactions, ranging from visits to prostitutes, to involvement with maidservants, to a recognized relationship with a mistress or lover, to common-law marriages. All of these relationships were decried by both Jewish and non-Jewish authorities alike, and offenders, particularly those involved in permanent or semi-permanent liaisons, were sometimes arrested by Church authorities, occasionally receiving the death penalty. The Church was more tolerant of Christian men having affairs with Jewish women, probably because Jewish mistresses were likely to adopt their lover's faith; indeed, the seduction/conversion of a Jewish girl by a Christian suitor became a popular theme in Christian literature. Not surprisingly, Jewish authorities objected far more strenuously to such relationships than they did to Jewish men keeping Christian or Muslim mistresses or maintaining sexual involvements with non-Jewish servants. This topic remains relatively unexplored, for as Salo Baron has written:

> Regrettably, not only illicit relations which, by their very nature, were secretive, but also more overt unions by marriage or concubinage are recorded only in connection with criminal prosecutions. There must have been numerous other offenders who escaped detection or whose prosecution left no traces in the extant documents, particularly wherever social relations between

[47] On this letter, see Franz Kobler, ed., *Letters of Jews Through the Ages*, Vol. 1: *From Biblical Times to the Renaissance* (New York-Philadelphia: East and West Library, 1952), 148–50; and Norman Golb, "Jewish Proselytism — A Phenomenon in the Religious History of Early Medieval Europe," *Tenth Annual Rabbi Louis Feinberg Memorial Lecture in Judaic Studies* (Cincinnati: Judaic Studies Program, University of Cincinnati, 1987).

[48] *Sefer Hasidim*, Bologna edition, paragraph 377.

Jews and Gentiles were very close, as in Spain, the Provence, or Renaissance Italy.[49]

Concern about Jewish-Christian sexual liaisons was certainly among the factors leading to efforts by the Church to isolate Jews from Christians by whatever means possible, and was among motivations behind the expulsion of the Jews from Spain in 1492, and the establishment of Jewish ghettos in the course of the sixteenth century.

Marriage Customs

During the Middle Ages, particularly in Europe, many of the customs connected with the celebration of Jewish marriages became standardized. By the twelfth century, it was common for the celebration of betrothal (*'erusin*) and the actual marriage (*nissu'in*) to take place at the same time. This was probably a reflection of the uncertain circumstances of Jewish life, where numerous difficulties could arise when a man and woman were considered legally married (as they were following the betrothal ceremony) but did not yet live together. Similarly, the double celebrations required for both betrothal and marriage could constitute a significant expense.

A second medieval innovation was that marriage became an official public event which was authorized and attended by community leaders. The combined betrothal/wedding ceremony usually took place in a public space, either the synagogue itself or a communal hall. An earlier ceremony of escorting the bride to the groom's home was replaced with the symbolic public *huppah* ("marriage canopy"), under which the seven wedding benedictions were recited. Since the *huppah* had been the place of marital consummation in earlier eras, there was some question of whether the couple was still required to be isolated together following the ceremony. To avoid doubt it was decided that following the *huppah* ceremony the couple should have a brief private time together, *yihud* ("seclusion"), before joining their guests for a festive meal.

The combined betrothal/marriage, which became the norm throughout the Jewish Middle Ages, was generally preceded by a period of engagement. At the engagement ceremony (*shiddukhin*) a legal document (*tena'im* or "conditions"), fixing the terms of the marriage and defining the penalties and damages to be paid if one of the parties should wish to abandon the match, was signed. Sometimes the endorsement of the *tena'im*, which had been negotiated previously, was made just before the wedding.

---

[49] Salo W. Baron, *A Social and Religious History of the Jews,* vol. 11: *Citizen or Alien Conjurer* (New York: Columbia University Press, 1967), 84.

References to the *shadkhan*, or marriage broker, first appear in rabbinic literature in the thirteenth century. During the medieval period matchmaking was often undertaken by highly respected rabbis and scholars. Generally the *shadkhan*'s fee was a percentage of the dowry. Despite the institution of fairly standard nuptial formalities, marriages effected by intercourse, particularly in the context of elopements, remained a much deplored occasional feature of medieval and early modern Jewish life. According to Maimonides and other medieval authorities, such marriages were valid, but a man who married in this way should be flogged for rebelliousness so that he would not inspire others to similar inappropriate behavior.

Many features of the medieval Jewish wedding, such as the cloth canopy, or *huppah,* under which the marrying couple stood, the portable *huppah* canopy for weddings held outdoors, the wedding ring, the shattering of a glass cup, and the decorated marriage contract are almost certainly Jewish adaptations of similar Christian or Muslim customs. During the early Middle Ages, weddings in Italy, Germany, and France were usually held inside the synagogue where the *huppah* was simply a cloth or *tallit* (fringed ritual garment) spread over the bride and groom. This custom may have its origins in the early medieval Church where a cloth was sometimes spread over a bridal couple during the nuptial Mass. The portable canopy, which seems to have originated in the sixteenth century, and was usually set up in the outside courtyard of the synagogue, was probably adapted from Catholic practice, where a portable canopy for outdoor Church rituals was used since early medieval times.[50] Jewish weddings in Spain, Portugal, and the Muslim world tended to take place indoors in a communal hall rather than the synagogue.

Shattering a glass as part of the Jewish wedding ceremony has no biblical or talmudic precedents but apparently was already common in the Rhineland by the twelfth century. It was probably influenced by Christian wedding customs in Germany of smashing drinking vessels. This practice, which presumably had the original purpose of frightening or propitiating evil spirits, was justified by fourteenth-century Jewish sources as symbolizing the destruction of the Jerusalem Temple. Later authorities also suggested that the custom is a reminder of the fragility of life.[51] The use of a ring as a binding symbol in the betrothal ceremony appears to have been introduced in medieval Europe as part of the combined *'erusin-nissu'in* ceremony, and was established practice by the twelfth century. In Muslim lands the exchange of a coin remained the norm in medieval times.

---

[50] Joseph Gutmann. "Jewish Medieval Marriage Customs in Art: Creativity and Adaptation," in *The Jewish Family*, ed. Kraemer (New York: Oxford University Press, 1989): 47–62, here 48.

[51] Gutmann, "Jewish Medieval Marriage Customs in Art," 52.

Decorating the *ketubbah* appears to have been adapted from Islam. The earliest examples date from Egypt and Syria-Palestine of the eleventh and twelfth centuries; their geometrical and floral decorations follow patterns found in contemporary illustrated Muslim marriage contracts.[52] Decorated *ketubbot* exist from Christian Spain of the thirteenth to fifteenth centuries. With the dispersion of Spanish Jews beginning in 1492, the practice spread to Turkey and Italy. In Italy the beautifully decorated *ketubbah* was not only displayed but was read as part of the wedding, separating the *'erusin* and *nissu'in* ceremonies. Joseph Gutmann writes that wealthy families in early modern Italy competed so fiercely to commission magnificent *ketubbot* that rabbis issued sumptuary legislation in an attempt to limit the amount of money that could be spent.[53]

Conclusion

In medieval Judaism marriage provided both a vehicle for ethnic continuity and a haven for personal intimacy. In a religious community where marriage was the norm for all adults and human sexuality was recognized and valued, legal mandates grounded in rabbinic Judaism spelled out the rights, responsibilities, and appropriate roles for each spouse, while strong ethical norms advocated harmonious unions in which partners were linked by mutual respect. Nevertheless, divorce was always an option for couples with irreconcilable differences. The influence of the host cultures in which Jews lived was also a significant factor in shaping the norms and practices of Jewish marriage, from the establishment of monogamy among Jews in Christian lands to the adoption of various wedding customs in both Muslim and Christian realms, many customs of which continue to be part of contemporary Jewish nuptial ritual.

[52] Gutmann, "Jewish Medieval Marriage Customs in Art," 55.
[53] Gutmann, "Jewish Medieval Marriage Customs in Art," 56.

At Marriage End: Girolamo Savonarola and the Question of Widows in Late Fifteenth-Century Florence

Konrad Eisenbichler

In premodern Europe, marriage ended with the death of one of the two partners. Because of medical and sanitary conditions at the time, adult women often died fairly young, in their twenties and in childbirth. Those who survived childbearing generally found themselves widowed in their thirties because, especially in Italy, marriage patterns among the merchant and banking class tended to couple women in their late teens with men in their early to mid-thirties.[1] The Florentine tax census of 1427 (the *catasto*) reveals that one in four adult women in Florence was a widow.[2] This is a staggering figure, not only because of the high number of women it represents, but also because of the economic and social burden such a group placed on the city and its charitable organizations. Not surprisingly, the government, the Church, families, and even concerned individuals sought to remedy this situation or somehow come to suitable terms with it.

In many ways, however, the problem was irresolvable within current social structures and customs. Marriage and dowry practices among the Florentine middle and upper classes fostered, if not encouraged, the age anomaly that inevitably led to women being widowed at a young age. Family economic strategies used widowed women to their own ends, often with little or no concern for the individual's personal preferences. Even the Church, supposedly the protector of the weak, did not provide a realistic alternative solution; all it could do was either to lead women back into marriage or to enclose them in a convent. In this

---

[1] For marriage ages in Tuscany, see David Herlihy and Christine Klapisch-Zuber, *Tuscans and their Families: A Study of the Florentine Catasto of 1427* (New Haven: Yale University Press, 1985), 87 and passim; C. Klapisch-Zuber, *Women, Family, and Ritual in Renaissance Italy*, trans. Lydia G. Cochrane (Chicago: University of Chicago Press, 1985), 19–20, 27–30, 109–11 and passim. For Venice, see Joanne M. Ferraro, *Marriage Wars in Late Renaissance Venice* (Oxford: Oxford University Press, 2001), 62–64. For northern Europe, see Merry Wiesner, *Women and Gender in Early Modern Europe* (Cambridge: Cambridge University Press, 1993), 56–58. For a look at widows in England in the sixteenth and seventeenth century, see Barbara J. Todd, "The Remarrying Widow: A Stereotype Reconsidered," In *Women in English Society 1500–1800*, ed. Mary Prior (London and New York: Methuen, 1985), 54–92. For a general overview of the bibliography (though now dated), see Ida Blom, "The History of Widowhood: A Bibliographic Overview," *Journal of Family History* 16:2 (1991): 191–210.

[2] Herlihy and Klapisch-Zuber, *Tuscans and Their Families*, 205, 216–17, 221 and passim.

article, I will look at some of the general attitudes towards widows in Tuscany in the fourteenth and fifteenth centuries, consider some of the alternatives available to widowed women at the time, survey Girolamo Savonarola's advice to widows in the first text he ever published, and close with a brief look at the Orbatello, a Florentine hospice for widows that was centuries ahead of its times. My conclusion will be that both spiritual and material interests in the city honestly sought to find solutions to what was, in fact, a dismal situation for widowed women, a situation that was, unfortunately, the inevitable result of that society's firmly established and generally sanctioned marriage patterns.

The natural end of a marriage could be either disastrous or empowering for a woman — disastrous if personal, social, or economic factors dramatically lowered the quality of her life; empowering if she was able to buck the general trend and gain control of her resources and of her life beyond the levels she had previously enjoyed. For Alessandra Macinghi Strozzi (1407–71), for example, the loss of her husband Matteo — first by virtue of his exile for political reasons from Florence, and then because of his death from the plague in Pesaro — proved to be the catalyst for active involvement in the economic, social, and political fortunes of her family.[3] Under normal circumstances, she never would have assumed such a role. Obliged to take charge of her orphaned family, Macinghi Strozzi became the *de facto* head of the household. In this new role, Matteo's widow grew to be a formidable figure who was able not only to arrange for honorable marriages for her children — a difficult task, given that they were the scions of a political exile — but also to re-integrate her adult sons into Florentine society after they had been, one after the other, exiled at the onset of puberty because of the judgment bearing against their father.

The case of Alessandra Macinghi Strozzi does not, however, represent the norm. Most widowed mothers were not able to assume direct control over their personal lives and over the management of the family. Instead, they bowed to the established order and followed one of three paths: (1) they remained in their matrimonial family as a peripheral figure whose sole purpose was to raise the children of the deceased husband under the watchful authority of a male in-law, or (2) they abandoned their children with the in-laws in order to return to their parental family and be married off, once again, for the benefit of their immediate kin's interests, or (3) they left the world altogether and entered a convent. Life as an independent widowed woman was, generally speaking, not a possibility, let alone an option.

[3] On Macinghi Strozzi, see Ann Morton Crabb, "How Typical Was Alessandra Macinghi Strozzi of Fifteenth-Century Florentine Widows?" in *Upon my Husband's Death: Widows in the Literature and Histories of Medieval Europe,* ed. Louise Mirrer (Ann Arbor: University of Michigan Press, 1992), 47–68.

When widows did manage to remain independent of direct male control, popular imagination immediately colored them in broad strokes with the usual vices and frailties attributed to women: sensuality and foolishness. Part of the reason for this was that society viewed widows with ambivalence. Louise Mirrer pointed out some years ago that

> the widow was, par excellence, an ambiguous human sign. A woman neither chaste nor married who might claim special protection from Church and secular institutions alike but who might also act on her own, the widow was often portrayed as both needful of safeguards against men and as a formidable enemy of men. . . . In popular as well as in learned texts, the ambiguities of widowhood were drawn on to emphasize the frightening excess to which widows might potentially enjoy their independence. They were portrayed, for example, as requiring constant reminders of the virtues of continence, for their liberation from male control was dangerously played out in their overindulgence of sexual desire (widows were proverbially pictured on the lookout for a new sexual partner as soon as their husbands were buried — "Llorar poko i buskar otro" [cry a little and look for another (man)], to cite one example from the Castilian tradition).[4]

Tales of lusty widows who frolic with young men thus abound in late medieval narratives. In the *Decameron*, Giovanni Boccaccio tells of a young Florentine widow, Elena,

> who was fair of body, proud of spirit, very gently bred, and reasonably well endowed with Fortune's blessings. When her husband died prematurely, leaving her a widow, she made up her mind that she would never remarry, having fallen in love with a handsome and charming young man of her own choosing. And now that she was free from all other cares, she succeeded, with the assistance of a maidservant whom she greatly trusted, in passing many a pleasant hour in his arms, to the wondrous delight of both parties.[5]

Lest we should think of Elena in positive terms as a young woman who affirmed her independence and her love for a partner of her own choosing, Boccaccio quickly adds that Elena's coy glances at parties demonstrated that she "was not in the habit of keeping her eyes fixed upon the ground," but greatly enjoyed the

---

[4] See Louise Mirrer, "Introduction" to *Upon my Husband's Death*, 7–8. See also Klapisch-Zuber, *Women, Family, and Ritual*, esp. chap. 10, "'The Cruel Mother': Maternity, Widowhood, and Dowry in Florence in the Fourteenth and Fifteenth Centuries," 134–62.

[5] Giovanni Boccaccio, *Decameron*, trans. with an introduction by G. H. McWilliam (Harmondsworth: Penguin, 1972), 621 (Day 8, Tale 7).

attention her good looks attracted, and "swiftly singled out those men who were showing an interest in her" (622). In other words, Elena desired sensual pleasures with young men, thereby becoming a temptation and a danger for them. In fact, the *novella* turns on her mistreatment of a sincere admirer — she makes him spend an entire winter night vainly waiting for her in a snow-covered courtyard while she enjoys herself with her lover in a near-by bedroom — and on his eventual revenge on her — he makes her spend an entire day naked on top of a tower in full view of the townspeople.

For every lustful widow of late medieval literature, however, there is also a foolish, gullible widow who falls victim to the ruses of that other ambivalent pre-modern animal — the friar. In a tirade against friars, the narrator of Tedaldo's story (*Dec.* 3.7) recurs to a New Testament trope to illustrate the fundamental corruption of the Mendicant Orders:

> And like the fisherman who tries to take a number of fish from the river with a single throw of his casting-net, so these fellows [the friars], as they wrap themselves in the capacious folds of their habits, endeavour to take in many an over-pious lady, *many a widow*, and many another simpleton of either sex, this being their one overriding concern (emphasis added, 283).

One of the most famous such friars in Italian Renaissance literature is Fra Timoteo, the corrupt cleric from Niccolò Machiavelli's play *The Mandrake Root*. In a brief but compelling scene in which Fra Timoteo comforts a devout widow greatly worried about the well-being of her departed husband's soul and the advancing power of the Ottoman Turks (III.iii), Machiavelli illustrates just how easily such simple women can be manipulated and fleeced by an irresponsible clergy.

Not all widows, however, were lustful temptresses or gullible simpletons. Some were astute women with a keen sense of propriety. One of these is Boccaccio's Monna Piccarda, "a widow of gentle birth" who was able not only to refuse the advances of a priest who had fallen in love with her, but also to teach him a lesson and have him severely reprimanded by the local bishop (*Dec.* 8.4). It is perhaps not without significance that, although Monna Piccarda sets up the ruse that exposes the priest, it is her two brothers, "a pair of very worthy and polite young gentlemen," who deal with the bishop and explain the situation to him. Clearly, one of Boccaccio's points is that a "proper" widow deals with the authorities only through her male relatives.[6]

---

[6] For further study of Boccaccio and widows, see Eugenio Giusti, "The Widow in Giovanni Boccaccio's Works: A Negative *Exemplum* or a Symbol of Positive Praxis?" in *Gendered Contexts: New Perspectives in Italian Cultural Studies*, ed. Laura Benedetti, Julia Hairston, and Silvia Ross (New York: Peter Lang, 1995), 39–48.

The admiration (and the restrictions) evident in the story of Monna Piccarda reveal that pre-modern Tuscans greatly respected those widows who were able to retain their *onestà*, that is, their virtue. A widow's virtue lay not only in her chastity, but also in her maternal instincts and in her piety. The Florentine bookseller and biographer Vespasiano da Bisticci expresses on several occasions his society's and his own admiration for those widows who refused re-marriage so as to dedicate themselves completely to their children and to their soul, that is, to motherhood and religion.[7]

The respect and expectations enunciated by Vespasiano were echoed by the clergy, and especially by the preaching orders. Antonino Pierozzi (1389–1459), the ascetic Dominican preacher who became archbishop of Florence and was later canonized as St. Antoninus, considered widowhood a "spiritual state" (*stato spirituale*) and expected "true widows" to behave accordingly.[8] The popular definition of a widow as "that woman who, having had a husband and having survived him, disposes herself completely not to want another husband,"[9] is clearly not enough for him. In his letter to Ginevra de' Cavalcanti, recently widowed of Lorenzo de' Medici (brother of Cosimo the Elder and great-uncle of his more famous namesake), Antoninus expands and elevates the definition in order to claim that "one can call every devout soul for whom the world and sensual appetite are dead a widow, for this is the first husband a soul takes before it reaches the age of reason."[10] Not surprisingly, Antoninus begins his letter to Ginevra by recalling that the Fathers had described the Church itself as a widow because it has been deprived

[7] See Vespasiano da Bisticci, *Renaissance Princes, Popes and Prelates. The Vespasiano Memoirs, Lives of Illustrious Men of the XVth Century*, trans. William George and Emily Waters (New York: Harper & Row, 1963), 439–62 for Alessandra de' Bardi.

[8] "Et se mi domandassi [fol. 67v] chome spesso mi debbo confessare, ti rispondo, che il mese almeno una volta spetialmente a chj tiene stato spirituale — chome le vedove vere." Biblioteca Nazionale Centrale di Firenze, MS. Banco Rari 331, "Epistola," fol. 67r–v; transcribed (with modernized spelling and punctuation) in *I manoscritti palatini di Firenze*, ed. Francesco Palermo, 3 vols. (Firenze: Dall'I. e R. Biblioteca Palatina, 1853), 1:706. Unless otherwise indicated, all translations and transcriptions are mine. (The allusion is to 1 Tim. 5:3–5.)

[9] "Vedova propiamente si chiama dalla gente la donna la quale a avuto marito e, rimasta dietro allui in tutto si dispone di non volere più altro marito." BNCF, MS. Banco Rari 331, "Epistola," fol. 6r; transcribed in *I manoscritti palatini di Firenze*, 704.

[10] "Vendova si può dire ciaschuna anima divota se allei è morto il mondo e appetito sensuale, il quale è il primo marito che piglia l'anima, innanzi che vengha a uso di ragione, chome dice santo Agostino sopra santo Giovanni." BNCF, MS. Banco Rari 331, "Epistola," fol. 4r; transcribed in *I manoscritti palatini di Firenze*, 704. (The source Is Augustine, Tract. in Evang. Joan. 15.21 [PL 35.1518].)

of the bodily presence of Jesus Christ, its groom.[11] While making such claims, the saintly archbishop was also aware that not all widowed women could, or even would, seek to conform to such high expectations. He thus acknowledged that some women are widows only in body and not in spirit, for they still seek men and make themselves pretty in order to be attractive to them. Antoninus clearly disapproves of these women, saying that "familiarity with young men, or even with clerics and members of religious orders, is not appropriate for the widowed state." He therefore advises Ginevra not to speak with youths and clergymen "for disordinate affections often arise from this."[12]

Somewhat similar views and advice were advanced by Girolamo Savonarola, the Dominican friar who, two generations later, followed in Antoninus's steps as prior of the influential convent of San Marco. Savonarola's first published work is, in fact, a short treatise entitled *Book of the Widow's Life* (*Libro della vita viduale*). First published in Florence in 1491, it enjoyed immediate success and, within five years, already underwent four different editions of its own.[13] In the first half of the sixteenth century it appeared eight more times as part of the Milanese and the Venetian editions of Savonarola's *opera omnia* or in collections of his treatises. It then disappeared from the presses, with only one edition in the seventeenth century (1667), none in the eighteenth or nineteenth, and then two in the twentieth century (1952 and 1976). The work's immediate success, its continued editorial life for about fifty years, and then its sudden disappearance from circulation echo the wild enthusiasm, the continuing interest, and then the complete lack of interest in post-Renaissance Italy for Savonarola's message. It also suggests that in the sixteenth century society's view of widows was changing dramatically, so much so that the friar's advice ceased to be relevant just two or three generations after it was given and completely disappeared from circulation in the centuries that followed.

---

[11] "Vendova è detta la santa Chiesa da' dottori, però che priva [fol. 1v] fu della presentia corporale del suo nobile sposo Gesù Cristo quando morto In sulla croce & dappoi il terzo di risuscittato finalmente salj In cielo." BNCF, MS. Banco Rari 331, "Epistola," fol. 1r–v; transcribed in *I manoscritti palatini di Firenze*, 704.

[12] "A dire chella vedova dette andare a nozze e feste a chonviti mondani e luoghi di balli e di chanti pare superfluo [fol. 14r] però che ciaschuno intende queste chose non si chonface a stato vedovile. Massimamente la domestichezza degli giovani e non meno de cherici e religiosi fuor di chasa di chonfessione o di domandare chonsiglio quando acchorre alchuno dubbio di choscientia / non frequentare parlamenti chon essi però che di qua procedono spesso disordinate affetioni sotto spetie di divotioni le quali molto intepidischono l'anima dal vero fervore e amore di dio . . ." BNCF, MS. Banco Rari 331, "Epistola," fols. 13v–14r; transcribed in *I manoscritti palatini di Firenze*, 706.

[13] For a detailed description of these first four editions, see Mario Ferrara's summary in Girolamo Savonarola, *Operette spirituali*, 2 vols. (Roma: Angelo Belardetti Editore, 1976), 1:301–14

On first reading Savonarola's short treatise, one is struck by its severity, if not its inherent misogyny.[14] According to the friar, widows ought to give up all social contacts, retreat into solitude, and dedicate themselves completely to prayer. Echoing and expanding on his predecessor St. Antoninus, Savonarola urges the "true widow" to avoid contact not only with men and with priests or friars, but also with nuns, family members, and even blood relatives. A widow should then chastise herself through careful self-control and denial of the senses, guarding herself from all occasions for sin that derive from touch, sight, smell, hearing, and so forth. She should not remarry, nor should she dedicate herself to the memory of her deceased husband. Instead, she should forget him completely and devote herself fully to her spiritual husband, Jesus Christ.[15] Savonarola's ideal widow should, in a way, become a hermit, separated from society, constantly engaged in self-mortification, and fully dedicated to prayer. To a modern reader, such advice sounds like house arrest, if not even self-arrest.

On second reading, however, the severity of Savonarola's advice appears tempered with understanding and perhaps even with a certain degree of indulgence. He realizes, for example, that not all widows are able, capable, or even willing to follow his suggestions and become a practical hermit. In fact, from the very beginning, when he categorizes widows into various groups according to their interests and abilities, he reveals a profound appreciation for the variety of human experience. As St. Antoninus had already done, Savonarola also points out that some women are widows physically, but not mentally, because they miss having a husband and therefore are keen to remarry. In discussing this type of widow, Savonarola indicates that he appreciates, and even allows for, the sexual needs of young women. Drawing on St. Paul's letter to Timothy (1 Tim. 5:14), he says that such young women *ought* to remarry so as to avoid danger — that is, so as to avoid illicit sexual urges and activities. Citing St. Paul again, Savonarola points out that it is better to marry than to burn.[16] Although possibly surprising for the modern reader, such an attitude is not unexpected from a pre-modern Christian moralist and a clergyman fully imbued with Pauline theology and medieval Christian rationality.

---

[14] What follows draws in part on three earlier articles of mine: "Il trattato di Girolamo Savonarola sulla vita viduale," in *Studi savonaroliani, Verso il V centenario,* ed. Gian Carlo Garfagnini (Firenze: Edizioni del Galluzzo, 1996), 267–72; "Prima opera a stampa di Savonarola: I consigli per le vedove," in *Città di vita* 53:2–3 (1998): 161–68, published simultaneously in *Savonarola rivisitato (1498–1998),* ed. M. G. Rosito (Firenze: Edizioni Città di Vita, 1998), 65–72; and "Savonarola e il problema delle vedove nel suo contesto sociale," in *Una città e il suo profeta: Firenze di fronte al Savonarola*, ed. Gian Carlo Garfagnini (Firenze: SISMEL Edizioni del Galluzzo, 2001), 263–71.

[15] Savonarola, *Libro della vita viduale*, 1:34–41.

[16] Savonarola, *Libro della vita viduale*, 1:18–19 (citing 1 Cor. 7:9).

Savonarola's next suggestion, however, may be unexpected: after allowing remarriage for a woman who is still young and not interested in entering a convent, the preacher also recommends remarriage for economic reasons, that is, in case "the widow were to be in such a state that, because of material needs, or because she has no income whatsoever, or for various other circumstances, she cannot live otherwise."[17] In other words, Savonarola says that a widow may remarry for the sole reason of finding a man who will support her. Conscious of the morally dubious nature of such a practice, Savonarola rationalizes the problem away by saying that "even though this proceeds from a bad root, nonetheless, the result would be good" ("avvengaché questo proceda da cattiva radice, nientedimeno el fine sare' buono," 1:19). Savonarola's casuistical sophistry, which may lead scholars of Italian literature to connect him immediately with Machiavelli's infamous Fra Timoteo, is predicated by an economic reality more pressing than any moralist's wishful thinking about chastity or the purpose of marriage. At the same time, however, this is not mere sophistry. Savonarola accepts the economic factor in the case of dire need, but he does not accept it in the case of self-interested greed. In fact, he points out that

> if a widow should remarry or should want to remarry for lust or for avarice, or in order to go where she knows there is wealth, or for pride, or when she is sought after by a man of high degree, or because she has fallen in love, or for some other depraved and perverse reason, without a doubt this desire of hers would be a sin.[18]

What is worth noting is that, in this list of "depraved and perverse" reasons for remarriage (reasons that include the traditional capital sins of lust, avarice, and pride, but also the more modern sins of chasing after wealth and social mobility), Savonarola also includes love. In fact, the reason "because she has fallen in love" is the last entry in Savonarola's crescendo of "depraved and perverse" reasons for remarriage. In so doing, Savonarola clearly adheres to the mercantile middle-class and political upper-class view of marriage as a social contract to be

---

[17] Savonarola, *The Book on the Life of the Widow* in *A Guide to Righteous Living and Other Works,* trans. Konrad Eisenbichler (Toronto: Centre for Reformation and Renaissance Studies, 2003), 196. "quando la vedova fussi in tale stato che, per necessità delle cose temporali, o perché non ha redutto alcuno, o per diverse altre circustanzie, non può vivere altrimenti": Savonarola, *Libro della vita viduale*, 1:19.

[18] Savonarola, *The Book of the Widow,* 196–97. "Ma quando una vedova si rimaritassi o volessisi rimaritare per libidine o per avarizia, per andare dove sa che è della roba, o per superbia, quando è dimandata da uomo di alto stato, o per innamoramento, o per altra prava occasione e perverso fine, senza dubbio questo suo desiderio sarebbe peccato": Savonarola, *Libro della vita viduale*, 1:19.

entered upon rationally and by design for economic, social, or political reasons. He clearly does not espouse the twentieth-century view of marriage as an intimate bond between two persons who are emotionally and sexually attracted to each other.

Sexual love and marital love are, in fact, completely absent from Savonarola's treatise. Nowhere in it does he refer to conjugal love, or commiserate with widows on their loss of a husband. He seems unable to conceptualize, and therefore says nothing of, widows who choose not to remarry because they love their deceased husband so much that they cannot think of marrying another man. When he does suggest that in losing her husband a woman has also lost her "every consolation in this world," he is clearly referring not to companionship or affection, but to the fact that "amusements are no longer allowed for her."[19]

Although, in Savonarola's view, a husband provides a wife with the opportunity for "amusements," never in the treatise does the friar suggest that marriage could have been a joyous state. On the contrary, from the very beginning Savonarola points out that, for a recently widowed wife, a husband's death is a liberating event she should accept with joy as a gift from God. He even lists seven different reasons why a woman is better off widowed than married: (1) as a widow she is no longer under the power of her husband; (2) she is no longer a victim of his and her own lust; (3) she is no longer tied to children; (4) she is no longer tied to the management of a family; (5) she is no longer an easy prey to avarice and pride; (6) she is no longer obliged to attend morally dangerous social events; and (7) widowhood is a rein that keeps a widow on the path of righteousness.[20]

It is, in fact, this need to rein in, to control widowed women that becomes the underlining element in Savonarola's advice to widows. The first means of control is, of course, sexual. We have already seen how Savonarola's first category of widows is, in fact, determined by sexual activity — it consists of women who wish to remarry. Whether this wish is motivated by sexual or economic reasons is irrelevant, for in both cases a widow is led back into the sexual embrace of a man that puts her squarely back into the accepted social pattern of male control and domination.

Savonarola's second category of widows is again based solely on sexual activity and desire, and consists of women who remain widows in theory, but not in practice, "because they do not maintain chastity in their hearts and they also openly show themselves in such a way as to reveal to dissolute youths what

[19] Savonarola, *The Book of the Widow,* 206. "E però la vedova, considerando che già ha perso la consolazione del mondo avendo perso il marito, perché non gli è più lecito el sollazzare": Savonarola, *Libro della vita viduale*, 1:34.

[20] Savonarola, *Libro della vita viduale*, 1:14–18; Savonarola, *The Book of the Widow,* 192–96.

they desire."[21] If the first category was that of marrying widows, the second is clearly that of merry widows, of women who have no interest in marriage but plenty of interest in the pleasures of young men. Savonarola's third category consists of widows who remain chaste because of social pressures, or because of fear of being saddled with a terrible husband, or because it is "in their nature" to remain so.[22] The fourth category is determined this time not only by sexual considerations but also by social responsibility. It consists of widows who choose to remain chaste, but are unable to withdraw from society because of their obligations to their families. These may be called the working widows who look after children, grandchildren, and the family in general. Savonarola's fifth category continues to be determined by sexual and personal needs and consists of women who are both chaste and free from family obligations, but fail to take the ultimate step and withdraw from society because of "faint-heartedness" (*pusillanimità*) or "compassion" (*compassione*). Savonarola does not condemn these hesitant widows; he even seems to feel some sympathy towards them as individuals not quite strong enough to take the final step of separation from the world and from their kin. The sixth and last category, that of "true widows" (*vera vidua*, as he himself calls them, picking up on a Pauline term already used by St. Antoninus and others) consists of women who have the moral, physical, and spiritual strength to abandon the world and to dedicate themselves completely to a life of prayer and service to God. It is to this last group that Savonarola addresses his treatise.

This effort to categorize widows by virtue of their sexual desires and personal situation reveals that Savonarola is both fairly liberal — in that he is ready to allow sexually active or economically disadvantaged women to remarry — and also a strict moralist — in that he expects "true widows" not only to give up sex, but also to give up their families and all worldly activities in order to dedicate themselves completely to prayer.

Savonarola's attitude to women's sexual activity is, as expected, molded by long-standing western Christian views of sexuality in general and of female sexuality in particular. According to Savonarola, women should not show an interest in sex because sexuality in women is reprehensible both spiritually (that is, in the sight of God) and socially (that is, in the sight of man). Women should, instead, suppress their sexual desires and seek to practice continence. Inherent in this attitude is the long-standing association of carnality and lust with the devil himself.

---

[21] Savonarola, *The Book of the Widow,* 197; "perché non servano castitate nel secreto suo e in aperto ancora si dimostrano per tale modo che danno ad intendere alli dissoluti giovani quello che elle desiderano": Savonarola, *Libro della vita viduale*, 1:20.

[22] The phrase "perché così gli dà la sua natura" (1:20) is quite ambiguous, to say the least.

In this view, sexual activity and devotion to God are mutually exclusive — it is impossible, Savonarola says, to serve God and to be sexually active because carnality separates and distances an individual from God.[23] And while Savonarola is prepared to allow young, sexually active women to remarry (on the Pauline rationalization that it is better to marry than to burn), he is also careful to warn older women to keep their guard up against carnal temptation because, as he points out, the fire of lust burns in us as long as there is flesh and thus carnality remains a danger even in old age.[24]

At times Savonarola's recurrent advice to older widows to flee temptation by distancing themselves from young men may sound, to modern ears, preposterous — Savonarola's warning seems to suggest that Florence was home to a disproportionate number of young men who were sexually attracted to older women. However, given Florentine marriage practices, according to which most marriages were contracted between men in their mid-thirties and women in their mid-teens, and given the average lifespan of people at that time, it becomes clear that Savonarola's "older widows" are nothing more than women past their prime marriageable years, that is, past their teens, but still in their twenties or thirties. Savonarola is therefore not protesting against teenage males chasing after post-menopausal women (as a modern misreading might lead us to believe), but rather against young men in the prime of their adulthood lusting after women who may very well be their contemporaries. While the average Florentine male in his late twenties/early thirties would still be nubile and considered young (that is, a *giovane*),[25] the average Florentine woman at this same age would probably have been married already for ten or more years; she would be mother to several children, and possibly even a widow. While he was looking to start a family, she had already finished hers. Whatever their place in the social order, however, these nubile men and widowed women in their twenties or thirties were both still sexually alive and quite possibly even mutually attracted to each other. Savonarola's injunction to widows to beware of young men may, then, be nothing more than an injunction to women in the prime of their adult life to beware of their male

[23] Savonarola, *Libro della vita viduale*, 1:15–16; Savonarola, *The Book of the Widow*, 193–94.

[24] Savonarola, *The Book of the Widow*, 210; "el fuoco della concupiscenzia tanto in noi dura quanto dura la carne nel corpo nostro": Savonarola, *Libro della vita viduale*, 1:38.

[25] On the question of age classifications in Florentine society, see Ilaria Taddei, "*Puerizia*, *Adolescenza*, and *Giovinezza*: Images and Conceptions of Youth in Florentine Society During the Renaissance," in *The Premodern Teenager: Youth in Society 1150–1650*, ed. Konrad Eisenbichler (Toronto: Centre for Reformation and Renaissance Studies, 2002), 15–26; and Ludovica Sebregondi, "Clothes and Teenagers: What Young Men Wore in Fifteenth-Century Florence," in *The Premodern Teenager*, 27–50.

contemporaries, also in the prime of their adult life. The need to control the sexuality of widowed women thus becomes an important consideration for the social peace of a community that sought to marry teenage girls to men a generation older than they.

Sexual temptation and misbehavior were not the only problems associated with widows. Taking care of these widows was also a major concern for Florentine society. When women lost their husbands, many also lost the material, social, and even emotional support such husbands provided. If a widow was young enough, she could try to find another man willing to assume responsibility for her, that is, someone to marry her. Savonarola, as we have seen, strongly encouraged this solution. However, widowed women were not a high commodity on the Florentine marriage market and therefore remarriage was often not feasible. The alternative was to remove these women from the marriage market and to place them in a convent where they would be cared for by the institution's administration and by its network of charitable supporters. Inside a convent, widowed women became not only less of a drain on their family's wealth, but also less of a risk to the *onore* of both the paternal and the marital families.[26] The demographic explosion of the fifteenth century led to a proliferation of convents. Richard Trexler points out that "between 1470 and 1550 the number of religious houses for women doubled and their population grew to the point where in the mid-sixteenth century some 13 percent of the total female population of Florence lived behind their walls!"[27]

Trexler has also examined the creation, in the late fourteenth century, of a lay hospice for widowed working-class women, the Orbatello. Such an institution was unusual for its time. It was, to put it in modern terms, an "apartment complex" or, better still, a "gated community" where widows lived on their own, keeping and raising their children, going out during the day to work, and returning to it at night to lead a fairly normal family life with their children. At times, members of their extended family moved in with them and, at times, when they were old and alone, single women moved in with each other to form mutually supportive groupings of two widows living together. Adult males were not allowed in the Orbatello, and male children were expected to leave it once they reached adolescence. The women governed themselves and their community so well that, as Trexler points out, the "Orbatello owed some of its evident stability to the self-administration of its matrons."[28] The Orbatello was, in short, a matriarchy of widows.

---

[26] On the risk to both families, see Klapisch-Zuber, *Women, Family, and Ritual*, 119–20.

[27] Richard C. Trexler, *Power and Dependence in Renaissance Florence*, 2: *The Women of Renaissance Florence*. (Binghamton, NY: Medieval & Renaissance Texts & Studies, 1993), 89–90.

[28] Trexler, *The Women of Renaissance Florence*, 85.

But this was an exceptional case. The Orbatello provided a very limited solution to the problem because it cared for, at most, 250 women. The thousands of widowed women living in Florence were thus obliged to rely on more traditional alternatives: the family or the convent.

If we take all these factors into consideration, we realize that Savonarola's advice to widows was predicated both by the severity of the demographic crisis in the growing female population of the city and by the need to provide widows with living arrangements that were economically, socially, and morally acceptable to a thriving mercantile community with a profound sense of Christian spirituality. As we saw, his first response was for young widows to remarry. This immediately solved the economic and moral problem by directing widows back into the arms of a husband who assumed responsibility for them and thereby released the State and the Church from such an obligation. Remarriage, however, was not without its spiritual drawbacks, for it prolonged the dangers inherent in a life of carnal relationships. So, Savonarola's second suggestion was for widows to withdraw completely from society and to enter into a life of prayer away from worldly cares and temptations. Aware, however, that not all widows could pursue this path, Savonarola's third suggestion was for widows to remain in the marital household and to dedicate themselves to the care of their families. In Florence there were many widows who helped out in the management of the family and the household. Some even assumed complete and sole responsibility for the well-being of their children. Their shoulders carried the entire weight of the family. We have seen such a case in the working-class women of the Orbatello and among upper-class widows such as Alessandra Macinghi Strozzi. This last type of widow, however, was something Savonarola was clearly aware of, and something that he could accept as a reality of life, but it was not something he could recommend as an ideal. For him, as for St. Antoninus and most pre-modern Florentine men, the "true widow" was a woman who had renounced the world and contracted a spiritual marriage with the ultimate husband: the resurrected Jesus waiting for her in their heavenly home.

Lollardy and the Integrity of Marriage and the Family

Dyan Elliott

By the later Middle Ages, the church had secured a near hegemony over marriage, emerging as its uncontested and, in many ways, unstinting guardian. This position of control was not necessarily an obvious one. Due to a marked privileging of chastity and an incumbent disparagement of sexual activity, the church's interest in marriage and enthusiasm for the married state had vacillated between hostile avoidance and tepid support in patristic times, and only gradually picked up momentum in the Carolingian period. Ecclesiastical authority over marriage began to be consolidated in the twelfth century when, in response to the dualist threat presented by the heretical Cathars, the church launched a vigorous defense of marriage. Part of its protective strategy was the inclusion of marriage in what emerged as the canonized list of seven sacraments.[1] It was not long before the proposition that marriage was the business of ecclesiastical courts went largely uncontested.

England, in part sustained by its centralized government and strong episcopacy, had been spared the various waves of heresy that seemed to have afflicted the continent. But in the late fourteenth century England would develop its own indigenous heresy in the form of Lollardy, a puritanically-inflected reform movement that originated in the teachings of the Oxford theologian, John Wyclif.[2] Wyclif's reforming initiative was originally leveled against ecclesiastical luxury and large landholdings — a critique shared by other progressive academics. Yet by the end of his career, Wyclif's philosophical leanings and reforming instincts led him to challenge what he perceived as the innovations of the medieval church.[3] Eventually the church hierarchy, its courts and its laws, the monastic orders

---

[1] See Gabriel Le Bras, "La doctrine du mariage chez les théologiens et les canonistes depuis l'an mil," in *Dictionnaire de théologie catholique*, ed. A. Vacant et al. (Paris: Librairie Letouzey et Ané, 1927), 9:2196–2220.

[2] On Wyclif's career and reforming tendencies, see K. B. McFarlane, *John Wycliffe and the Beginnings of English Nonconformity* (London: English Universities Press, 1952), and Curtis Bostick, *The Antichrist and the Lollards: Apocalypticism in Late Medieval and Reformation England* (Leiden: Brill, 1998), 56–75. Also see the summary accounts in Richard Rex, *The Lollards* (New York: Palgrave, 2002), 25–51, and M. D. Lambert, *Medieval Heresy: Popular Movements from the Gregorian Reform to the Reformation*, 2nd ed. (Oxford: Blackwell, 1992), 225–42.

[3] See Gordon Leff, "The Place of Metaphysics in Wyclif's Theology," in *From Ockham to Wyclif*, ed. Anne Hudson and Michael Wilks, Studies in Church History, Subsidia 5 (Oxford: Blackwell, 1987), 217–32.

(particularly the mendicants), many of the sacraments, and devotional acts like pilgrimage or the veneration of saints were all rejected. Since the true church was seen as consisting of all good men predestined to salvation, Wyclif further advocated the translation of scripture into the vernacular, doing away with the mediation of clerical interpreters. For their own part, members of the laity were not only justified in refusing the ministrations of the priesthood but were even called upon to reform the church — forcibly, if need be.

Wyclif's reform very soon broke loose from its scholastic moorings, at which point it spread among the lower clergy and the semi-literate artisan class.[4] Its success with this audience presupposed considerable skill on behalf of the heretical preachers at adapting a rigorous intellectual heresy to popular tastes, a success largely achieved by rendering its polemic personal and concrete. In particular, the evils afflicting the ecclesiastical macrocosm were reconfigured to suit the microcosmic domestic circles to which Lollardy was now limited. At the very vanguard of this polemical transformation was the Lollard presentation of marriage and the family. The central strategy was to depict these intimate institutions as beleaguered and urgently in need of vigorous defense. This platform constrasted markedly with the positions of most continental sects which exhibited dualist or antinomian leanings, thus tending to devalue or undermine marriage. But when Lollardy reversed these coordinates the primary foe envisaged was not, of course, these other heretics but the very ecclesiastical authorities who stood as marriage's self-appointed guardians. This paper examines Lollard sermons and polemical literature with a view to understanding how this concern was wielded both as a device for unifying and consolidating its constituency and as a potent agent for proselytization.

Lollard polemics presented the church as not simply an unwitting destabilizing force but as a deliberate enemy of the family unit, bombarding it with a series of creative and unrelenting arguments. On a macrocosmic level, church hostility to marriage was conveyed through the ideology and implementation of canon law. Lollard apprehension of the church's judicial system was grounded in

[4] On the origins of Lollardy, see Anne Hudson, *The Premature Reformation: Wycliffite Texts and Lollard History* (Oxford: Clarendon Press, 1988), esp. chap. 3; Rex, *The Lollards*, 54–74, and Lambert, *Medieval Heresy*, 243–59. On the question of Lollard literacy and education, see A. Hudson, "'*Laicus litteratus*': The Paradox of Lollardy," in *Heresy and Literacy, 1000–1530*, ed. Peter Biller and eadem (Cambridge: Cambridge University Press, 1994), 222–36; and Rita Copeland, *Pedagogy, Intellectuals, and Dissent in the Later Middle Ages: Lollardy and Ideas of Learning* (Cambridge: Cambridge University Press, 2001), esp. 8–18, 114–124. For the kind of texts that disseminated the Lollard platform, see A. Hudson, "A Lollard Compilation and the Dissemination of Wycliffite Thought," in *Lollards and their Books* (London: Hambledon, 1985), 13–29. Also see Shannon McSheffrey, *Gender and Heresy: Women and Men in Lollard Communities, 1420–1530* (Philadelphia: University of Pennsylvania Press, 1995), esp. 58–60, 70–72.

the conviction that judgment was reserved for God alone. The dispensations allotted by ecclesiastical courts were, at best, meddlesome and blasphemous, but at worst destructive. The fact that there was no authorization in scripture for canon law sustained this position. The essential conservatism of the Lollard stance is expressed in the following passage:

> Thei chesen newe lawis maad of synful men & worldly & coueytise prestis and clerkis to reule the peple bi hem as most nedful and best lawis, & forsaken the perfiteste lawe of the gospel . . . for now hethene mennus lawis and worldly clerkis statutis ben red in vnyversitees, & curatis lernen hem faste with grete desir, studie & cost, but the lawe of god is litel studied . . . and lesse kept and taught.[5]

Marriage was thus the hostage of sinful and fallible men — devoid of any authority, motivated by greed and lust for power — who rejected scripture in favor of a pagan and worldly code. This was the weapon they wielded in order to penetrate and disrupt the most important aspects of family life.

The ecclesiastical courts' motives for sanctioning sinful affronts like adultery, incestuous marriages, and divorce were perceived as entirely mercenary. In the treatise *On the Seven Deadly Sins*, for example, marriage between blood and affinal relations is categorized under lechery; the ecclesiastical courts, for their part, are prepared to condone this abomination in return for financial gain.[6] The flipside of ecclesiastical support of invalid unions is the ease with which church jurists accommodated the dissolution of a marriage. Canon lawyers are repeatedly accused of facilitating divorce "bi false witnesse & othere cautelis (tricks), & [they] so reisen debatis & enemytes bitwene weddid men & here (their) wiwes bi many priue menys of anticrist."[7] The *Lanterne of Light* (1409–15) offers a cynical and explicit account of how the lechery of the laity and the avarice of the canonists work together to promote bigamy. The process is set in motion when the devil sows strife between the married couple:

> Thanne the man feyneth (fashions) a cause (reason); to go fro this womman . . . . He cumeth anoon to the chirche; that is clepid (called) laweles/ Not for the chirche. but for (because of) the officeris . . . . He chesith (chooses) him a notarie; & paieth him his wagis/ to make him an instrument; of his forgid lesing (false lying)/ thanne goith he to the maistris (i.e., canon lawyers); that sitten on her seetis (seats)/ with furid hoodis and fonned heedis (foolish heads); & gyueth hem (them) money greet plente/ and preieth hem

[5] *The Office of Curates* c. 25, *EW*, 157; cf. *Three Things Destroy this World*, *EW*, 184–85. On the Lollard critique of canon law, see Bostick, *The Antichrist*, 102–13.

[6] *On the Seven Deadly Sins* c. 29, *SEW*, 3:162.

[7] *Three Things*, *EW*, 185.

> to be his voketis (advocates) that this devorse were mad/ for he wole be redi at the laweles dae/ to ring forthe his twelueth hand aforn the iugge Sir Symound/ and make a good with al the court that he hath no rigt to the woman that he weddid for dedis don aforn/ Thanne sir Symound gyueth his doom (judgment); to dissolue trewe wedlock/ & autoriseth lecherie; in thise bothe partiees for to lyue in hoordam (whoredom); fro that dai forward/ & sendith hem forthe at dyuerse (different) doris; departid iche from othir.[8]

The cleric authorizing the divorce is appropriately named "Sir Symound," signifying that the orthodox clergy was rife with simony — the sin of trafficking in the gifts of the Holy Spirit. For many Lollards, this offense undercut the efficacy of the sacraments altogether. From the perspective of one polemicist, even the official insistence on banns prior to the exchange of vows, although implemented "for good entent," has now been "turned into coveitise and raveyn and symonye . . . . For prestis han many yeer seld thus this sacrament, therfore it is nowe lawe and privylegie of the Chirche." The awareness that ecclesiastical control over marriage was a gradual development accomplished over a prolonged period of time justifies the author's rejection of the church's hegemony. And since clandestine marriages were still considered valid, although only grudgingly so, canon lawyers would have been compelled to admit that the ecclesiastical presence was otiose.[9]

Thus the church blessing contributed nothing to the bond. In fact, a simoniacal ceremony could even be perceived as detrimental to the purity of the central exchange of promises, which is the essence of the sacrament. Significantly, this polemic did not challenge the sacramental status of marriage, an institution that most Lollard preachers sought to dignify, but rather the church's role in its formation. We can see an extreme articulation of this position in the actual trials of Lollards themselves. Thus Hawisia Moone, tried before the bishop of Norwich in 1430, would advance "that oonly consent of love betuxe man and woman, withoute contract of wordis and withoute solennizacion in Churche and withoute symbred askyng, is sufficient for the sacrament of matrymoyn."[10] Not only

---

[8] *The Lanterne of Light*, ed. Lilian Swinburn, c. 12, *EETS*, o.s. 151 (London: Kegan Paul, 1917; reprt. 1971), 124–25. Also with respect to both dispensations for marriage and divorce, see *The Leaven of Pharisees* c. 6, *EW*, 20; *The Chirche and hir Membris* c. 5, *SEW*, 3:348–49.

[9] See *The Grete Sentence of Curs Expouned* c. 6, *SEW*, 3:284–285; cf. the contestation over baptism and confirmation (*SEW* c. 6, 3:285). On clandestine marriages, see Michael Sheehan, "The Formation and Stability of Marriage in Fourteenth-Century England: Evidence of an Ely Register," in idem, *Marriage, Family, and Law in Medieval Europe* (Toronto: University of Toronto Press, 1997), 45, 55–62.

[10] *Heresy Trials in the Diocese of Norwich, 1428–31*, ed. Norman Tanner (London: Royal Historical Society, 1977), 141.

does Hawisia dispense with banns and ecclesiastical sanction, but she also eliminates the articulation of vows: the bare necessities for the canonists' definition of *matrimonium de praesenti*.[11] A severe minimalist, Hawisia even regards the verbal agreement as extraneous in view of the couple's inner harmony. Hawisia's dismissal of the sacrament of baptism should probably be placed on a continuum with her radically simple, but exalted, view of marriage insofar as the children of believers would already be full members of the Christian community.[12]

The Lollard critique extended beyond the larger framework of ecclesiastical institutions to include the failings of individual clerics as well. Hence the Lollard indictment of clerical celibacy turned upon the cases of abuse fostered by the practice. Generally, Lollardy was prepared to recognize that celibacy was, at least in theory, a higher path than marriage — a position which Wyclif himself probably shared.[13] The author of the treatise *Of Weddid Men and Wifis* makes this admission readily and at length.[14] Yet while clerical celibacy may have remained unchallenged as the nobler path, the Lollards tended to maintain that the very fragility of human nature made this level of perfection impossible for most. As the author of *The Order of Priesthood* observes, it is folly for a frail priest to take a vow of celibacy since St. Paul himself could scarcely withstand the temptations of the flesh.[15] Some of the calamitous results eventuating from these misguided vows were already made explicit in the *Twelve Conclusions of the Lollards*, a declaration nailed to the doors of Westminster Hall during the 1395 session of Parliament. The third conclusion perceives clerical continence as prejudicial to women and productive of sodomitical relations; the eleventh conclusion alleges that vows of continence among women eventuate in abortion and infanticide.[16]

---

[11] On exchange of consent *de praesenti*, see M. Sheehan, "Marriage Theory and Practice in the Conciliar Legislation and Diocesan Statutes of Medieval England," in idem, *Marriage, Family, and Law*, 154–66.

[12] Tanner, ed., *Heresy Trials*, 140.

[13] See H. C. Lea, *The History of Sacerdotal Celibacy*, 3rd rev. ed. (London: Ballantyne and Co., 1907), 1:474–75.

[14] *Of Weddid* c. 1, *SEW*, 3:190; cf. *De papa* c. 8, *EW*, 474.

[15] *The Order of Priesthood* c. 9, *EW*, 170.

[16] *SFEWW*, 25, 28. The Latin text appears in the collection attributed to Thomas Netter, *Fasciculi zizaniorum magistri Johnannis Wyclif cum tritico*, ed. Walter Shirley (London: Longman, Brown, Green, Longmans, and Roberts, 1858), 360–69. On the different Latin and vernacular versions of the *Conclusions*, see Hudson, *Premature Reformation*, 49 and nn. 225, 226. Hudson argues for the primacy of the English version. Note that an orthodox rejoinder to the Twelve Conclusions accused the Lollards themselves of sodomy. See Carolyn Dinshaw, *Getting Medieval: Sexualities and Communities, Pre- and Postmodern* (Durham, NC: Duke University Press, 1999), esp. 67 ff.

An unchaste cleric was automatically implicated in a grim series of adulteries which were enacted on both temporal and spiritual planes. Transgressing against his commitment to God, such a cleric is frequently compared with loose women — a fornicating queen, a strumpet, a rebellious wife.[17] "For, right as a wiif in a worldli mannys house, rebel agenst hir lord or housbonde, most teneth and troublith the lord and his meyne, so hit is of the rebel clerge that schuld [be] the most obedient and seruiable parte in Cristis spouse, that is his chirche."[18] The sexually active priest violates his own marriage with Christ in favor of Antichrist so that, in the opinion of one reformer, "more foule devorse was nevere none made."[19] In a similar vein, the treatise *De officio pastorali* denounces a clergy bound neither by legitimate human marriage, nor the wedding with the church inherent in the office, nor even by the soul's marriage with God. Such offenders should be disciplined by a lay boycott of their masses, a remedy pioneered by the Gregorian reformers of the eleventh century.[20] The treatise *De precationibus sacris* even cites the original canon issued by Nicholas II in 1059 almost verbatim.[21] Yet while such drastic measures were originally taken with a view to centralizing the church around the reforming papacy, the Lollard implementation of the lay boycott was for opposite, centrifugal ends. The fornicating priest, moreover, harmed much more than his own soul: "here blessynge turneth into cursyinge, and here preiere turneth into synne," drawing his own Donatist and, hence, quasi-heretical, conclusions on this score.[22]

From a quasi-Donatist perspective, all clerical incontinence, be it heterosexual or same-sex activity, had the potential to denigrate the sacraments and wreak spiritual havoc on Christendom. But the Lollard preachers chose to stress heterosexual abuses — a decision that was both on a continuum with the traditional taciturnity surrounding sodomy and consistent with their concern for the integrity of the family unit.[23] Illegitimate clerical households, supporting long-term concubines and their offspring, were perceived as a drain on the laity's resources and

[17] *Titus Tract, The Works of a Lollard Preacher*, ed. Anne Hudson, EETS, o.s. 310, pt. 2 (Oxford: Oxford University Press, 2001), 189.

[18] *Titus Tract, Works of a Lollard Preacher*, ed. Hudson, 184.

[19] *On the Seven Deadly Sins* c. 30, *SEW*, 3:163.

[20] *De officio pastorali* c. 19, *EW*, p. 435. The lay boycott was advocated by Wycliff. See Lea, *History of Sacerdotal Celibacy*, 1:460, 473–74.

[21] *De precationibus sacris* c. 3, *SEW*, 3:224; Romanum Concilium, 1059 c. 3, ed. G. D. Mansi, *Sacrorum conciliorum nova et amplissima collectio* (Paris: Hubert Welter, 1902), 19:878.

[22] *De precationibus* c. 3, *SEW*, 3:224.

[23] See Mark Jordan, *The Invention of Sodomy in Christian Theology* (Chicago: University of Chicago Press, 1997), 106, 111, 150–51.

were bitterly resented. For "it is yvel to kepe a wast hors in stable to destrie pore mennus godis, but it is worse to have a womman with-ynne or with-oute at racke & at manger, for this holding is more costly & more wast to body & soul."[24] It was widely advocated that tithes be witheld from such offenders.[25]

But more dangerous still were the clerics who perpetrated covert seduction upon the unwitting households of their spiritual charges. Staggering under the insupportable burden of clerical celibacy — a discipline with no biblical warrant that was all too often used to disparage marriage — clerics, particularly friars, become the seducers of other men's wives.[26] In many ways, the Lollard critique of the mendicant orders conformed to the contours of antifraternal sentiment in orthodoxy.[27] Once again, however, the Lollard reformers succeeded in outstripping their orthodox counterparts even on a quantitative level. A recent count reveals that the greatest number of antifraternal poems in the English tradition were produced by the Lollards.[28] Doubtless a count of Wycliffite sermons would reveal a similar ratio. Their prolixity was matched by their vehemence — a vehemence that went beyond orthodox limits.

The charges against the friars threatened to become as ubiquitous as the friars themselves were perceived to be. A sermon, the foundational scriptural text for which is Christ's warning against "the leaven of Pharisees, which is hypocrisy" (Lk. 12:1), renders a particularly fulsome account of seduction. Like the mendicant Daun John of Chaucer's Summoner's Tale, although stripped of all humor, the Lollard-confected friars play on women's native fatuousness and credulity. While perpetrating sodomy among themselves, they also

> . . . seyn to nyse (foolish) wymmen that it is lesse synne to trespase with hem than with othere weddid men . . . . Thei studien on the holy day aboute experymentis or wiche craft or veyn songis and knackynge (tricky music) and

[24] *De officio pastorali* c. 19, *EW*, 435.

[25] See, for example, the constant repetition of this point in *De officio pastorali* c. 8, 10, 19, *EW*, 418, 421, 436. Adherents such as Hawisia Moone were also of this opinion (Tanner, ed., *Heresy Trials*, 141).

[26] See, for example, *Of the Leaven* c. 2, *EW*, 6–7; *Of Prelates* c. 35, *EW*, 100. Cf. Thomas Renna, "Wyclif's Attacks on Monks," in *From Ockham to Wyclif*, ed. Hudson and Wilks, 267–80.

[27] One friar even appears in Langland's *Piers Plowman* as Sire *Penetrans domos*. See Wendy Scase, *Piers Plowman and the New Anticlericalism* (Cambridge: Cambridge University Press, 1989), 1, 15–16, 32–39. The name is an allusion to 2 Timothy 3:1–6, which denounces the haughty religious "who make their way into houses [*qui penetrant domos*] and captivate silly women": Penn Szittya, *The Antifraternal Tradition in Medieval Literature* (Princeton: Princeton University Press, 1986), 1.

[28] Szittya, *Antifraternal Tradition*, 195.

> harpynge, gyternynge (strumming) & daunsynge & othere veyn triflis . . . . Thei feynen (pretend) hem sotil (cunning) of fisik and knowynge of wymmenys complexcion and preuyte (secrets), seiynge that siche siknesse or deth schal com to hem in absence of here housbondis but yif (unless) thei haue mannus helpe, and thus defoulen (defile) on and other . . . . Thei leden a-wey mennus wyues or wenches in here newe habitis, to do lecherie bi hem as hem liste . . . . Thei maken wyues and other wymmen hure (their) sustris bi lettris of fraternite and othere iapes (tricks), and geten children vpon hem.[29]

The mendicants are thus viewed as mobilizing every prerogative associated with their vocation for their nefarious purposes. Thus they speciously argue that the woman sins less with a cleric than with the husband of another, trading on their celibate state to recommend themselves as superior lovers. Their privileged access to medicine afforded them by their university training (an institutional instrument of the devil, according to some moralists)[30] is wielded to give them special knowledge, and hence power, over women's bodies.[31] The friars' encouragement of women pursuing a religious vocation in secular society through the tertiary orders, indicated in their bestowal of "newe habitis" and their efforts to "maken wyues . . . hure sustris," is recast as yet another transparent ploy for seduction.

Auricular confession — regarded by Lollard moralists as a pseudo-sacrament since it also lacked an explicit biblical foundation — was believed to be frequently bent to the friars' lecherous ends, resulting in the spread of bastardy.[32] And the

[29] *Of the Leaven* c. 2, ed. Matthew, *EW*, 6; c. 3, 8–9; c. 3, 10; c. 3, 12.

[30] See a letter in which "Satan" describes how he gradually debauched the friars, first tempting them to abandon poverty, then to beg for alms, "and sone aftur thei went to scoole and began to savor of our lernyng, and than thei preachyd because men shuld haue them in more fauor" (*Epistola Sathanae ad cleros*, in *SFEWW*, 92).

[31] On the medical interest in the woman's body in theological circles, see the anonymous Dominican's incredibly misogynistic *Women's Secrets: A Translation of Pseudo-Albertus Magnus's 'De secretis mulierum' with Commentaries*, trans. Helen Rodnite Lemay (Albany: State University of New York Press, 1992).

[32] *The Grete Sentence* c. 13, *SEW*, 3:304. Also see *Of Confession, EW*, 329–35; cf. serm. 209, *EWSer*, 3:254. On confession as an innovation of the papacy, see serm. 52, *EWSer*, 1:460; *Of Mynystris in the Chirche, EWSer*, 2:361. This was also one of the *Twelve Conclusions (SFEWW*, no. 9, 27; Netter, ed., *Fasciculi zizaniorum*, 365). Also see Gradon and Hudson's discussion in *EWSer*, 4:44–47. The canon lawyer Panormitanus (d. 1445) conceded that there is not any overt authority indicating divine institution of confession to a priest (*Commentaria in quartum et quintum Decretalium Librum* [London: Cum privilegio regis Philippo Tinghio, 1586], vol. 3, fol. 256r, ad X.5.38.12, *Omnis utriusque* [= Lat. IV, c. 21]). On the introduction of auricular confession in the high Middle Ages, see Dyan Elliott, *Proving Woman: Female Spirituality and Inquisitional Culture in the Later Middle Ages* (Princeton: Princeton University Press, 2004), 9–14.

extraneous nature of confession is, in fact, an area in which the church was extremely vulnerable. Auricular confession was only made mandatory for Latin Christendom at the Fourth Lateran Council of 1215 under Innocent III, who also sanctioned the formation of the mendicant orders.[33] The mendicants were immediately required to supplement the parochial clergy's labors in their newly acquired task of hearing confession and were, thus, particularly implicated in the emergence of this sacrament.[34] Moreover, the Lollards were not alone in their fear of the potential sexual opportunities afforded under the pretext of confession. Confessors' manuals were constantly presenting ingenious ways to minimize contact between the confessor and their female penitents.[35] Pastoral theologians simultaneously exhibited considerable concern that the affective bond which often developed between confessor and penitent might exceed the limits of spiritual love.[36]

---

[33] Lat. IV, c. 21 in Norman Tanner, ed., *Decrees of the Ecumenical Councils* (London: Sheed and Ward, 1990), 1:245.

[34] For the relation between preaching and hearing confession, see Roberto Rusconi, "De la prédication à la confession: transmission et contrôle de modèles de comportement au XIIIe siècles," in *Faire Croire: Modalités de la diffusion et de la réception des messages religieux du XIIe au XVe siècle* (Rome: Ecole Française de Rome, 1981), 67–85; and Lester Little, "Les techniques de la confession et la confession comme technique," in *Faire Croire*, 88–89.

[35] Raymond of Peñafort, *Summa de poenitentia et matrimonio* 3.34.30 (Rome: Joannes Tallini, 1603), 464–65; Jean Gerson, *De cognitione castitatis*, in *Oeuvres complètes*, ed. Palémon Glorieux (Paris: Desclée, 1973), 9:63; Antoninus of Florence, *Confessionale Anthonini* 3.11 (Paris: Jehan Petit, 1507?), fol. 28r. Antoninus' solution is not unlike one Lollard compromise proposed: recommending that two priests be present for a woman's confession (*Of Confession*, *EW*, 335–36). See Alexander Murray, "Counselling in Medieval Confession," in *Handling Sin: Confession in the Middle Ages*, ed. Peter Biller and Alastair Minnis, Studies in Medieval Theology 2 (York: York Medieval Press in association with Boydell and Brewer, 1998), 72–73; Dyan Elliott, "Women and Confession: From Empowerment to Pathology," in *Gendering the Master Narrative: Women and Power in the Middle Ages*, ed. Maryanne Kowaleski and Mary Erler, (Ithaca: Cornell University Press, 2003), 31-51, here 44.

[36] Thomas of Cantimpré relates many hortatory anecdotes on the dangers besetting so-called spiritual relationships between the sexes. See his *Bonum universale de apibus* 2.30.44–47 (Douai: B. Belleri, 1627), 348–53. The dangers of confusing spiritual with carnal love is also an important theme in the literature of spiritual discernment. See Henry of Friemar, *De quatuor instinctibus*, in *Insignis atque preclarus de deliciiis sensibilibus paradisi liber: cum singulari tractatu de quatuor instinctibus* (Venice: Iacobus Pentius, 1498), 4th sign. fol. 61r; Jean Gerson, *De probatione spirituum*, in *Oeuvres complètes*, ed. Glorieux, 9:180, 184 (bis); trans. Paschal Boland, *The Concept of 'Discretio spirituum' in John Gerson's 'De probatione spirituum'* (Washington, D.C.: Catholic University Press, 1959), 30, 36–37.

Moreover, to a society obsessed with lineage, the fear of an adulterous wife covertly introducing a spurious heir was omnipresent. Authors of confessors' manuals had also agonized over what to advise the female penitent who confessed to having secretly practised such a deception.[37] In pursuing this vexed issue, Lollard preachers were playing upon anxieties that were deeply rooted in clerical and lay society alike. Furthermore, rhetorically seeking to heap insult on injury, the anonymous writer of *The Leaven of Pharisees* even suggests that the lecherous friar acted with malicious intent "to maken false heiris and to for-do the kynde of men." The wretched offspring of such illicit unions are expressly conceived for the purpose of replenishing these despised religious orders.[38] Little wonder that among the charges against the Lollard defendant Richard Wyche was the alleged assertion that bastards, particularly those of the clergy, cannot be saved.[39]

Not content with furtively undermining the family through the bastards begotten on other men's wives, however, the mendicants perpetrated yet another form of seduction by abducting the legitimate offspring for the purpose of perpetuating their own kind. With the relentless success of a Pied Piper, the friars approached children who were under the age of consent and tempted them with feasts, apples, money, or else beguiled them with lies about the superiority of their order and a secure guarantee of salvation.[40] An older, more worldly, child may have been promised worldly honor and welfare, or even "wombe ioie and ydelnesse." The child was often led to "ferre contres fro here frendis and [thei] holde hem cloos til thei ben professid agenst here will, an than thei suffre hem not to goo out thoug thei ben vnable to kepe this religion."[41] The end result was always the same: the once innocent child became a "child of helle" who often was "worse than her bewperis (ecclesiastical superiors)."[42] The abandoned family was, in turn, depicted as emotionally and economically destitute: "For sumtyme thes

[37] See Robert Courson's discussion of this predicament in V. L. Kennedy, ed., "Robert Courson on Penance," *Mediaeval Studies* 7 (1945): 320–21, c. 10.

[38] *Of the Leaven* c. 2, *EW*, 6–7; also see c. 3, 12. Note the repeated legislation enacted to remove the stigma of illegitimacy by both ecclesiastical and, to some extent, secular authorities. The impediments against such a child entering holy orders were also gradually lifted (Lea, *History of Sacerdotal Celibacy*, 1:416–21).

[39] Netter, ed., *Fasciculi zizaniorum*, 367–68; 380–81.

[40] *De blasphemia, contra freris* pt. 2, SEW, 3:416; *Of Poor Preaching Priests*, EW, 278; *Epistola Sathanae*, SFEWW, 92.

[41] *How Religious Men Shoulde Kepe Certayne Articles* c. 29–31, EW, 22; cf. *Of Poor Preaching Priests*, EW, 278.

[42] *The Ecclesiastical Hierarchy*, SFEWW, 76.

children frendis fallen in mornynge to deth; & sumtyme bi myschef ben dede where here children thus stolen schulden ellis helpe hem."[43]

The mendicants' greed was perceived to be fully equal to their lust. In their tireless pursuit of alms, presented as yet another form of seduction, the friars make overtures to various members of the family, encouraging "wyues, prentis (apprentices), seruauntis and children to stele fro here housbondis, maistris and fadir and modir,"[44] all the time revelling in this domestic anarchy. One treatise bearing the revealing title *Fifty Heresies and Errors of the Friars* thus simulates mendicant delight over the moral and financial ruin of the lay family.

> Lete olde curatis waxe roten in synne, and lete hom not do hor offis by Gods lawe, and we wil lyve in lustis so longe, and waste veyneliche and nedeles sixty thousande marke by yeere of tho pore comyns of tho lond; and so at tho laste make discencioun bytwene hom and hor childre, for dymes (tithes) and offringes that we wl gete prively to us by ypocrisie.[45]

Thus the mendicant orders were understood to be in tacit competition with the family. The latter's loss was the friars' gain.

Women are perceived as the most willing and profligate of almsgivers and therefore the single most important factor in the depletion of familial resources. Moreover, their frivolity extends beyond the family unit, harming the few good priests who remain in the church. Thus when the title of a treatise poses the probing question *Why Poor Priests have no Benefice*, one of the answers put forward is that ladies prefer priests who can dance, hunt, hawk, play summer games, flatter, and send gifts.[46] Wives are especially susceptible to solicitations when their husbands are away from home.[47] Hence, it naturally follows that widows are an especially easy mark since, according to *The Lanterne of Light*: "wommen that ben weddid; and vndir the power of mannes daunger dore not gyue thise wordli goodis; withouten counseile of her housbond . . . . Widowes ben ful of pite to give whanne thei ben pitousli axid. and han no man to werne this dede."[48] The widow's potential vulnerability had traditionally won her a place alongside of the orphan as a *miserabilis persona* —a disadvantaged individual who enjoyed the special protection of the church. But widows and orphans needed shielding from their predatory

---

[43] *How Satan and His Priests* c. 3, *EW*, 269.

[44] *Of the Leaven* c. 3, *EW*, 11; cf. *De officio pastorali* c. 22, *EW*, 439–40; *The Grete Sentence* c. 13, *SEW*, 3:302.

[45] *Fifty Heresies* c. 50, *SEW*, 3:401.

[46] *Why Poor Priests have no Benefice* c. 1, *EW*, 246.

[47] *Of Weddid* c. 5, *SEW*, 3:199; *Of the Leaven* c. 6, *SEW*, 3:10.

[48] Swinburn, ed., Lanterne c. 4, 52.

guardians.[49] In keeping with their acquisitive ethos, however, the friars only approached rich widows: the truly helpless and destitute were heartlessly ignored.[50]

Constantly seeking to reveal and denounce the evils of the contemporary church, the negative tenor of Lollard polemic is inescapable. When Lollard reformers attempted to develop a positive kerygma, however, they were frequently distracted. The treatise *Of Weddid Men and Wifis* is typical in this respect. As one might suspect, the author puts to good use whatever positive nuptial imagery can be gleaned from scripture, in many ways paralleling standard orthodox fare. The creation of marriage in paradise, Christ's presence at Cana, and the Pauline imagery of marriage as a figure for Christ's union with the church all receive due attention. Likewise, the important issues of mutual consent, marital chastity, and indissolubility are treated.[51] But in the course of a multi-tiered justification of marriage, apology transgresses against its rhetorical boundaries, crossing over into bitter invective. Any implicit tension between marriage and chastity is accordingly transformed into open warfare. The insistence that God himself made the order of matrimony, but did not make the order of friars, is one in a series of aggressive sallies.[52] Christ's resolve to be born in wedlock, his mother's marriage at the time of conception (versus a simple betrothal), and his presence at Cana (mentioned for a second time) provide further ammunition.[53] But the author soon veers off target to Christ's warning against the heretics who will arrive toward the end of the world forbidding marriage (1 Tim. 4:1-3), followed by a lengthy denunciation of the evils of clerical celibacy. Thus "bi ypocrisie of fendis and fals men, manye bynden hem to presthod and chastite, forsaken wifies bi Goddis lawe." Yet such fulminations are preparatory to the conflicted admission that celibacy is, in fact, the higher state.[54]

---

[49] See *Of Clerks Possessioners* c. 20, *EW*, 129; cf. James Brundage, "Widows as Disadvantaged Persons in Medieval Canon Law," in *Upon My Husband's Death: Widows in the Literature and Histories of Medieval Europe*, ed. Louise Mirrer (Ann Arbor: University of Michigan Press, 1992), 193–206. Anthropologist Jack Goody's interpretation of the church guardianship of widows corresponds exactly with the Lollard reading. See his controversial *The Development of the Family and Marriage in Europe* (Cambridge: Cambridge University Press, 1983).

[50] *How Satan and His Children* c. 6, *EW*, 216. Also see *Tractatus de Pseudo-Freris* c. 4, *EW*, 304; *De officio pastorali*, *EW*, 417; *Images and Pilgrimages*, *SFEWW*, 85; *Vae octuplex*, *EWSer*, 2:368; *Fifty Heresies* c. 27, 3:387–88; Swinburn, ed., *Lanterne* c. 1, 106.

[51] *Of Weddid* c. 1, c. 3, *SEW*, 3:188–89, 194; for the doctrinal issues, see *SEW* c. 2, 3:191–92. On orthodox polemics, see D. L. d'Avray and M. Tausche, "Marriage Sermons in *ad status* Collections in the Central Middle Ages," *Archives d'histoire doctrinale et littéraire du moyen âge* 47 (1980): 71–119.

[52] *Of Weddid* c. 1, *SEW*, 3:189. Cf. *De blasphemia*, pt. 2, *SEW*, 3:417.

[53] *Of Weddid* c. 1, *SEW*, 3:189; cf. serm. 89, *EWSer*, 2:200; serm. 102, *EWSer*, 2:256. The authority of Ambrose is invoked.

[54] *Of Weddid* c. 1, *SEW*, 3:190.

Although the Lollard identity was largely constructed from what the reformers sought to stigmatize, there were certain select subjects about which they were prepared to be positive. One of these was the role of the husband. And this is to be expected. Perceiving the leadership of the church as failing, Wyclif himself had looked to the secular lords for the reformation of the church. The ultimate moral responsibility for the family and, on a larger scale, for society itself, was perceived as residing in the male head of household. Hence injunctions regarding his familial obligations are almost interchangeable with his responsibilities in government. *A Schort Reule of Lif*, for example, outlines the lord's responsibilities in the following way. First, he must attend to himself, controlling his five senses and keeping God's commandments. Then he must govern his wife, children, and servants accordingly as their souls are under his protection and he, in turn, would be damned for their evil lives. The third duty is to provide a merciful government and an excellent moral example for his tenants. Finally, it is his task to see that all those who break God's laws are appropriately chastised, while God's true servants should be protected — a task clearly requiring considerable discretion. Not only is it a grievous offense against God to maintain "Antichristi discipulos," but the lord is further enjoined to "warne the pepul of here grete synes, and of fals prestis and ypocritis that disceyvyn Cristen men."[55]

Thus the very substantial power already accorded the husband as head of household traditionally by secular and ecclesiastical authorities alike would be further augmented in Lollardy by his annexation of the spiritual leadership usually reserved for the priesthood. This could entail an even more circumscribed role in marriage for women than is prescribed in orthodox circles. The treatise *Of Weddid Men and Wifis* enlists every conceivable biblical text that points to the wife's requisite subordination to her spouse, drawing heavily upon the conservative pastoral epistles.[56] Although the husband's headship is sacrosanct, he is nevertheless urged not to abuse his position — notably with regard to the sex act. The wife, for her part, is warned against angering her husband and exhorted to persuade him to a virtuous and peace-loving life.[57]

---

[55] *Schort Reule*, *SEW*, 3:206–7. Similar responsibilities are outlined in *Of Servants and Lords*, *EW*, 227–43.

[56] *Of Weddid* c. 3, *SEW*, 3:193–94.

[57] *Of Weddid* c. 5, *SEW*, 3:197–98. Cf. a similar call for sexual restraint in orthodoxy in Dyan Elliott, "Bernardino of Siena versus the Marriage Debt," in *Desire and Discipline: Sex and Sexuality in Premodern Europe*, ed. Jacqueline Murray and Konrad Eisenbichler (Toronto: University of Toronto Press, 1996), 168–200. The advice to the wife parallels orthodox teaching. See particularly Sharon Farmer, "Persuasive Voices: Clerical Images of Medieval Wives," *Speculum* 61 (1986): 517–83.

Women are thus permitted a vague influence, but no real power. Therefore the widespread belief that women found a more equitable role in heresy, a view which receives some vindication on the continent, seems to be confounded by Lollard polemic. In practice, Lollard women were accorded an equally circumscribed role within the sect.[58] The fact that the family, not the church, was the Lollard vehicle of salvation put its seal on women's limited position within the sect — an allotment constantly reinforced by the representation of women as the weak link in the chain of familial integrity. Sometimes this conviction is stated explicitly. The treatise *Of Weddid Men and Wifis* identifies what the author refers to as three common flaws to married life, two of which explicitly target women: that women are prone to mourn their deceased children excessively; and, more to the purpose, that they are inclined to waste "here husbondis goodis" while he is away on business.[59] Yet, despite the wife's alleged shortcomings, she is generally spared the kind of antifeminism which stalks her in orthodoxy.[60] Certainly woman never becomes the occasion for the kind of satire one sometimes glimpses in the Hussite movement — the Czech exponent of Wycliffite ideas.[61] Lollardy's restraint in this respect corresponds with the desire to dignify marriage. Hence Lollard preachers saw no advantage in excessively denigrating either husband or wife. But there is also a sense in which the woman, caught between powerful husband and rapacious friar, is understood to be sufficiently powerless and

---

[58] Cf. McSheffrey's parallel assessment in *Gender and Heresy*, 80–87. McSheffrey's study also suggests that the heightening of patriarchal control is in line with the limited role for women in the Lollard sect (see especially 55–61). Cf. the more estimable role for women in the continental Waldensians, who anticipated the Lollards in many of their reform initiatives (Lambert, *Medieval Heresy*, 160–61).

[59] *Of Weddid* c. 5, *SEW*, 3:199.

[60] Some of the key texts in the orthodox antifeminist tradition have been collected by Alcuin Blamires in *Woman Defamed and Woman Defended: An Anthology of Medieval Texts* (Oxford: Oxford University Press, 1992). The Lollards still make the occasional jibe at the woman's predilection for finery (*Ave Maria, EW*, 205). Moreover, they continue to inhabit the same symbolic framework as orthodoxy, one steeped in antifeminism. Thus, one sermon associates man's errant flesh with a "femele asse" for its frailty, stupidity, and endurance. Its strength is all in the hindquarters. See Gloria Cigman, ed., *Lollard Sermons*, EETS 252 (Oxford:EETS, 1989), no. 1, 5–6.

[61] Katherine Walsh, "Wyclif's Legacy in Central Europe in the Late Fourteenth and Early Fifteenth Centuries," in *From Ockham to Wyclif*, ed. Hudson and Wilks, 397–417. See particularly Alfred Thomas's translation and commentary of a poem depicting a female Hussite attempting to convert a young cleric and Elliott's response ("'The Wycliffite Woman': Reading Women in Fifteenth-Century Bohemia," in *Voices in Dialogue: New Directions in Women's Cultural History*, ed. Kathryn Kerby-Fulton and Linda Olson [Notre Dame, IN: University of Notre Dame Press, forthcoming].

vulnerable as to escape censure altogether. In discussions of adultery, the friars inevitably shoulder the blame that would routinely have been assigned to women in orthodoxy: Lollards cast unfaithful wives as pathetic victims rather than lascivious harlots. Moreover, alleged mental incapacity helps to exculpate women's unfortunate initiative with regard to endowments and alms: "For wymmen ben of schort wyt, thei ben menys to suche dedis; but foly and lustus of men ben ofte more to blame than wymmen. As, yif wymmen knowe not Godus lawe in dowyng of prestus, and it semeth to wymmenys wyt bothe almes and mercy, and thei mouven lordis herto, as thes wymmen duden Eroude, — this synne is in the[s] proctouris, but more in thes lordis."[62] "Thes wymmen" refers to Salome and her mother Herodias, the wife of Herod. Herodias had benefited from her daughter's sexual power over Herod to secure the death of her critic John the Baptist, who denounced Herodias for marrying Herod while her former husband (who happened to be Herod's brother) was still living. The husband who succumbs to uxorial pressures to give alms shares in Herod's susceptibility to the whims of depraved women: bestowing alms is equated with beheading John the Baptist. Moreover, it is the husband Herod who is really to blame for allowing himself to be dominated by women.

The above comparison opens a door onto some of the unacknowledged suppressions that still haunt Lollard rhetoric, suppressions which help to explain part of Lollardy's appeal to heads of households. For if the husband is depicted as Herod, then Salome, the immediate instigator of the Baptist's execution, represents the Lollard wife. Therefore the cleric directing the wife's behavior is tacitly associated with the mastermind behind Salome's seductive antics, Herodias — an illegitimate wife, perhaps, but a true mother. It is not unusual to find the clergy metaphorically embodied by the wife in Lollard letters.[63] But the clergy's gendered role in this particular scenario is extremely germane because, as with the evil Herodias and her equally evil daughter, there is another way of understanding women's relations with the clergy — one in which they emerge as not the clergy's victims, but their co-conspirators. The husband's strategy for holding together the fragile vision of family integrity was by denying the wife's complicity and heaping all the blame on the cleric. But whoever was ultimately understood as culpable,

---

[62] *EWS*, serm. 115, 2:298.

[63] Such analogies were not necessarily disparaging. The conjugal unit is also used as an idiom for conveying the all-important motif of lay access to scripture. John Purvey, secretary to Wyclif, metaphorically evokes how "the housebonde, and the wiffe seyn come; and he that hereth seith he cometh" (Apoc. 22:17), aligning Christ with the husband and the doctors and preachers with the wife. Thus the wife-priest is supposed to second the husband-Christ's invitation to the laity (Margaret Deanesly, ed., *The Lollard Bible* [Cambridge: Cambridge University Press, 1966], app. 2, 439–40).

it was nevertheless the responsibility of the Lollard husband to govern and discipline both of his unruly wives. Thus on the domestic level, he needs to curtail the wife's injudicious impulse to give alms; on a national level, he must discipline the clergy by withholding tithes and divesting them of their vast estates.

There is much to be said for this conspiracy theory. Although the church played a vital role in consolidating the husband's control over his wife, it had also traditionally provided various means for evading this very control by endorsing female piety. Much of Lollardy's negative polemic systematically seeks to undermine these mechanisms. The disparagement of celibacy is a case in point. Although it is impossible to argue that the ecclesiastical idealization of the celibate state worked to the advantage of most women, the church's very disparagement of human sexuality underwrote the efforts of women like Christina of Markyate (d. after 1155), Margery Kempe (d. after 1438), or Margaret Beaufort (d. 1509) to convert their husbands to perpetual chastity — transitions that generally coincided with a relaxation of masculine rule.[64] Initiation into the mendicant tertiary orders and other penitential movements, indicated in the derogatory reference to the "newe habitis" and "sustris bi lettris of fraternite," generally corresponded with a transition to a stricter sexual code, observing the traditional penitential periods.[65] And it was women who were perceived as agitating for these changes.

The denunciation of confession as a sacrament simultaneously abolished the premise for the relations that often ensued between confessors and their penitents. One sermon in particular targeted the habit of great ladies who retained their own private confessors and chaplains, frequently men who were famous in their own right.[66] And yet, as the lives of any number of religiously inclined women of the later Middle Ages suggest, these relationships sometimes benefited both parties. In the case of mystics and their confessors, the spiritual gains were often reciprocal. As John Coakley has demonstrated, the confessor had the effect of validating a given mystic's vocation and provided ready access to the sacraments. The woman, for her part, provided the priest with a special charisma that he lacked.[67] This kind of coalition even offered unprecedented opportunities in public life to a select few. Bridget of Sweden, a recently canonized matron whose cult was immensely popular in England, is a case in point.[68] But these relations

[64] Elliott, *Spiritual Marriage*, 208–9, 211, 251–56.

[65] Elliott, *Spiritual Marriage*, 196–99.

[66] *Of Confession*, *EW*, 334.

[67] John Coakley, "Gender and the Authority of Friars: The Significance of Holy Women for Thirteenth-Century Franciscans and Dominicans," *Church History* 60 (1991): 453–56.

[68] Her revelations were widely circulated in Middle English. See, for example, William Cumming, ed., *The Revelations of Saint Birgitta: Edited from the Fifteenth-Century MS.*

were frequently enriching in other ways as well, again providing a *quid pro quo* that benefited both parties. Thus John Fisher's funeral oration for his pious penitent, Margaret Beaufort, is informed by the ongoing desire to be generous with the woman who had always been so generous with the church.[69] Nor is it surprising that, from an orthodox pastoral perspective, the comparatively smooth edifice of the husband's control was most likely to be eroded over the question of alms. Some authorities even permitted the wife to circumvent the husband's explicit prohibition when it came to almsgiving.[70] A parallel incentive can be discerned in the English Church's efforts to alter Common Law, thus securing a wife the right to make binding wills (some of which would surely benefit the church) without her husband's permission — an initiative that was ultimately defeated.[71]

In short, Lollardy strove to undercut the orthodox coalition between women and the clergy by misrepresenting the nature of the relation; to depict female almsgivers as victims rather than agents was to strip them of their power. Any experimentation with traditional gender roles, a tendency frequently associated with heresy, was likewise eschewed. What Lollardy sought to offer women instead was a protected role within an embattled but resilient family unit in which every member knew their place.

in the Garrett Collection. EETS, o.s. 178 (London: Oxford University Press, 1928; repr. Millwood, N.Y.: Kraus, 1987). The Brigittine order was also extremely popular. See Nancy Warren, *Spiritual Economies: Female Monasticism in Later Medieval England* (Philadelphia: University of Pennsylvania Press, 2001), 44–58.

[69] On Margaret Beaufort, see Brooke, *The Medieval Idea of Marriage*, 34–38. For Fisher's sermon, see John Mayor, ed., *The English Works of John Fisher, Bishop of Rochester*, EETS, e.s. 27, pt. 1 (London: Trübner, 1876), 289–310.

[70] Raymond of Peñafort, *Summa de poenitentia* 2.8.9, 252. See Elliott, *Spiritual Marriage*, 189–90.

[71] M. Sheehan, "The Influence of Canon Law on the Property Rights of Married Women," in idem *Marriage, Family, and Law*, 16–30.

Abbreviations

EETS	Early English Text Society. London: Kegan Paul et al., 1864–.
EW	Matthew, F. D., ed. *The English Works of Wyclif*, 2d ed., EETS, o.s., 74. London: Kegan Paul, 1880; rev. 1902.
EWSer	Hudson, Anne, ed. *English Wycliffite Sermons*. Oxford: Oxford University Press, 1983.
SEW	Arnold, Thomas, ed. *Select English Works of John Wyclif*. Oxford: Clarendon Press, 1871.
SFEWW	Hudson, Anne, ed. *Selections from English Wycliffite Writings*. Cambridge: Cambridge University Press, 1978.

Germanic Marriage: The Case of Medieval Iceland

Jenny Jochens

Medieval Iceland possesses an abundance of sources in narrative genres and in legal texts that describe marriage arrangements in detail. Some narratives, the famous family sagas or sagas of Icelanders, are centered on the pagan pre-literate age. Others, the so-called contemporary sagas, describe the world of the authors of both genres in the thirteenth and fourteenth centuries.[1] The laws were inscribed from the beginning of the twelfth century but had been performed orally for almost two hundred years, and were eventually replaced with newer versions.[2] In other words, the available sources seem to describe pagan as well as Christian times and should make it possible to ascertain the influence of Christianity on the institution of marriage. The problem with this theory is, of course, that pagan Icelanders had not yet made the crucial step from orality to writing. With the exception of skaldic poetry, which is of little use for the purpose of examining marriage, no sources can be said to speak authentically about the pagan age. Christians wrote the texts I have mentioned, and a certain degree of mediation from the new religion is unavoidable. Nonetheless, I shall use the Icelandic sources as evidence for pagan marriage not only among Nordic people, but I shall argue that they may be applicable to the entire Germanic family.

The meager sources available from the Anglo-Saxons and the Continental tribes — like the Nordic evidence this material is divided into narrative and legal texts — conform well to the picture provided by the much richer Icelandic sources. In other words, from the Icelandic evidence it is possible to construct a pagan marriage model that may be valid for the entire Germanic world.

Before we can examine the Germanic marriage model as found in medieval Iceland, it is necessary to investigate whether marriage as an institution was possible there. Norwegians began settling in Iceland from the end of the ninth century. In the manner of Vikings, they first brought few women with them, as

---

[1] The corpus of the family sagas as well as the short stories (*þættir*) can be found in English translation in *The Complete Sagas of Icelanders including 49 Tales*, ed. Viðar Hreinsson, 5 vols. (Reykjavík: Leifur Eiríksson, 1997). The most important contemporary saga, the complex known as *Sturlunga Saga,* is translated into English in *Sturlunga Saga*, trans. Julia H. McGrew and R. George Thomas, 2 vols. (New York: Twayne Publishers, 1970–1974).

[2] The two most important laws are *Grágás* and *Jónsbók*. The former is available in English translation in *Laws of Early Iceland*, trans. Andrew Dennis, Peter Foote, and Richard Perkins, 2 vols. (Manitoba: University of Manitoba Press, 1980–2000). Jana K. Schulman is working on a translation of *Jónsbók*.

evidenced from a remarkable document, the so-called *Landnámabók*, or "The Book of Settlements." First composed in the beginning of the twelfth century, it lists the original settlers and some of their descendants. Among almost 450 named settlers only 90 were women.[3] With this kind of demographic profile one might well ask how the original settlers managed to marry and reproduce. The answer lies in the number of Celtic women who arrived on the island as slaves, wives, or concubines of settlers. Some of these women may not have come directly from Norway, but were the offspring of Vikings who had settled in the Western lands. This Celtic element that is still visible in the Icelandic population demonstrates that from the very beginning a sufficient number of women made it possible for male settlers to enter stable marital unions in Iceland in the manner they knew from Norway.[4]

It is true, of course, that during warfare and wanderings men frequently obtained women through abduction, rape, and other forms of violence. Such stormy beginnings may have led in many cases to permanent marriage.[5] This observation has led German scholars to postulate an original "marriage by capture" or *Raubehe*, in opposition to the later "marriage by purchase" or *Kaufehe*. Since the former is clearly dysfunctional in a settled society, the institutionalized form of marriage among the Germanic tribes, and hence also among the Norwegians, became "marriage by purchase."[6] This is the marriage model described in sources that span from the Roman historian Tacitus in the first century to the Icelandic sagas of the thirteenth century. In other words, just as the Romans had developed a stable form of marriage before their encounter with Christianity — a form which the Church accepted with only few modifications — so the pagan Germanic tribes created their form of a stable marriage pattern in which churchmen in turn tried to make changes.[7] In the following pages, I shall first

[3] See Judith Jesch, *Women in the Viking Age* (Woodbridge: Boydell, 1991), 79–83.

[4] See Gísli Sigurðsson, *Gaelic Influence in Iceland: Historical and Literary Contacts*, Studia Islandica 46 (Reykjavík: Bókaútgáfa Menningarsjóðs, 1988); Jenny Jochens, "Race and Ethnicity in the Old Norse World," *Viator* 30 (1999): 79–103; eadem "Vikings Westward to Vínland: The Problem of Women and Sexuality," in *Cold Counsel: The Women of Old Norse Literature and Myth*, ed. Sarah May Anderson (New York: Garland, 2001), 129–58.

[5] A good illustration is Álfhildr, a noble woman who had been abducted from her native England and brought to Norway by Vikings. She married a Viking and gave birth to a child. Later she became the mistress of King Óláfr and mother of Magnús, his only son and successor. See Jenny Jochens, "The Politics of Reproduction: Medieval Norwegian Kingship," *American Historical Review* 92 (1987): 327–49.

[6] See Suzanne Fonay Wemple, *Women in Frankish Society: Marriage and the Cloister, 500–900* (Philadelphia: University of Pennsylvania Press, 1981), 31–50.

[7] On Roman marriage, see Susan Treggiari, *Roman Marriage: "Justi Coniuges" from the Time of Cicero to the Time of Ulpian* (Oxford: Clarendon Press, 1991).

identify a few distinct features for each of the two marriage models, the pagan and the Christian, and at the end examine to what degree the Christian model was implemented.

Pagan Marriage

Pagan marriage was first and foremost characterized by a contract.[8] The term "marriage by purchase" does not imply that a man bought a wife in the way he might buy a cow, but it does emphasize that pagan marriage essentially was a commercial contract. The couple's families agreed to provide a specified amount of property, thereby enabling this couple to establish a new household and care for the children they were expected to produce. Since only legitimate children could inherit from their parents, this form of marriage ensured the orderly passing of property from one generation to the next. Two distinct steps, the engagement and the wedding, were required to bring about this arrangement.[9] Negotiations occurred between two men of equal social standing, the father or other guardian of the bride, and the spokesman for the groom or — more frequently — the groom acting on his own behalf. The father of the bride could not take the initiative, however, but had to wait for a suitable candidate to appear. According to custom, the groom would visit the father of the girl he wished to marry, bringing with him a group of several kinsmen. The party was not supposed to bring up the errand for several days, but eventually the groom would present his request for the daughter of the house, specifying the bride price (*mundr*), that is, the amount of money or wealth he and his family were willing to invest in the new household. If the father liked the candidate and was satisfied with the conditions, he would inform the groom of the amount he was ready to give his daughter as her *heimanfylgja*, literally "that which would follow her from home," in other words, her dowry or her inheritance. If they reached an agreement, witnesses were called, the two men repeated the conditions, and, to seal the bargain, they shook hands. The commercial character of the transaction is clear from the fact that the ritual — the agreeing on a price, the witnesses, and the handshake —

---

[8] For a comprehensive treatment of love and marriage in Norse society, see Björn Bandlien, *Å finne den rette: Kjærlighet, individ og samfunn i norrön middelalder* (Oslo: Den Norske Historiske Forening, 2001). An English translation is forthcoming. See also Jenny Jochens, *Women in Old Norse Society* (Ithaca: Cornell University Press, 1995), 17–36; and Roberta Frank, "Marriage in Twelfth- and Thirteenth-Century Iceland," *Viator* 4 (1973): 473–84.

[9] On engagement, see Jana K. Schulman, "Make Me a Match: Motifs of Betrothal in the Sagas of Icelanders," *Scandinavian Studies* 69 (1997): 296–321.

was also used to negotiate three other important acquisitions, of land, of a chieftainship, and of an ocean-going vessel.

The concern for property also explains the relatively few restrictions in pagan marriage. No lower age limit was set for either partner, but the law did limit a bride price allowed for an eighty-year old man, and further disinherited any subsequent children, unless he had received permission from his present heirs. Moreover, poor people were not allowed to marry. Fear of proliferating poor people mandated minimum property requirements beyond the everyday clothes on their backs. Similar concerns permitted the castration of beggars. People undertaking this task were not punished, even if they seriously wounded or even killed the victim. Furthermore, if a foreigner fathered a child by an Icelandic woman and left the country, the baby was to be entrusted to a compatriot and taken to the father. Pagan society banned sexual relations within the immediate nuclear family, but most of the rules restricting marriage and sexual activity were prompted more by practical concerns of safeguarding property from reproductive despoliation than by personal and social considerations.

The two men who arranged the engagement also set a date for the wedding. The interval between the two events could range from a few days to several months and stretch to three years in cases of young men who wanted to secure brides before going abroad. In contrast to the engagement in which property considerations were paramount, the wedding was dominated by themes of sex and reproduction. The ceremony normally took place at the bride's house and consisted of an elaborate banquet, at the end of which the groom was led to the bride who waited for him in bed. Assuming that a proper engagement had already occurred, the wedding was legal if six witnesses saw the husband openly go to bed with the wife. The festivities lasted several days, and when the guests departed, they were provided with important gifts.

The second notable feature in the pagan marriage is the absence of female involvement. The engagement was arranged entirely between the two men, and although the woman naturally had the greatest interest in the negotiations, she was totally absent. Indeed, no meeting between the two young people was required. The law nowhere implies that a woman in pagan times was asked for her approval but clearly states the father's right to force his daughter into a marriage he desired. According to an addition to the law made probably around 1200, a father was prohibited from coercing his daughter to marry if she wanted to become a nun. With only two nunneries in Iceland, this possibility could not have accommodated many women, but the regulation is one of the churchmen's first attempts to ameliorate the female premarital condition. It implies, however, that paternal enforcement was normal and accepted in other situations. A few cases appear in the sagas of Icelanders to suggest a notion of pagan consent — and I shall return to these — but it is notable that the majority of the marriages were arranged completely without the women's knowledge, let alone approval. In one case a woman did not even know she was getting married until the wedding guests arrived.[10]

The third feature worth mentioning in a pagan marriage is married men's sexual behavior. Although pagan marriage stipulated only one legal wife, it did not preclude other sexual unions. In fact, given the numerous prohibitions in the law against illegal intercourse, it is clear than men engaged frequently in this activity. Furthermore, the legal classifications and the vocabulary make it clear that this custom was of pagan origin. Identifying a series of sexual crimes, ranging from stealing kisses to sleeping with and impregnating women, the law prescribed varying penalties from payment of fines to outlawry, culminating in granting the right for a man to kill on the spot any male caught in *flagrante delicto*, that is, having intercourse with one of six women under the avenger's jurisdiction: his wife, daughter, mother, sister, foster daughter, or foster mother. The failure to distinguish between married and unmarried women in this sequence, or in other words, between adultery and fornication, clearly indicates its pagan origin. It also shows that the law construed sexual crimes as being committed against the families who controlled women's sexual and reproductive capabilities, not against women as individuals.

The narratives provide specific information about these additional sexual partners. According to the family sagas or sagas of the Icelanders, the most famous of the narratives, relatively few married men had concubines. In fact, the sagas include hundreds of married couples living seemingly peaceful, monogamous lives. The problem of mistresses, however, seems much more serious in the saga authors' own world described in another, less well-known genre, the so-called contemporary sagas. I shall return to the problem of the difference between these two genres. In addition to wives and the few recorded mistresses, the pagan world did, however, provide men with other sexual outlets, as is clear from the frequent theme of "the illicit love visit." During their youths, free men exhibited a great deal of sexual aggression toward women of their own class, visiting and impregnating them against the will of the girls' families, thereby naturally provoking hostilities and feuds.[11] Furthermore, men had unlimited access to slaves and servants. The unavoidable illegitimate births issuing from these extramarital activities were controlled through infanticide — a problem also under male jurisdiction.

[10] This is the case of Steingerðr's marriage to Bersi in *Kormáks Saga*; see *The Complete Sagas*, 1:188–90.

[11] On this problem, see Jenny Jochens, "The Illicit Love Visit: An Archaeology of Old Norse Sexuality," *Journal of the History of Sexuality* 1 (1991): 357–92.

Christian Marriage

If pagan marriage thus can be characterized briefly as a commercial contract arranged by men offering no choice for the woman concerning her partner, and not restricting male sexual behavior, it is obvious that Christian marriage presented a stark contrast.[12] Again, I shall single out just a few features. The most fundamental difference between the pagan and the Christian model concerns the nature of the agreement. Churchmen did not object to the traditional financial agreements in marriage, which, of course, families continued to negotiate. However, they insisted that Christian marriage was not a contract but a sacrament, a bond comparable to the mystical union between Christ and his church. If that concept was accepted, churchmen were willing to compromise with pre-existing rules. Little is known about the earliest form of Christian marriage, but it seems originally to have followed the Roman custom and consisted of a single act. Influenced, however, by the system found among the Continental Germanic tribes whom churchmen wanted to convert, they were willing to accept their marital scheme. Therefore, like the Norse model I have outlined, Christian marriage came almost from the beginning to consist of two steps, although these were not formulated until much later. From the middle of the twelfth century, canon lawyers in Europe distinguished between what they called *verba de futuro* and *verba de presenti*, of which the former, the engagement, entailed a promise of future marriage, and the latter, the wedding, an immediately binding contract. The problem is controversial, but there is little evidence that engagement existed in Roman and early Christian marriages. It was most likely adopted by churchmen from the Germanic model to become the first step also in Christian marriage. On the surface, therefore, the marital program later brought to the north by the Church conformed to the twofold Germanic model already familiar to the Nordic people.

To the simple pagan ban on sexual relations within the nuclear family, churchmen added prohibitions against marriage and procreation within a vast network of relatives and friends, determined by the three principles of consanguinity (relations by blood), affinity (relationship by marriage), and spiritual kinship (relationship through the sacraments). Although the limits were reduced over time, these rules still circumscribed more severely than the old system the number of marital candidates.

The outward form of the Christian marriage thus presented no obstacles to the Icelanders because it conformed to their own native system. Problems occurred, however, when churchmen wished to apply their specific sacramental principle to this model. I shall single out just two of these applications: consent and fidelity. Churchmen cherished the notion of consent above others in their program because

[12] See Jochens, *Women*, 36–54.

it accommodated and facilitated two ideas held in high regard in principle, if not always in practice, that of gender equality and the extension of the Christian family beyond inherited tribal and social restrictions.[13] They had borrowed the idea from Roman law, but here it meant the consent of parents to the marriage, not of the couple itself. In contrast to the Romans, Germanic young men escaped parental influence at puberty. Among their privileges was the freedom to choose their marital partner themselves. It is this aspect churchmen wanted to extend to women. Formulated by canon lawyers on the Continent by the middle of the twelfth century, female consent was promulgated in Norway and Iceland already by the 1180s. In 1189 the archbishop of Trondheim in Norway declared in a letter to the two Icelandic bishops that full matrimony was established as soon as a man has betrothed a woman "with her own yes-word," as the text states, in the presence of witnesses. The idea was later incorporated into Christian legislation. Judged by these texts, the change from the older ceremony would have been striking. The pagan woman did not even witness the two men's solemn handshake that sealed her fate. Silently and passively, she was transferred from her father to her husband. The Christian formula, by contrast, did not mention relatives but placed the woman at the center of the stage, and whose clearly heard "yes-word" became the "speech-act" — in J. L. Austin's words — that loudly and publicly instituted marriage.

While female consent was truly a radical idea, the other Christian aspect of marriage, that of marital fidelity, is less an innovation than a logical extension of the fundamental notion of the Christian marriage as a sacrament. Comparing the marriage bond to the mystical union between Christ and his church, churchmen implied that — like that union — marriage was eternal and exclusive. Promising fidelity for life — indeed a faith corresponding to a religious belief — the young couple voluntarily entered into a monogamous and indissoluble union. A Christian marriage therefore restricted sexual interaction to a monogamous couple that had entered the union voluntarily and expected it to last for life.

These ideas — marriage as a sacrament with the concomitant consequences of consent, fidelity, and indissolubility — presented the grand model of an ambitious marital program promulgated by churchmen throughout Europe. Local problems, however, caused them to emphasize different aspects at different times. On the Continent, for example, they focused on the notion of indissolubility and worked hard to curtail divorce, a problem I shall not discuss here.[14] In the North, their

---

[13] On consent, see Jenny Jochens, "Consent in Marriage: Old Norse Law, Life, and Literature," *Scandinavian Studies* 58 (1986): 142–76; and "Með Jákvæði Hennar Sjálfrar: Consent as Signifier in the Old Norse World," in *Consent and Coercion to Sex and Marriage in Ancient and Medieval Societies*, ed. Angeliki Laiou (Washington DC: Dumbarton Oaks, 1993), 271–89.

[14] See Jochens, *Women*, 54–61.

prime concerns were the two aspects we have been dealing with, consent and marital fidelity. Were they implemented?

The letter of consent I quoted earlier written by the Norwegian archbishop to his Icelandic colleagues might suggest that consent became the law of the land. The reality is far less simple. It is true that the idea was incorporated into the so-called Christian laws both in Norway and in Iceland. According to these, a man was to go directly to the woman he wanted to marry, and declare that he betrothed her in accordance with the law of God. The witnesses were to hear the woman's "yes-word, because it was prohibited according to God's law that a man should marry a woman or maiden against her will." Apparently, the idea that a woman might speak on this occasion was so novel that many remained silent, and lawmakers were forced to add that the marriage was valid also if the bride said nothing, concluding, however, "but if she says no, the marriage cannot be concluded legally."[15] Even these elaborate rules do not allow the conclusion that consent had been accepted. The Christian laws, in which the idea was inserted, pertained to matters under the jurisdiction of churchmen. Unfortunately, the secular laws were also being revised. In 1262 Iceland lost independence to Norway and was forced to accept a new law, the so-called *Jónsbók* to replace the old *Grágás*. Dealing with marital arrangements, the new law included a watered-down notion of female consent, giving it, not to the bride, but to her mother, who now together with her own husband was responsible for arranging their daughter's marriage. A more ominous threat was found in the section that regulated the transfer of property. Here it is stated that if a woman married without her kin's consent, she would lose her inheritance to the next in line. Surely, this was a powerful deterrent for any woman inclined to follow her own wishes, but it was doubtless considered necessary because of the new freedom offered by ecclesiastic legislation. The idea was evidently so radical that lay society felt compelled to protect itself.

When historians use laws as evidence of past society, they are faced with the problem of whether these texts are descriptive or prescriptive, that is to say, do they describe society as it was, or as its leaders would like it to be in the future. To clarify this problem I turn again to the narratives. Consent is rarely mentioned in the sagas that describe the thirteenth century, the genre I referred to earlier as the contemporary sagas. Dealing with prominent political leaders, they include women who are summarily married by their fathers or brothers to further the men's own political plans.[16] But the authors of the family sagas were also

[15] For references to these citations, see Jochens, *Women*, 45–46.

[16] For a specific case involving Snorri Sturluson (1178–1241), author, law speaker, and politician, see J. Jochens, "Wealth and Women in Snorri's Life," *Sagnaþing helgað Jónasi Kristjánssyni sjötugum 10. apríl 1994*, ed. Gísli Sigurðsson et al., 2 vols. (Reykjavík: hið Íslenska bókmenntafélag, 1994); 455–63.

at work during this period. In their narratives they included several prominent saga heroines who they claimed had been allowed to approve of the candidates proposed by their fathers. This is truly remarkable because the women and their marriages belonged to the pagan era of the tenth and eleventh centuries. Not only was Christianity barely known in Iceland, but the notion of consent had not yet been formulated by church leaders anywhere. That thirteenth-century authors awarded consent to their pagan foremothers must be seen as clerical influence incurred by the authors during their training by churchmen. The fictional aspect of this consent is suggested by the fact that these marriages eventually were concluded according to the fathers' wishes. Agreeing with churchmen that female consent was a desirable goal, the authors attributed this Christian privilege to a few of the most prominent heroines in the pagan society. They were described so lovingly in the hope, undoubtedly, of creating a model that their listeners and readers might emulate. The assertion that female consent already existed during paganism thus was the first result, albeit only literary, of local churchmen's attempts to curtail male control in marriage. Consent, therefore, presents one of the issues in the family sagas where Christian mediation is noticeable despite the otherwise smooth pagan surface. Nonetheless, it is possible to demonstrate from other types of evidence — literary as well as linguistic — that female consent became accepted in the North, perhaps starting among people with little wealth.[17] Furthermore, beginning in the twelfth century, self-determination became an integral part of marriage throughout the Western world, in contrast, for example, to Asiatic cultures where, even now, both men and women enter marriages arranged by their families.

Although it is difficult to outline the exact path, it seems clear that churchmen scored a victory on the issue of consent. In contrast, their defeat in enforcing marital fidelity is unquestionable. It is perhaps not to be wondered at, since churchmen themselves refused to obey the rule of celibacy. Most Icelandic bishops and priests were regularly married and produced large families. When they were forced to abandon their wives, they responded, not by accepting celibacy, but by taking permanent concubines. Jón Arason, for example, the last Catholic bishop of Iceland before the Reformation, had several mistresses, of whom the last — who was considered the First Lady of the country — gave birth to his six children. It is true, of course, that the rule of celibacy placed the greatest control of sexuality, that of total abstention, on clergymen. Nonetheless, the failure of Icelandic churchmen to conform to this rule undoubtedly lent an aura of hypocrisy to their efforts to enforce on the laity the milder regulation of marital fidelity.

I mentioned earlier that although the family sagas rarely referred to concubines, the law indicates that illegitimate sexual intercourse was of pagan origin.

[17] See "Linguistic Evidence" in Jochens, "Consent in Marriage," 167–69.

That this behavior persisted into Christian times is evident from the genre known as the contemporary sagas. Less known than the family sagas, they convey vivid pictures of the political life of the twelfth and thirteenth centuries. As mentioned, the law code *Grágás* was in effect until 1262, but if its rule of outlawry had been obeyed, requiring all men who had fathered illegitimate children to be absent from the country for three years, the island would have been bereft of grown males. In fact, promiscuity was so rampant that the right to kill on the spot any man caught in the act with one of six women under the avenger's jurisdiction was disregarded and replaced in the new law with a simple fine. Prominent married men had several mistresses, and ordinary folk ignored marriage altogether and lived in informal but stable unions.

Churchmen responded with excommunication and other sentences to make people comply. Women were singled out for special opprobrium because they carried the visible proof of extramarital sexual activities in the form of pregnancies and illegitimate children. They were denied the use of a candle with which married women were greeted on the festive occasion when they were readmitted to church after their confinement. Men were refused the Eucharist unless they gave up their concubines, but sick unmarried women were denied the last sacrament — a deprivation undoubtedly considered more serious than missing the Eucharist — unless their lovers promised to marry them, or the women agreed to separate from them if they got well. This sexual behavior is not an aberration of contemporary society, as is sometimes claimed, but the continuation of a pattern deeply ingrained in the pagan past. The relative absence of concubines from the family sagas must therefore be seen as another sign of Christian mediation. Painfully aware of their own and their contemporaries' shortcomings, the authors embellished the stories of their forefathers to conceal this aspect of the pagan social world, thereby adjusting it to the Christian program of monogamy in their own era, again perhaps in the hope of emulation.

Despite churchmen's fulminations and authors' prettified view of the past, sexual crimes in the form of illegitimate births and incest continued unabated for centuries within Iceland's isolated farmsteads.[18] The cessation of slavery may have reinforced a native reluctance against infanticide and facilitated the acceptance of churchmen's prohibition of this custom. The resulting increase in the number of surviving illegitimate offspring necessitated accommodations in the laws of inheritance, thereby further blurring the lines between formal marriage and informal unions.

[18] Incest appears in sources only later, but it was undoubtedly also common during the Middle Ages. See Már Jónsson, *Blóðskömm á Íslandi 1270–1870* (Reykjavík: Háskóli Íslands, 1993).

Conclusion

By way of a conclusion I shall return to the church laws stipulating that a Christian marriage was valid as soon as witnesses had heard the bride accept the groom. Mutual consent presented the essence of a Christian marriage. Extended to its logical conclusion, it meant that secret marriages were valid. In part to prevent this development, churchmen created public ceremonies, which in Iceland came to preface the native festivities. Simple in the beginning and performed outside the church door, the ritual was eventually brought inside. In Western society we take for granted that the bride and groom choose each other without intrusion from either family. Whether a couple opts for a church wedding or a civil ceremony the bride has had the opportunity to say yes or no to the person standing next to her. These features clearly belong in the Christian context. But it is worth recalling the ritual that precedes the "yes-word." In a church wedding the bride is still led to the altar by her father who hands her over to her future husband. It is ironic that this last vestige of the old Germanic marriage custom is preserved in ceremonies celebrated in churches.

The Many Loves of Philip Augustus

John W. Baldwin

Sex is a no-win subject for the historian of the high Middle Ages. What is best known is not representative; what is representative is scarcely known. We are better informed about the sexual thoughts and lives of the clergy, who wrote copiously in Latin, but were not supposed to have sex, than the laity, who were illiterate and wrote very little, but were expected to have sex. Among the laity we know more about kings and queens than our average knight and lady, not to speak of peasant man or woman. How representative is the sex life of Charlemagne, Henry VIII, or William Jefferson Clinton? Not very, we may hope, or can we be sure? How representative are the loves of Philip Augustus who ruled France around 1200?

The scandals that surrounded Philip Augustus's marriages enable us to know more about his sexual life than about almost any other person of his time. The problems of Philip Augustus's second marriage to Ingeborg of Denmark attracted the attention of the major chroniclers of the period and could not remain unnoticed among the inhabitants of the royal domain where the pope levied an interdict and closed the churches for nearly a year.[1] Despite this unusual publicity, however, historians continue to have difficulty in gaining access to the king's private life. As a public personage, Philip's actions were widely known, but chroniclers could rehearse only common opinion and often remained unaware of private realities. Because the marriage to Ingeborg was contested in the church courts, it generated direct testimony from the king and the Danish princess, but as is normal in such disputes they contradicted each other. (We have become inured to the litany of "he said — she said" recited in such cases.) Evidence was reported in the letters of the pope to the principals and the judges, but these records were drafted to serve lawyers who argued the legal merits of their clients.[2] In focusing on Philip's amatory life, I shall attempt to make sense out of the surviving evidence.

---

[1] The fullest discussion of the Ingeborg marriage may be found in the older studies: Hercule Geraud, "Ingeburge de Danmark, Reine de France," *Bibliothèque de l'Ecole des Chartes* (1844): 3–27, 93–118; Robert Davidsohn, *Philipp II. August von Frankreich und Ingeborg* (Stuttgart: J. G. Cotta, 1888); and Alexander Cartellieri, *Philipp II. August, König von Frankreich*, 4 vols. (Leipzig: Dyksche Buchhandlung, 1899–1922). A version of this paper was published in French in *Mariage et sexualité au moyen âge: Accord ou crise?*, ed. Michel Rouche, Cultures et civilisations médiévales 21 (Paris: Presses de l'Université de Paris-Sorbonne, 2000). English version printed by permission.

[2] The *Regesta* of the letters of Innocent III are available in two editions: (1) *Die Register Innocenz III.*, ed. O. Hageneder, A. Haidacher et al., Publikationen der

The most solid evidence on Philip's sexual life appears in response to questions posed by demographers: the date and age of partners in marriage and the date of birth of children. From two legitimate marriages and two known concubines the king acknowledged four (perhaps seven) births over a lifetime of forty-three years of potential fertility. These demographic conclusions present — to be sure — an absolute minimum of Philip's sexual experience, but they do offer an initial framework that can be expanded for the purposes of investigation. I would propose that Philip underwent six different sexual behaviors during his lifetime: (1) at age fourteen a youthful marriage with Isabelle de Hainaut with the goal of obtaining an heir, (2) at age twenty-five a close masculine bonding with Richard Coeur de Lion, (3) at age twenty-eight acute sexual trauma with his second wife Ingeborg of Denmark, (4) at age thirty-one mature sexual harmony with a concubine, Agnès de Méran, (5) by age thirty-nine sexual consolation with a mistress from Arras, and (6) at age forty-eight resignation to a non-sexual relationship with Queen Ingeborg, in which state he died at the age of fifty-eight.

Youthful Marriage with Isabelle de Hainaut

Six months after his coronation, Philip (age fourteen) married Isabelle de Hainaut (age ten) in April 1180.[3] (Fourteen for boys and twelve for girls were the minimal ages prescribed in canon law.) The choice of the girl was imposed by the count of Flanders who dominated the Capetian court, but the young king's own preoccupation was undoubtedly to produce a male heir as soon as the youthful couple could achieve fertility. It had taken his father twenty-eight years of marriage and three wives to arrive at this goal. Four years later, however, the king precipitously proposed to divorce the fourteen-year-old queen. Political considerations rather than the absence of a child doubtlessly lay behind the surprising move. The chronicler Gislebert de Mons, who was commissioned by Isabelle's brother and was well informed about the family, maintained that after the couple's reconciliation the king continued to refuse to communicate with his wife in bed or perform

Abteilung für historische Studien des Österreichischen Kulturinstituts in Rom (Graz: Böhlau, 1964–), cited hereafter as ed. Vienna; vols. 1, 2, 5–7 have appeared; and (2) *Patrologiae cursus completus . . . series latina*, ed. J.P. Migne (Paris: Migne, 1844–1903), vols. 214–216 (cited hereafter as *PL*), and calendared in *Regesta pontificum romanorum*, ed. A. Potthast (Berlin: Rudolphide Decker, 1874), cited hereafter as Potthast.

[3] *Oeuvres de Rigord et de Guillaume le Breton*, ed. H.-F. Delaborde (Paris: Librairie Renouard, 1882), 1:21, 180; *La Chronique de Gislebert de Mons*, ed. L. Vanderkindere (Brussels: Kiessling, 1904), 101, 129–30, Cartellieri 1:64.

his conjugal duties.[4] The desirability of a male heir nonetheless remained an underlying preoccupation. The royal chronicler Rigord noted its absence in 1185, but when a son Louis was born in September 1187, both Rigord and Gislebert reported widespread rejoicing among the population.[5] Whatever his former hesitations, the king had evidently returned to his conjugal duties. When the queen died unexpectedly at the age of twenty in March 1190, one chronicler reported that it was the result of stillbirth from twins.[6]

Philip and Richard, the Love of Kings

Philip was not only preoccupied with engendering a male heir, but he also defended himself against the hegemony of the English King Henry II by enticing Henry's disaffected sons as allies. In 1187 while Queen Isabelle was carrying the future Prince Louis, Philip was occupied with winning the friendship of Richard, duke of Aquitaine. The English chronicler Roger de Howden described their relations in a well-known passage:

> After peace was made, Richard, duke of Aquitaine and son of the English king, resided with Philip, king of France, who so honored him for so long that they ate together each day at the same table and from the same plate, and in the evenings they were not separated in the bed. And the king of France loved him with his soul; and they loved each other so much that the king of England (Richard's father) was profoundly struck by the violent love that existed between them and wondered what it could signify. To take precautions for the future he delayed his plans to return to England in order to determine what intrigues the sudden love could foretell.[7]

[4] Gislebert de Mons 152, Cartellieri 1:138. A later chronicler, Baudouin d'Avesnes (before 1281), claimed that the grounds for divorce were the lack of an heir. Text in Cartellieri 1: Beilage 13A, 87–88.

[5] Rigord 1:48, 81–82, Guillaume le Breton 1:186, Gislebert de Mons 199.

[6] *Ex Genealogia comitum Flandriae, Recueil des historiens de la France* (Paris, 1734–1934), cited hereafter as *RHF*, 18:562. It is noteworthy, however, that this information is absent in Rigord and Gislebert, the most interested and best informed of the chroniclers: Rigord 1:97–98, Gislebert de Mons 245. Raoul de Diceto (*Historical Works*, ed. W. Stubbs. [London: Longman and Company, 1876], 2:77) attributed her death to childbirth.

[7] First version in Benedict of Peterborough in *Gesta Regis Henrici Secundi*, ed. W. Stubbs (London: Longmans, Green, Reader, and Dyer, 1867), 1:7; shortened version in Roger de Howden, *Chronica*, ed. W. Stubbs (London: Longman, 1869), 2:318.

This text has attracted modern comment because it appears to suggest a homosexual dalliance to our sensibilities.[8] Understood in a twelfth-century context, however, such a reading is unwarranted. Originating in Cicero's ideal of friendship and articulated by court poets since the time of Alcuin, Philip's love here was the love of kings for their subjects, which was limited to aristocratic men (therefore excluding the lower elements and women), was entirely public (and therefore open), honorable (he honored him so much), and therefore it was virtuous, and not sexual (he loved him as his own soul). Howden's studied and public evocation of the common dish and bed entirely excluded the private, ignoble, dishonoring, and sexual properties of the vice of sodomy.[9] King Henry's severe reaction against this violent love was political and entirely justified. Two years later it was responsible for his own defeat and death.

The Trauma of Queen Ingeborg

Louis's birth resolved the problem of royal succession only temporarily because the queen's death in 1190 and the prince's grave illness a year later reopened the question. When the king returned from the crusade in 1191, one of the urgent matters of business was to find a new wife and to reinforce the royal lineage. His choice of the Danish princess Ingeborg in 1193 remains difficult to understand. English chroniclers who were sensitive to King Richard's vulnerability while he was in a German prison saw the marriage as a means to enlist the claims of the Danes to the English throne and their army and navy to invade England, but the expedition was scarcely feasible when Normandy remained faithful to Richard. The best Philip received from Denmark was a wife of royal blood and a dowry of 10,000 marks of silver.[10] The princess arrived at Amiens on 14 August 1193, and the couple was immediately married. During the coronation ceremonies the next day the king became extremely agitated. At the conclusion he announced that he was sending his bride back to Denmark and would seek to have the marriage dissolved.[11] Evidently

[8] John Boswell, *Christianity, Social Tolerance, and Homosexuality* (Chicago: University of Chicago Press, 1980), 231–32.

[9] C. Stephen Jaeger, "L'amour des rois: Structure sociale d'une forme de sensibilité aristocratique," *Annales ESC* 46 (1991): 547–71; and idem, *Ennobling Love: In Search of a Lost Sensibility* (Philadelphia: University of Pennsylvania Press, 1999), 11–13. Philip's and Richard's friendship attracted the attention of other chroniclers who ignored any sexual implications. See Gervase of Canterbury, *Historical Works*, ed., W. Stubbs (London: Longman, 1879), 1:371.

[10] William of Newburgh, *Historia rerum Anglicarum* in *Chronicles of the Reigns of Stephen, Henry II, and Richard*, ed. R. Howlett (London: Longman, 1884), 1:368.

[11] Rigord 1:124–25, Guillaume le Breton 1:195, *Gesta Innocentii III, PL* 214: cxiii–iv.

something had gone terribly wrong on the wedding night of 14–15 August between a bridegroom of twenty-eight and a bride of eighteen, the one who spoke no Danish, the other no French, and both a bare minimum of Latin.

Once again, the English chroniclers provided the explanations that came first to mind (bad breath, for example, a hidden defect, or lack of virginity),[12] but all other chroniclers defended the bride's beauty and virtue. The attempts of modern historians to illuminate the event remain only speculations. Whatever the explanations, there is no doubt that Philip's aversion to Ingeborg was profoundly personal, indeed sexual. Throughout his life he steadfastly refused to receive the queen into his bed, for which he endured the censures of the papacy, even interdict upon his lands. The Ingeborg affair threatened to destroy the important achievements of his reign. Refusing to return home, Ingeborg, for her part, defended her rights as a legitimate wife and a fully consecrated queen. She paid for her obstinacy with twenty years of sequestration in abbeys and royal castles and deprivation not only of her royal dignity but even of the normal amenities of life.

For our purposes, however, her most important decision was to appeal her case to the papacy in famous, if elementary Latin: *Mala Francia, mala Francia, Roma, Roma.*[13] Five years later she found an energetic defender in Pope Innocent III who asserted exclusive jurisdiction over the matrimonial dispute and attempted to resolve it in the ecclesiastical courts. Thanks to the survival of Innocent's collection of letters we have, despite some important lacunae, a substantial dossier of testimony on the marriage of Philip and Ingeborg.[14] Previous scholars have thoroughly exploited this material to trace the history of the judicial process; I shall limit my search to the testimony on the sexual life of the king and queen.

Philip's initial argument for dissolving the marriage was founded on Ingeborg's alleged kinship with his first wife Isabelle de Hainaut. He instructed his uncle, the archbishop of Reims, to call a council at Compiègne composed of bishops and magnates, most of whom were the king's relations or in royal service. They declared under oath that the two queens were related in the fourth and fifth degrees of consanguinity. According to canon law these impediments of consanguinity-affinity, if sufficiently proven, offered a legitimate recourse for annulling the marriage. As Philip pointed out, they were sufficient in the past to dissolve his father's marriage to Eleanor of Aquitaine and those of his contemporaries, the Emperor Frederick Barbarossa and King John.[15] Since the Danes were quick to respond that the genealogies compiled by the royal chancery were

[12] William of Newburgh 1:368.

[13] *Gesta Innocentii, PL* 214:xcv.

[14] Unfortunately the Registers are missing for the crucial years of 1200–1201.

[15] Innocent III, *Regestum* V, no. 49 (50), ed. Vienna, 5:94, Potthast no. 1712 (1–5 June 1202).

crucially defective, the king's lawyers were thereby forced to change their legal strategy. From arguments of consanguinity and affinity which were relatively simple to demonstrate, they passed to the issue of non-consummation, proof of which was more difficult. In other words, recalling the wedding night of 14–15 August, Philip began to assert that he had been unable to consummate the marriage; from the outset, however, Ingeborg declared that he had.[16] As long as both parties stood by their testimonies, how was the question to be resolved?

Canon law offered a solution. Although the French canonists hesitated, the Bolognese canonists, following Gratian, were prepared to dissolve a marriage on the grounds of non-consummation due to the impediment of frigidity or impotence of one of the partners.[17] Philip, of course, had not been impotent during his previous marriage and was soon to lose this alleged disability in a future union with Agnès de Méran, as shall be seen, but the canon lawyers were able to accommodate his situation by recognizing two forms of impotence. In addition to natural causes, which were permanent and directed to all partners, was a second manifestation that could be temporary and directed to a specific person. Its most common form was through female witches or sorceresses permitted by God but instigated by the devil.[18] This was doubtless the practice later called "nouer l'aguillette" in French customary folklore.[19] Rigord and Guillaume le Breton, the Capetian royal chroniclers, introduced this accusation into their accounts of what happened on the fateful night in August. "Remarkable to say," Rigord exclaimed, "on that same day by the instigation of the devil and with concurrence of certain witches, the king was prevented through sorcery. The wife he had desired for so long now became odious to him."[20] The anonymous biographer of Innocent, who took up Ingeborg's cause, deferred the incident to a later date at the abbey of

[16] This is clearly the picture in *Gesta Innocentii*, *PL* 214:xciv.

[17] The authoritative texts were collected in Gratian, C.33 q.1, ed. A. Friedberg, *Corpus iuris canonici* (Leipzig: Bernhardi Tauchnitz, 1879), vol. 1, and X: 4. 15, *De frigidis et maleficiatis et impotentia coeundi*, ed. A. Friedberg, *Corpus iuris canonici* (Leipzig: Bernhard Tauchnitz, 1881), vol. 2. For recent discussion see James Brundage, "The Problem of Impotence," in *Sexual Practices and the Medieval Church*, ed. Vern Bullough and idem (Buffalo: Prometheus Books, 1982), 135–37; and James Brundage, *Law, Sex, and Christian Society in Medieval Europe* (Chicago: University of Chicago Press, 1987), 290–92, 224–25, 376–78, 457. Robert de Courson, who was a papal judge delegate in the affair in 1212, considered at length the various arguments about impotence and sorcery in his *Summa* XLII, 16, Paris, BnF, MS. lat. 14524, fol. 142vb–143vb.

[18] Gratian, C.33 q.1 c.4 *Si per sortiarias* was the authoritative text.

[19] Thomas of Chobham (*Summa confessorum*, ed. F. Broomfield, *Analecta mediaevalia Namurcensia* 25 [1968]: 184) reported a contemporary form of the custom at Paris.

[20] Rigord 1:124, Guillaume le Breton 1:195.

Saint-Maur-des-Fossées where the queen had been sequestered. "The king entered her bed but departed shortly, despising her so much that he could not even bear the mention of her in his presence. Thereafter the queen affirmed that the king had known her carnally, but the king asserted on the contrary that he had not been able to do so."[21]

The impediment of impotence through sorcery, however, did not enter the judicial pleading until later. Innocent himself first raised the issue as a possible accusation against Ingeborg in 1200 and later repeated it to the archbishop of Reims in 1202.[22] It was not until 1205, however, after the affinity argument appeared to be useless, that the king's lawyers themselves proposed this impediment. "The king believes, and many others concur," Innocent reported to Ingeborg, "that he was perpetually prevented by witches" and thereby sought a separation.[23] Two years later Philip was even prepared to try to have sexual relations with Ingeborg in order to confirm the impediment by witchcraft, but without prejudice to his suit should he fail. Innocent granted the proviso but reminded the king that according to canon law such an experiment must be accompanied by prayers, alms, and oblations to break the power of the devil before such an impediment could be allowed.[24] Apparently the pope did not apply the normal stipulation of canon law that the couple must pursue this regime for three years before a separation could be decreed.[25] The papal legate was nonetheless instructed to add sorcery to

[21] *Gesta Innocentii, PL* 214:xciv.

[22] Innocent III, *Regestum* III, no.11, ed. *PL* 214:883, Potthast no. 1153 (22 October 1200); Innocent III, *Regestum* V, no. 48 (49), ed. Vienna 5:92, Potthast no. 1712 (3 June 1202).

[23] Innocent III, *Regestum* VIII, no.113, ed. *PL* 215:680, Potthast no. 2560 (5 July 1205).

[24] Innocent III, *Regestum* X, no. 176, ed. *PL* 215:1266, Potthast no. 3259 (15 Nov.–31 Dec. 1207). See Gratian, C.33 q.1 c.4 and the commentary of Etienne de Tournai, *Summa über das Decretum Gratiani*, ed. J. F. von Schulte (Giessen: E. Roth, 1891), 245; and Rufinus, *Summa decretorum*, ed. H. Singer (Paderborn: F. Schöningh, 1902), 497. These conditions were recognized in a memorandum on the legal strategy for the divorce recorded in the royal chancery registers: *Registres de Philippe Auguste*, ed. J. W. Baldwin et al., *RHF*, Documents financiers et administratifs 7 (Paris: Imprimerie nationale Diffusion de Boccard, 1992), 553.

[25] Rufinus, 497; *Summa Parisiensis*, ed. T. P. McLaughlin (Toronto: Pontifical Institute of Mediaeval Studies, 1952), 249; Bernardus Papiensis, *Summa decretalium*, ed. E. A. T. Laspeyres (Regensburg: G. J. Manz, 1860), 177; *Glossa ordinaria* to *nequibunt* C.33 q.1 c.4. The canonists' discussions assumed that the bewitched was the husband and that it was the wife who sought to dissolve the marriage and take another husband, usually to have children. Although it was Philip who was impotent and the motives were the same, in this case it was the husband who sought to dissolve the marriage.

the other grounds for annulling the king's marriage.[26] It appears, however, that the king did not dare to perform this experiment. By 1208 he had added a third ground for separation, that of Ingeborg's voluntary entry into a monastery.[27] In response, Innocent once again reminded Philip of the requirements of canon law. Only if the couple had never had carnal relations could a separation be granted to the spouse who remained in the world. Although Philip maintained that he had not had sex with Ingeborg, she had confessed in law before the papal legates that the king had known her carnally through the "mixing of the sexual organs."[28] Four years later in 1212 a final attempt was made to resolve the issue of consummation before the papal judge delegates. Once again the queen swore that the marriage had been consummated. This time those who offered oaths for the king swore that even if "the mixing of the sexual organs had occurred in carnal commerce, a mixing of the seeds had not taken place in the female receptacle." Since church law made no distinction between the mixing of genitals and that of seeds, the pope considered this explanation an insane error and considered the issue of non-consummation closed.[29]

In her one surviving letter to Innocent, Ingeborg wrote in 1203: "This consolation I seek from you: as I and my clerics have insisted, that if, driven by threats and terror, I should propose anything through feminine weakness against the rights of my marriage, it should not be accepted in prejudice of that marriage. Certainly not by you who are the avenger of forced confessions."[30] Ingeborg's steadfast and consistent declaration that her marriage had been consummated was finally victorious over the shifting arguments of consanguinity-affinity, sorcery,

[26] Innocent III, *Regestum* XI, no. 86, ed. *PL* 215:1403, Potthast no. 3425 (29 May 1208).

[27] Innocent III, *Regestum* XI, no. 180, ed. *PL* 215:1493 (Oct 1208). *Recueil des actes de Philippe Auguste*, ed. J. Boussard (Paris: Imprimerie nationale, 1956), 3, no. 1051. This issue generated a large number of papal decretals collected in X: 3.32 *De conversione coniugatorum*. In principle only unconsummated marriages could be dissolved by entry into the monastic life, and separation was only by mutual consent. The few exceptions to the condition of non-consummation would not have benefited Philip as long as Ingeborg did not consent to taking the veil. See Brundage, *Law, Sex,* 296, 375–76.

[28] "quod tu eam carnaliter per commistionem sexuum cognovisti": Innocent III, *Regestum* XI, no. 182, ed. *PL* 215:1496, Potthast no. 3557 (9 Dec. 1208).

[29] Ingeborg: "quas conjugium declaratur carnali copula consummatum": Innocent III, *Regestum* XV, no. 106, ed. *PL* 215:617, Potthast no. 4529 (9 June 1212). Philip: "quod reginam uxorem suam carnaliter non cognovit, pro eo forte quod etsi commistio sexuum in eorum carnali commercio intercessit, commistio tamen seminum in vase muliebri non extitit subsecutiam": *Regestum* XV, no. 107, ed. *PL* 215:618, Potthast no. 4530 (9 June 1212).

[30] Innocent III, *Regestum* VI, no. 85, ed. Vienna, 6:134 (May 1203).

and monastic profession offered by her husband. If she had won her suit in law, did she also prove it in fact? Not necessarily, despite the weakness of Philip's legal strategies. The truth of consummation depended solely on two contradictory testimonies without other corroboration. Against the queen's unmoveable insistence, the king's lawyers may have proposed a redefinition of sexual consummation in an effort to break the impasse, but it also failed. Although the passage of centuries has eliminated further evidence, what remains clear to historians is the equal determination of either party: Ingeborg's persistence is matched by Philip's equally persistent and profound aversion to his new bride which rendered his marriage impossible for the purposes of engendering a second heir. This repugnance accounted for his lawyers offering one legal argument after the other. In an age of arranged marriages, no aristocrat could have insisted upon finding love within matrimony, but this king could not tolerate even the minimal sexual activity required for propagating the Capetian dynasty.

The pope not only asserted jurisdiction over this marital dispute, but also insisted that the queen be restored to her original position before a final decision could be rendered. In his first letter to Odo de Sully, bishop of Paris and the king's cousin, Innocent instructed the bishop to urge the king "to strive to readmit the queen to the fullness of her royal grace and to treat her with marital affection."[31] Restoring Ingeborg both as queen and as wife was a constant theme throughout the papal letters. I shall not concern myself here with the royal prerogatives, but turn to the concept of marital affection.[32] Previous popes, most notably Alexander III, had frequently proclaimed the church's duty to compel delinquent husbands to return to their discarded wives and treat them with marital affection.[33] The concept of *maritalis affectio*, which popes applied, originated in Roman law and was adopted in canon law by Gratian. Not precisely defined, it was not restricted to a single element, but included a cluster of related aspects. Its fullest scope was expressed in the tautology: to treat a wife as befitted a wife. The term *affectio* emphasized a state of mind or the emotion of love and respect. Following the apostolic command (Col. 3:19), the church urged spouses to love each other. While marital affection included sexual relations, the latter were not essential to its fulfillment. Mary and Joseph, for example, had been united through marital affection but not through sexual cohabitation. In letter after letter Innocent

---

[31] "ut predictam reginam in plenitudinem gratie regalis admissam maritali studeat affectione tractare": Innocent III, *Regestum* I, no.4, ed. Vienna, 1:11, Potthast no. 13 (9 Jan.–Feb. 1198).

[32] The fundamental study of this concept is John T. Noonan Jr., "Marital Affection in the Canonists," *Studia Gratiana* 12 (1967): 479–509.

[33] See the examples collected in *X*: 4.1.9 *Ex parte*, 10 *Ex literis Silvani*, 13 *Veniens*; 4.9.2 *Proposuit nobis*; 4.19.5 *Ex literis tuis*.

urged Philip to treat Ingeborg with "marital affection," often pairing it with "conjugal grace," or substituting "conjugal affections."[34] In contrast to the frequency of "marital affection" never did the pope apply directly to the king the phrase "render the marital debt" which was the biblical term for the "conjugal debt" or sexual relations in marriage.[35] Rehearsing the complaints of Ingeborg in 1203, Innocent reminded Philip "that she had left her brothers and sisters so that she could adhere to you in matrimony, and you two would be one flesh, united as two persons in conjugal affection. If the marital debt had eluded her, if your left arm was not under her head and your right has not embraced her as she had hoped, should she be thereby deprived of other things or the other recompense for which she left all others?"[36] Two years later he confessed to Ingeborg his failure to persuade the king to show such affection toward her. "We have not been able to inspire love in his soul, since only God can do this."[37] Finally in 1208 in response to the king's charges that he was treated too harshly, Innocent protested vigorously: "Although we have often warned you to restore to your wife her due privilege and to treat her with royal honors, we have not yet compelled you to do it with apostolic power. Although we often asked you to return to her the conjugal debt, diligently warning you many times, we never compelled you with ecclesiastical censure." In other words, the pope had stopped short of applying the ultimate sanction. Explaining that even though he had published an interdict over part of the kingdom, the pope said he had not applied personal excommunication either to the king or to his concubine.[38] In Innocent's interpretation, therefore, sexual relations were desirable but not necessary in fulfilling the requirements of marital affection.

---

[34] For examples: *maritali affectione*: Innocent III, *Regestum* I, no.4, ed. Vienna, 1:11, Potthast no. 13 (9 Jan.–Feb. 1198); III, no.11, ed. *PL* 214:882, Potthast no. 1153 (22 Oct 1200); III, no. 16, *PL* 214:893, Potthast no. 1150 (22 Oct 1200); VIII, no.113, ed. *PL* 215:680, Potthast no. 2560 (5 July 1205). *Gratia conjugali*: I, no. 171, ed. Vienna, 1:245, Potthast no. 199 (17 May 1198); I, no. 347, ed. Vienna, 1:518, Potthast no. 361 (15–31 Aug. 1198); I, no. 348, ed. Vienna, 1:519, Potthast no. 362 (15–31 Aug. 1198); II no. 188 (197), ed. Vienna, 2:361, Potthast no. 855 (Sept.–Oct. 1199); III, nos. 11, ed. *PL* 214:882, Potthast no. 1153 (22 Oct 1200); III, 16, ed. *PL* 214:893, Potthast no. 1150 (22 Oct 1200); X, no.42, ed. *PL* 215:1135, Potthast no. 3071 (2 Apr. 1207). *Affectione conjugali*: X, no.42, ed. *PL* 215:1135 (2 Apr. 1207); XI, no.181, ed. *PL* 215:1493, Potthast no. 3551 (7 Dec. 1208). *Debito affectu*: I, no. 347, ed. Vienna 1:518, Potthast no. 361 (15–31 Aug. 1198).

[35] Only the bishop of Soissons introduced the term in a letter of 1200 to the pope: Innocent III, *Regestum* III, no. 14, ed. *PL* 214:886 (22 Oct 1200).

[36] Innocent III, *Regestum* VI, no.180 (182), ed. Vienna, 6:299–300, Potthast no. 2036 (9 Dec 1203). (The second allusion is to Cant. 2:6.)

[37] Innocent III, *Regestum* VIII, no. 113, ed. *PL* 215:680, Potthast no. 2560 (5 July 1205).

[38] Innocent III, *Regestum* XI, no. 182, ed. *PL* 215:1497, Potthast no. 3557 (9 Dec. 1208).

Marital Harmony with Agnès de Méran

Since the king refused to have sexual relations with the queen, he was obliged to search elsewhere for the urgent task of reinforcing the Capetian lineage. After believing that his marriage to Ingeborg had been annulled at Compiègne in 1193, Philip did not find a willing partner until June 1196 when he married Agnès, daughter of the duke of Andechs-Meranien.[39] However impotent Philip had been with Ingeborg, Agnès quickly cured the king of his disability, delivering him a daughter Marie in 1198 and in 1200 a son Philip. Both were raised in the royal nursery at Poissy, not far from Paris.[40] Apparently the German bride also enjoyed the king's marital affection that was withheld from the Danish princess. Innocent's biographer acknowledged that the king found Agnès very beautiful and just as acceptable as the queen was loathsome.[41] A full generation later the vernacular chronicler Philippe Mousket reported that Agnès was beautiful and intelligent and dearly held by the king.[42]

To the papacy, however, Agnès was not a legitimate wife but a *superinducta*, that is, someone brought in from the outside, a concubine, at best. Since the king had been forbidden to marry anyone other than the queen and had refused to give up Agnès for Ingeborg, in January 1200 Innocent placed the royal lands under interdict. Among the conditions for lifting the sanctions, Philip was commanded not only to receive Ingeborg publicly as queen but also to separate himself from Agnès physically and geographically and to promise that he would not know her or see her until a decision had been reached on the queen's marriage.[43] The king, however, refused to accept the papal condition. Since Agnès was pregnant with the young Philip and the day of delivery was approaching, she was removed from the royal domain but not beyond the boundaries of the kingdom.[44] Agnès served

[39] Rigord 1:135; Guillaume le Breton 1:199; Anonyme de Béthune, *Chronique des rois de France*, ed. L. Delisle, *RHF* 24:757; Philippe Mousket, *Chronique rimée*, ed. Le Baron de Reiffenberg (Brussels: M. Hayez, 1836), 2, vv. 20, 475–504, Cartellieri 3:131–32.

[40] The expenses for their clothing were recorded in the surviving accounts of 1202/03: *Le premier budget de la monarchie française*, ed. F. Lot et R. Fawtier, Bibliothèque de l'Ecole des Hautes Etudes, Sciences historiques et philologiques, 259 (Paris: H. Champion, 1932), clvi (2), clxxxiii (2), cci (1, 2).

[41] *Gesta Innocentii, PL* 214:xcvi, xcix.

[42] "C'on tenoit à biele et à save . . . Icele dame mout cière ot": Philippe Mousket, *Chronique rimée*, vv. 20, 480–82.

[43] Innocent III, *Regestum* III, no. 15, ed. *PL* 214:889 (8 Sept. 1200). The *Gesta Innocentii* (*PL* 214:c) rehearses the terminology of the letter and adds that the *superinducta* was to be removed from the king's embraces.

[44] Innocent III, *Regestum* III, no. 16, ed. *PL* 214:892, Potthast no. 1150 (22 Oct. 1200). Again, the *Gesta Innocentii, PL* 214:ci repeats the letter.

the king well, however, not only by providing a second male but also by dying not long after on 18–19 July 1201, thus relieving him of the embarrassment of bigamy.[45] (A later report that she died giving birth to a third child has found no other confirmation.)[46] Philip memorialized his affection for her with an endowment for the nuns of Saint-Corentin at Mantes where she was buried.[47]

Three months after Agnès's death Innocent took the astounding step of legitimizing her children. Explaining this action to the bishops of France, the pope declared that in addition to Louis, the firstborn son, from his first wife King Philip had no other progeny except for the boy and girl whom the noble daughter of the duke of Méran, now deceased, had produced. Believing that his marriage to Ingeborg had been nullified by the archbishop of Reims because of affinity, he assumed that he had wedded Agnès in legitimate marriage. If the affinity had been proven, then the queen would not have been his wife, and as a consequence, his second nuptials legal and his children legitimate. On Philip's good faith, therefore, Innocent declared the young Philip and Marie dispensed of their bastardy.[48] Rigord commented that the decision displeased many at the time, chief of whom must have been Ingeborg who could only have considered the legitimization of her rival's children as a brutal betrayal of her own cause. Among the explanations modern historians have offered for Innocent's bewildering action, the most convincing links it with German politics. Concurrently the pope was attempting to enlist Philip's support for Otto of Brunswick as candidate for the imperial throne.[49] The strengthening of the Capetian succession at the expense of the unfortunate Danish princess was the price the pope was willing to pay. But he could have saved Ingeborg her grief because, despite the legitimizing of Agnès's children, Philip never offered support for Otto.

---

[45] Rigord 1:150, Guillaume le Breton 1:206, *Gesta Innocentii, PL* 214:cii, Cartellieri 4:82–83.

[46] Baudouin de Ninove (after 1254), *Chronicon, Monumenta Germaniae Historica, Scriptores*, 25:536.

[47] Guillaume le Breton 1:206.

[48] Letter to Philip: *PL* 214:1191–94. This letter was not enregistered but referred to in a letter to the count of Montpellier. Innocent III, *Regestum* V, no. 127 (128), ed. Vienna, 5:249–55, Potthast no. 1794 (1–10 Dec. 1202). Rigord 1:151, Guillaume le Breton 1:206, Anonyme de Béthune 757.

[49] *Regestum Innocentii III papae super negotio Romani imperii*, ed. F. Kempf, Miscellanea historiae pontificiae 12 (Rome: Pontificia Università Gregoriana, 1947) nos. 63–64.

Consolation with the Demoiselle from Arras

Bereft of his beloved Agnès, but secure in two legitimate sons, Philip was free to take sexual consolation from whom he could find it. A later chronicler noted that neither the exhortation of king, dukes, or other friends, nor ecclesiastical censure could induce him to return to his legitimate wife, but he did not shrink from summoning concubines to his bed as long as he lived.[50] Only one of these instances can be confirmed. A boy named Pierre Charlot, born in 1208 or 1209, was acknowledged by the king and assigned a career in the church as treasurer of the chapter of Saint-Martin-de Tours for which he was dispensed of illegitimate birth by Pope Honorius III in 1217.[51] Pierre's mother was not identified until more than a generation later when Philippe Mousket's *Chronique rimée* noted that the king of France took delight with a demoiselle from Arras and produced Pierre Charlot. From the position of this passage in the chronicle it appears that the liaison began around 1204.[52]

A Chaste Marriage with Ingeborg

When Philip's legal strategies for repudiating Ingeborg failed in 1212, he once again broke off negotiations with Innocent, but less than a year later he suddenly announced that he would receive the queen into his grace. Explanations for this final denouement, like the other surprises in the king's marital history, remain conjectural. The most satisfactory is that while Philip faced his two major enemies, John of England and Otto of Brunswick — two roaring lions on either side, as one chronicler put it — the one outstanding obstacle between him and the church was the estrangement with his wife.[53] With that problem resolved he could prepare for the forthcoming battle of Bouvines with the blessing of the pope. The royal chronicler Guillaume le Breton reported great rejoicing among the people for whom the king had no other fault than the withholding of the marital debt from his wife.[54] There is no doubt that Ingeborg was subsequently treated as queen. Whether Philip did render the conjugal debt is less certain.

[50] Baudouin de Ninove, 536.

[51] Cartellieri 4:277–78, 534. Guillaume le Breton, who was his tutor, said he was fifteen in 1223 or 1224 when he dedicated the *Philippidos* to him: Guillaume le Breton 2:4, 383. He later rose to be bishop of Noyon.

[52] Philippe Mousket, vv. 20, 723–32.

[53] Pierre des Vaux de Cernay, *Hystoria Albigensis*, ed. P. Guébin et E. Lyon (Paris: Champion, 1926), 1:73–74.

[54] Guillaume le Breton 1:247, Philippe Mousket vv.23, 434–44.

Guillaume mentioned the king's grace to which Robert d'Auxerre added "conjugal affection," which did not require sexual relations.[55] It remains unlikely that the forty-eight-year king who had refused his wife for twenty years was prepared to offer the thirty-eight year Ingeborg any more than "marital affection," which was all that the pope had ever demanded of him. Public appearances nonetheless were cordial. In his testament of 1222 Philip addressed her as "our dearest wife, queen of France;" in her charters Ingeborg reciprocated with "our dearest husband Philip, glorious king of the French."[56]

At the king's death ten years later Philippe Mousket pictured the funeral as attended by the queen in deep mourning surrounded by Philip's progeny, all children of other wives: Louis, the legitimate son of Queen Isabelle and heir to the throne; Philippe, count of Boulogne and Marie, duchess of Brabant, both legitimized children of the deceased Agnès de Méran; and finally even the bastard Pierre Charlot, son of an unidentified lady from Arras.[57] The chronicler's scene conveys plausibility because, except for Marie, the above-mentioned were provided for in the king's final testaments.[58] Their presence at this concluding family gathering recapitulates and emblematizes the varieties of the old king's many loves.

[55] Robert d'Auxerre, *Chronicon*, ed. O. Holder-Egger, *Monumenta Germaniae Historica, Scriptores* 26 (Hannover: Hahniani, 1890), 279.

[56] *Recueil des actes de Philipppe Auguste*, ed. M. Nortier (Paris: Imprimerie nationale, 1979), 4: no. 1796. Texts in Davidsohn, Philipp II. August, 326 (1224), 327 (1231).

[57] Philippe Mousket vv, 23, 885–900.

[58] Cartellieri 4:559–60, 565–67.

Scenes from a Marriage: Hospitality and Commerce in Boccaccio's *Tale of Saladin and Torello*

Cristelle L. Baskins

A pair of panels, painted in Florence in the 1420s, illustrates the tale of Saladin and Torello from Giovanni Boccaccio's *Decameron*, day 10, story 9 (figures 1 and 2).[1] Boccaccio's tale blends fact and fantasy, drawing on a host of earlier romances, poems, and anecdotes about Salah al Din (1138–1193 C.E.), the Muslim ruler of Egypt and Syria, who drove the Crusaders out of the Holy Land.[2] The panels have received scant attention and little analysis beyond clarifying the narrative source. Bruce Cole, for example, proposes a general, didactic reading; for him the pictures convey virtuous messages through action and suspense in an exotic location.[3]

---

[1] The panels are Florence, Museo Nazionale del Bargello inventory number 160, and Venice, Collection Vittorio Cini, inventory number 994. There are several versions of the Bargello composition but only the Cini example illustrates the second half of the story. Tancred Borenius was the first scholar to read these panels as paired illustrations of *Decameron* 10.9; see "The Oldest Illustration of the Decameron Reconstructed," *Burlington Magazine* 35 (July 1919): 12. See also Ellen Callmann, "Subjects from Boccaccio in Italian Painting, 1375–1525," *Studi sul Boccaccio* 23 (1995): 19–78; and Paul Watson, "A Preliminary List of Subjects from Boccaccio in Italian Painting, 1400–1550," *Studi sul Boccaccio* 15 (1985–86): 149–66. For domestic painting in the first quarter of the fifteenth century, see Jerzy Miziolek, *Soggetti classici sui cassoni fiorentini alla vigilia del rinascimento* (Warsaw: Instytut Sztuki Polskiej Akademii Nauk, 1996). For discussion of the authorship of the panels and an attribution to Francesco di Michele, see Everett Fahy, "Florence and Naples: A Cassone Panel in the Metropolitan Museum of Art," in *Hommage à Michel Laclotte: Etudes sur la peinture du Moyen Age et de la Renaissance*, ed. J. Avril (Milan and Paris: Electa/Reunion des musées nationaux, 1994), 231–43.

[2] For an overview see Americo Castro, "The Presence of the Sultan Saladin in the Romance Literatures," in *An Idea of History: Selected Essays of Americo Castro* (Columbus: Ohio State University Press, 1977), 241–69; and John V. Tolan, "Mirror of Chivalry: Salah Al-Din in the Medieval European Imagination," in *Images of the Other: Europe and the Muslim World before 1700*, ed. D. Blanks (Cairo: American University in Cairo Press, 1997), 7–38; idem, *Saracens: Islam in the Medieval European Imagination* (New York: Columbia University Press, 2002) . See also Victoria Kirkham and Maria R. Menocal, "Reflections on the Arabic World: Boccaccio's Ninth Stories," *Stanford Italian Review* 7 (1987): 95–110; and Janet Levarie Smarr, "Other Races and Other Places in the *Decameron*," *Studi sul Boccaccio* 27 (1999): 113–36.

[3] Bruce Cole, *Italian Art 1250–1550* (New York: Harper & Row, 1987), 20–21. For a critique of conventional readings of domestic painting, see Cristelle L. Baskins, *Cassone Painting, Humanism and Gender in Early Modern Italy* (New York: Cambridge University Press, 1998).

But Cole's reading does not take into account the material, cultural, or political factors shaping images of Saladin and Torello. In fact, fifteenth-century Florentines renewed their fascination with the Levant, "Saracens," and Saladin at a critical moment in the development of overseas trade and commercial privileges with the Mamlukes.[4] Representations of Saladin and Torello visualize relations between East and West as a domestic event, an encounter that results in fabulous gift exchange and courteous hospitality. The pictures translate immediate concerns, risks, and vulnerabilities into reassuring successes. Boccaccio's tale inspires images that merge the foreign and the familiar: ransom and marriage, crusade and commerce, trade and magic.[5]

Each of the panels features three polygonal fields framed by interlacing bands and gilt foliage in relief. The overall effect is reminiscent of decorative arts imported from Spain, North Africa, or the Levant. At the left of the first panel we see Torello, a Pavian knight, dressed in a pink mantle and helmet. He offers hospitality to Saladin and his companions, unaware that they are touring Europe disguised as Cypriot merchants in order to gain information about plans for a Christian crusade.[6] Saladin, wearing a yellow garment, tips his hat in greeting; Torello takes him firmly by the hand, leading him to his residence in the countryside. Boccaccio mentions that the Saracens happened to be fluent in Italian and that therefore language was no barrier to the exchange of compliments, chivalrous courtesy, and table talk at the banquet that Torello hastily arranges for his guests.

---

[4] For the Renaissance in global perspective, see *Circa 1492: Art in the Age of Exploration*, ed. Jay A. Levenson (New Haven and London: Yale University Press, 1991); Lisa Jardine, *Worldly Goods: A New History of the Renaissance* (London: W. W. Norton & Company, 1996); Lisa Jardine and Jerry Brotton, *Global Interests: Renaissance Art Between East and West* (Ithaca: Cornell University Press, 2000); and Rosamond E. Mack, *Bazaar to Piazza: Islamic Trade and Italian Art 1300–1600* (Berkeley: The University of California Press, 2001).

[5] For a helpful discussion of approaches to Boccaccio, see Albert Ascoli, "Boccaccio's Auerbach: Holding the Mirror up to *Mimesis*," *Studi sul Boccaccio* 20 (1991–92): 377–97. See also the critique of realism in Frederic Jameson, *The Political Unconscious: Narrative as a Socially Symbolic Act* (Ithaca: Cornell University Press, 1981), 17–102.

[6] Medieval popular tales feature Saracen spies dissuading Saladin from attacking Christian troops; see Roger S. Loomis, "The *Pas Saladin* in Art and Heraldry," in *Studies in Art and Literature for Belle da Costa Greene*, ed. D. Miner (Princeton: Princeton University Press, 1954), 83–91. In the Palazzo Galganetti (now Palazzo Arcivescovile), Colle di Val d'Elsa, a late fourteenth-century fresco shows Saladin and famous Crusaders from the *pas saladin*; see C. Jean Campbell, *The Game of Courting and the Art of the Commune of San Gimignano, 1290–1320* (Princeton: Princeton University Press, 1997), 253.

In the central scene, we see the events of the following day. Torello had sent word to his wife, Adalieta, to prepare their city residence for the arrival of his guests. The painter distinguishes the domestic architecture in the second scene from the fortified walls of the first. The assembled figures now stand before a Pavian townhouse while Torello's wife and their two children are shown accompanied by a maidservant. Adalieta begs the strangers, after they have bathed and eaten, not to refuse or to despise her "trifling" gifts:

> She then sent for two pairs of robes for each of the guests, one lined with silk and the other with fur, all of a quality more suited to a prince than to any merchant or private citizen. And these she presented to the gentlemen, along with three silken jackets and small-clothes, saying: 'Take these robes; they are like the ones in which I have arrayed my husband.'[7]

Saladin, shown wearing a turban and sporting a scimitar, reaches out to receive a dark, figured silk garment while the maidservant holds the remainder of the clothes to be given to his two companions. In the text, Boccaccio says that the Saracens could "scarcely believe their eyes . . . and for a moment they suspected, seeing that the robes were more sumptuous than those of any merchant, that [Torello] had seen through their disguise." The hospitality of the Pavian knight and his wife, including new garments for their servants, a tour of the city, fresh horses, and another magnificent feast, continues to impress the strangers. Saladin concludes that "there was never a more perfect gentleman than this, nor any more courteous or considerate." Saladin observes that if all Christian knights were like Torello they would be invincible. The Saracens depart for Alexandria with Saladin vowing someday to repay Torello's hospitality, or as he puts it, "to show him the quality of his merchandise."

The third scene from the first panel shows the departure of Torello for the long-anticipated crusade. We see Torello on horseback, accompanied by fellow soldiers, while his wife and maidservant bid them farewell on the threshold of

[7] Boccaccio, *The Decameron*, trans. G. H. McWilliam (New York: Penguin, 1972), 800; all further references will be to this edition. The standard Italian edition is *Decamerone*, ed. Vittore Branca (Firenze: Sansoni, 1966). For an analysis of clothing in the *Decameron*, see Elissa Weaver, "Dietro il vestito: La semiotica del vestire nel *Decameron*," in *La novella italiana: Atti del convegno di Caprarola 19–24 settembre 1988* (Roma: Salerno, 1989), 701–10. For the clothing industry in Florence, see Carole Collier Frick, *Dressing Renaissance Florence* (Baltimore: Johns Hopkins University Press, 2002). See also *Encountering Medieval Textiles and Dress: Objects, Texts, Images*, ed. Desiree G. Koslin and Janet Snyder (New York: Palgrave, 2002); and Ann Rosalind Jones and Peter Stallybrass, *Renaissance Clothing and the Materials of Memory* (New York: Cambridge University Press, 2000).

their palace. Torello's cape matches the fabric of his wife's dress, as well as the magnificent garment she had given to Saladin; sumptuous figured silk thus links the three main protagonists. In the event of his death while on campaign, Torello makes Adalieta promise to wait a year, a month, and a day before remarrying. Despite her promise of fidelity, Torello knows that his wife's brothers and kinsfolk will be unable to avoid contracting a second marriage for a woman so young, beautiful, of good lineage, and exceptional gifts. The scene then illustrates Adalieta taking a ring from her own finger, presenting it to Torello, and kissing his other hand. If they never meet again, at least the ring will serve to remind Torello of his faithful wife.

The second panel opens at left with Torello in prison in Alexandria after having been captured during the crusade (figure 2). While in captivity he learns to train hawks and is eventually made the Sultan's falconer. The artist represents the moment when Saladin finally recognizes that his captive falconer is actually his old host, Torello. Saladin asks Torello if he recognizes the garments he is wearing, and Torello responds that they remind him of clothes he once wore himself and clothing that he had given to some travelling merchants. Overjoyed at the prospect of repaying Torello's generosity, Saladin dresses him in regal robes and declares him no longer a servant but co-ruler of the realm.

While Torello is enjoying his extraordinary reversal of fortune, his wife receives false reports of his death. The requisite waiting period has all but elapsed and she is about to be given in marriage. Torello hears of the impending wedding and begs Saladin to be allowed to return home. The middle scene of the second panel shows how Saladin's magicians transported Torello on an enchanted bed to the church of San Pietro in Ciel d'Oro at Pavia. The bed appears incongruously in the midst of the church where three monks gaze fearfully at the spectacle of Torello wearing a turban and Saracen clothing, reclining on velvet pillows, cloth of gold mattresses, and a quilt embroidered with gemstones. Further going-away gifts from the Sultan appear beside him: a crown, sword, brooch, golden bowl overflowing with coins, rings, belts, pearls, and a ruby ring of inestimable value. Saladin's ring parallels Adalieta's; it is another token of everlasting affection. The parallel rings remind us that the homosocial bond between the men — played out in identities ranging from host and guest, master and slave, or co-rulers — competes with the conjugal bond between spouses. A groom viewing the painted imagery of this wedding chest might well have recalled with nostalgia his carefree single days, hunting in the company of wealthy, powerful men, exempt from the cares of business or a household.

The third scene illustrates the happy conclusion in which Torello attends his wife's marriage feast still in disguise. Torello wants to test his wife's behavior and attitude before revealing his identity. Although Adalieta does not know who he is, Boccaccio says that she cannot stop looking at his extraordinary clothing.

Satisfied as to her reluctance to marry again, Torello then drops the ring that she had previously given him into her chalice; after drinking from the cup she recognizes the ring and realizes that the stranger is none other than her husband, Torello. Adalieta is shown boldly leaning across the table to kiss her disguised husband. In Boccaccio's text she even overturns a table in her haste to embrace him and her actions are described as "berserk." The text explains that the unlucky bridegroom concedes Adalieta to Torello. Not only does she return the groom's marriage gifts, but Torello further compensates him for the cost of the banquet. Presumably the seated man to the right of the scene, shown conversing with a lady dressed in pink, represents the spurned bridegroom who knew better than to dispute Torello's claims.

In the story of Saladin and Torello, material goods, textiles, and gifts effortlessly criss-cross the Mediterranean as tokens of hospitality, affection, and worthiness. Whereas the tale appears to equate the courtesy of Christian and Saracen, demonstrating their essential similarity, Boccaccio characteristically undercuts such idealism in the conclusion. There the narrator Panfilo warns that those who are inept in carrying out courtesy may find that their deeds do *not* redound to their credit, and that the cost of courtesy may exceed its value. Panfilo's final word invites the reader and viewer to take another look at the systems of exchange dramatized in the tale of Saladin and Torello and to speculate about the production of credit and value in late medieval Florentine domestic pictures.[8]

Marriage Gifts

The Saladin and Torello panels appear on domestic furniture, the wedding chests or *cassoni*, produced for wealthy merchants and patricians in late medieval Florence. The pictures not only illustrate gift exchange and magnificent changes of clothing, but the chests themselves were gifts commissioned by the bride's father or, as later became the norm, by the groom.[9] The chests were lavishly decorated with expensive pigments and gold leaf. The average cost for a *cassone* ensemble was

[8] For irony as a radical reading strategy, see Guido Almansi, *The Writer as Liar: Narrative Technique in the* Decameron (London and Boston: Routledge and Kegan Paul, 1975). For another destabilizing reading by a *Decameron* narrator, see Cristelle L. Baskins, "Griselda, or the Renaissance Bride Stripped Bare by her Bachelor in Tuscan *Cassone* Painting," *Stanford Italian Review* 10 (1991): 153–76.

[9] On workshop practice, commissions, and costs, see Ellen Callmann, *Apollonio di Giovanni* (Oxford: Clarendon Press, 1974); and Kent J. Lydecker, "Il patriziato fiorentino e la committenza artistica per la casa," in *I ceti dirigenti nella Toscana del Quattrocento*, ed. Donatella Rugiadini (Firenze: Papafava, 1987), 209–21.

sixty-five florins, or the equivalent of a working man's annual salary. The sumptuous enchanted bed that conveys Torello to Pavia might also have reminded contemporary viewers of the other key piece of furniture purchased for new couples. Artists decorated not only bedsteads and chests but also birth trays known as *deschi*, or wainscotting called *spalliere*, with scenes from ancient history, mythology, and vernacular literature. The works of Boccaccio and Petrarch remained popular as sources for domestic pictures well into the fifteenth century.

Wedding chests and their contents were subjected to intense scrutiny during the public procession in which they accompanied the bride to her new residence. *Cassoni* served as containers for the trousseau — the underclothes, linens, towels, gloves, belts, and ribbons — that the bride brought with her to her new home. The wedding procession itself could become a flash point for would-be suitors, who might threaten to kidnap the bride unless they were paid a ransom. In his tale, "The Precious Jewel," Agnolo Firenzuola describes how a clever bride convinces some gullible youths to accept a counterfeit ring in exchange for allowing her bridal procession to continue on its way.[10] Not only does she escape the encounter unmolested, but the youths suffer public humiliation for their stupidity and greed. Even if such mock kidnappings were highly choreographed street theater, they allowed participants to defuse aggression and to curb excessive competition over women and money.

As Christiane Klapisch-Zuber has suggested, the *cassoni* were a material reminder of the dowry received by the groom from the bride's father; whereas dowry payments could be delayed by investments, rents, or business proceeds, the decorated wedding chests carried visible and tangible goods. In return for the dowry, the groom provided a counter-dowry, the bride's outer clothing, and dresses often with elaborate, detachable sleeves displaying the arms or heraldry of the groom's family.[11] When Adalieta returns her marriage gifts to the suitor and Torello pays him for the marriage banquet, contemporaries would have

[10] Brucia Witthoft, "Marriage Rituals and Marriage Chests in Quattrocento Florence," *Artibus et Historiae* 5 (1982): 43–59. See *Tales of Firenzuola*, ed. Eileen Gardner (New York: Italica Press, 1987), 73–81.

[11] The public wedding cavalcade was no longer routine after the mid-1460s when the belongings of the bride were moved in simple baskets. See Christiane Klapisch-Zuber, *Women, Family and Ritual in Renaissance Italy* (Chicago: University of Chicago Press, 1985), 213–46, and eadem, "Le zane della sposa: La fiorentina e il suo corredo nel Rinascimento," *Memoria* 11–12 (1986): 12–23. See also Jane Fair Bestor, "Marriage Transactions in Renaissance Italy and Mauss's *Essay on the Gift*," *Past & Present* 164 (1999): 6–46; and Evelyn Welch, "New, Old, and Second-Hand Culture: The Case of the Renaissance Sleeve," in *Revaluing Renaissance Art*, ed. Gabrielle Neher and Rupert Shepherd (Aldershot: Ashgate, 2000), 101–20.

recognized the complexity of gift exchanges and the amounts of money necessary for a wedding that would confer honor on both families involved.

The depiction of gifts of clothing on the Saladin and Torello panels recalls the exchange of dowry and counter-dowry between bride and groom, but it would be a mistake to think of the pictures as merely reflecting social custom. In Boccaccio's story and in the *cassoni* pictures, patrician Florentines encountered a pointed reversal of late medieval gender expectations. It is Adalieta, the wife, who gives silk and fur-lined clothing to her husband, as well as to Saladin and his companions (figure 1). Furthermore, whereas a contemporary bride might receive jewelry and rings from her relatives, it is Adalieta here who bestows a ring on Torello. It is not just the exotic Saracens who are strange in the story, but domestic conjugal identities are also estranged through the representation of atypical gift-giving. When wives take on the prerogatives of husbands, could they also be imagined as adulterous? After all, Adalieta comes very close to marrying another man while her first husband still lives. Perhaps even more titillating or threatening for contemporaries would have been the final scene in which Adalieta boldly kisses a man who appears to be an alien, a Muslim among Christians, a Saracen among the citizens of Pavia (figure 2). Even if viewers of the panel knew that Adalieta recognized her husband beneath the exotic costume, the image still visualizes miscegenation, and thus gives rise to the play of transgressive fantasy.

Domestic Enemies

What would an average Florentine citizen of the 1420s know about Saladin, Muslims, or inhabitants of the Levant? Boccaccio's story portrays fictional Saracens travelling through northern Italy *incognito*. But in the early fifteenth century, Florence hosted actual travelers from the East, including Manuel Chrysoloras, emissary of the Byzantine emperor Manuel II. Chrysoloras occupied the first salaried chair of Greek at the University of Florence from 1397–1400 and he helped to train the next generation of Florentine classicists. The opening years of the fifteenth century also witnessed high hopes for an alliance of Mongols and Europeans to crusade against their common foe, the Turks; Timur, the Mongol leader, encouraged commercial ties as well as an alliance with the West. Even after his death in 1405, Timur was celebrated by humanists who placed him among exemplary "*uomini famosi*" like Alexander the Great, Augustus Caesar, or Charlemagne. Florentine authors such as Petrarch, Giovanni Villani, Andrea da Barberino, and Fazio degli Uberti included information about Islamic culture in their chronicles, poems, and romances. While such texts certainly relied on stereotypes and were fueled by Christian polemics and crusade fervor, Gloria Allaire reminds us that they could occasionally impart accurate details about topography, landmarks, people, and customs in the region of the Levant.[12] Saracens might be characterized as having blue skin and worshipping improbable gods, but an author like Andrea da Barberino might also give a reliable description of a beverage made by steeping raisins in water or of the particular features of the buildings known as "*mosche*" or mosques.

Although the division between Christian and Muslim was theoretically fixed and absolute, identities could be more fluid in practice. Alterity was not so much a given, as an effect continually being produced and reinforced through social practices, including the making and viewing of precious objects like *cassoni*. Florentine patrician youths might encounter mock Saracen enemies while participating in military brigades or when looking at pictures. An anonymous mid-fifteenth-century *cassone* panel shows young men honing their skills by tilting at the "*Saraceno*" or quintain erected in the Piazza della Signoria (figure 3).[13] The quintain appears as a truncated male figure on a pole. Armed with a shield, helmet, and staff, the *Saraceno* is racially distinguished from its opponents by dark skin coloration. Curious women are shown leaning out of windows hung with carpets and rugs, domestic goods imported from the Levant, to watch the men compete in the piazza.

Another early fifteenth-century *cassone* panel attributed to Gherardo di Jacopo, known as Starnina, may represent an historical battle set in the Middle East or North Africa (figure 4).[14] Starnina went to Spain, working in Toledo and Valencia from 1393 to 1401, and he may have drawn details of costume and physiognomy from first-hand knowledge of Muslims. But Starnina's picture also recalls the mock battles between Moors and Christians that were staged during religious

---

[12] For the question of cross-cultural influence, see Maria Rosa Menocal, *The Arabic Role in Medieval Literary History: A Forgotten Heritage* (Philadelphia: University of Pennsylvania Press, 1987); see also Nancy Bisaha, "Petrarch's Vision of the Muslim and Byzantine East," *Speculum* 76 (2001): 284–314; Gloria Allaire, "Portrayal of Muslims in Andrea da Barberino's *Guerrino il Meschino*," in *Medieval Christian Perceptions of Islam*, ed. John V. Tolan (New York: Garland, 1996), 243–69; and eadem, "Noble Saracen or Muslim Enemy? The Changing Image of the Saracen in Late Medieval Italian Literature," in *Western Views of Islam in Medieval and Early Modern Europe*, ed. David R. Blanks and Michael Frassetto (New York: St. Martin's Press, 1999), 173–84.

[13] Richard C. Trexler, *Public Life in Renaissance Florence* (Ithaca: Cornell University Press, 1991), 233. See Richard Barber and Juliet Barker, *Tournaments: Jousts, Chivalry and Pageants in the Middle Ages* (New York: Weidenfeld and Nicolson, 1989), 86, 163. The *cassone* panel is untraceable; see *The Image of the Black in Western Art*, ed. Jean Devisse (New York: William Morrow and Co., Inc., 1979), vol. 2:2, 210.

[14] Frederick Antal, *Florentine Painting and its Social Background* (reprint Cambridge, MA: Harvard University Press, 1986), 367.

festivals throughout late medieval Europe.[15] Beneath their alien costumes, the supposed Saracen enemies represented in Starnina's picture or those participating in a Florentine pageant could turn out to be one's own neighbors or kin. Torello's exotic disguise, as represented on the Cini panel (figure 2), perhaps reminded contemporary viewers of the role-playing they enjoyed in mock battles, jousts, and civic pageantry.

Eastern "Tartar" slaves were also a common sight in late fourteenth- and early fifteenth-century Florence; Petrarch's term for these resident aliens brought to Italy from the Black Sea region was *domestici hostes*, or domestic enemies.[16] The vast majority of such imported slaves were female, women and girls intended for domestic service. The maidservant who appears with Adalieta twice in the Bargello *cassone* panel could perhaps be a reminder of such Tartar slaves (figure 1). Whereas Boccaccio's tale presents Torello dramatically taken into slavery during a Crusade, the actual traffic in slaves was mundane, commercial, and regulated. The Florentine Statutes of 1364 specify the conditions and terms of the trade with special provisions for the treatment of slaves, their potential wrongdoing or disobedience, and for those who might become fugitives.[17] The prices of Tartar slaves varied but they could equal the cost of a pair of decorated wedding chests, i.e. sixty-five florins. It was not unusual for a domestic slave to be included in a bride's dowry along with other objects of conspicuous consumption. But after the fall of Constantinople in 1453 and Turkish domination of the Levant, Tartar slaves were no longer readily available; those who could afford the increased expense of slaves looked to North African traders or to prisoners of war to supply their needs.

Unlike the royal, courteous, and chivalric Saladin featured in literature, actual Tartar slaves were considered uncivilized and prone to violence and lust. Boccaccio's Saladin, who already speaks Italian, lacks only a change of clothing

[15] Loomis, "The *Pas Saladin*," 88; Joyce Kubiski, "Orientalizing Costume in Early Fifteenth-Century French Manuscript Painting (*Cité de Dames* Master, Limbourg Brothers, Boucicault Master, and Bedford Master)," *Gesta* 40 (2001): 176; and Max Harris, *Aztecs, Moors, and Christians: Festivals of Reconquest in Mexico and Spain* (Austin: University of Texas Press, 2000), 31–63.

[16] See Iris Origo, "The Domestic Enemy: The Eastern Slaves in Tuscany in the Fourteenth and Fifteenth Centuries," *Speculum* 30 (1955): 321–66. See also Franco Angiolini, "Schiave," in *Il Lavoro delle Donne*, ed. A. Groppi (Rome and Bari: Laterza, 1996), 92–115; and Lauren Arnold, *Princely Gifts and Papal Treasures: The Franciscan Mission to China and its Influence on the Art of the West* (San Francisco: Desiderata Press, 1999). There is a new study by Steven A. Epstein, *Speaking of Slavery: Color, Ethnicity, and Human Bondage in Italy* (Ithaca: Cornell University Press, 2001). For female domestics in Florence, see Klapisch-Zuber, *Women*, 165–77.

[17] For a translation of the document, see *The Society of Renaissance Florence: A Documentary Study*, ed. Gene Brucker (New York: Harper & Row, 1971), 222.

to resemble his host Torello. Tartar slaves, on the other hand, were not so easily socialized. Their facial features, tattoos, or pox scars, as well as their strange clothing and unpronounceable names were obvious signs of difference. In order to absorb Tartar slaves into Florentine households, they were converted, baptized, and given new Christian names as well as a new set of clothes. Sumptuary legislation limited slave garments to a simple linen head scarf and a plain dress with low, flat shoes. The domestic slave pictured in the Bargello *cassone* panel can be differentiated from her mistress, Adalieta, by just such a plain white veil and red dress. Adalieta, in contrast, wears a figured silk garment trimmed with ermine while her hair is loose and crowned with a garland. The servant accompanying Adalieta represents the ideally acculturated, submissive and obedient slave that Florentines seldom enjoyed in practice. Instead, their letters complain about theft and threats of violence. Many Florentine mistresses expressed fear for their safety with Tartar slaves in the house.

Whereas in Boccaccio's story Saladin happily frees Torello after recognizing his former host, late medieval Florentines were ambivalent about emancipating female slaves and reluctant to recognize the children they might have fathered with them. The fictional Saladin helps Torello to return home to Pavia and to his legally sanctioned marriage, but Florentine men were only too interested in extramarital sex with their female slaves. In the Cini panel (figure 2), in contrast, it is the wife, Adalieta, who loses control and makes the first move on what appears to be a Saracen but turns out to be her own husband, Torello.

Bawdy carnival songs testify to the stereotypical lust and duplicity especially associated with Russian and Circassian slave women. A stanza from a typical sonnet by Antonio Pucci (d.1390) describes the potential for domestic conflict when the man of the house indulges in sexual relations with a slave:

> The slave is paid for and brought [home - *implicit*] first;
> She doesn't wear a wedding ring on her finger,
> But she satisfies her appetite better
> Than her mistress, whom she checkmates.[18]

---

[18] My translation. The poem is cited in Italian in Origo, "Domestic Enemy," 363–64; see also Ferruccio Ferri, *La poesia popolare in Antonio Pucci* (Bologna: L. Beltrami, 1909), 196. For the erotic significance of chess, see Maribel König, "Die profanen Fresken des Palazzo Davanzati in Florenz: Private Repräsentation zur Zeit der Internationalen Gotik," *Mitteilungen des Kunsthistorischen Instituts in Florenz* 34 (1994): 245–48; and Pat Simons, "(Check)Mating the Grand Masters: The Gendered, Sexualized Politics of Chess in Renaissance Italy," *Oxford Art Journal* 16 (1993): 59–74. On the excess pleasure of alien others, see Jeffrey J. Cohen, "On Saracen Enjoyment: Some Fantasies of Race in Late Medieval France and England," *Journal of Medieval and Early Modern Studies* 31 (2001): 113–46.

Pucci's *double-entendre* employs the images of food and gaming to describe how a slave might dominate her owner and intimidate her mistress. Of course, such an image of the pampered, spoiled slave derives its power from the anxiety, jealousy, and fear of wives who might be expected to tolerate concubines in the home and to raise their husband's "natural" children as their own.

The ubiquity of slaves in early fifteenth-century Florence makes it likely that the Saladin and Torello *cassone* panels resonated for contemporary viewers; but the pictures do not "reflect" social practice as much as they reshape it. In reality, Florentine slavery was based on class domination, racial prejudice, and gender subordination. In domestic painting, however, slavery could be pictured as a fantasy of decorum, of mutual friendship between men who exhibit the same degree of princely generosity, and chivalric spirit.

Council of the Sea

Boccaccio scholars have always noted the mercantile interests of the *Decameron*, but they have tended to assume that the text realistically illustrates aspects of contemporary business and commerce. The Saladin and Torello *cassoni* instead reveal a more complex relationship between cultural context and pictorial representation. Against the contingency and volatility of fifteenth-century international trade, the pictures present an appealing image of easy exchange, effortless travel, and fabulous profit. The *cassone* panels feature episodes that take place in Pavia, northern Italy, but the location shifts across the Mediterranean to Alexandria, Egypt, before it returns to Pavia again for the conclusion. The pictures reveal nothing of the physical effort and expense involved in making such a journey in the 1420s. The second panel shows Torello returning to his hometown not on a ship but rather on an enchanted bed; the trip is magical and instantaneous rather than requiring months at sea. And unlike those Florentine merchants who had to outsmart competitors and negotiate their way into foreign markets, Torello receives magnificent gifts and treasure out of friendship rather than as the result of business acumen.

Florentine viewers of the Torello and Saladin *cassoni* had reason to be especially attentive to the representation of Levantine travel and to the exchange of luxury textiles. While trading networks had operated between the Mediterranean and the Levant throughout the middle ages, landlocked Florence only gained control over the port of Pisa in 1406 and of Livorno in 1421. In order to compete with the maritime republics of Genoa and Venice the Florentines established a state galley system in 1422.[19] Representatives from the major guilds formed the *consoli del mare*;

[19] For the development of this new state enterprise, see Michael E. Mallett, *The Florentine Galleys in the Fifteenth Century* (Oxford: Clarendon Press, 1967). See also Gene Brucker, *The Civic World of Early Renaissance Florence* (Princeton: Princeton University Press, 1977).

these Counselors of the Sea had to administer the building, financing, and outfitting of galleys, preside over a commercial court, as well as send trade embassies to foreign ports ranging from Southampton to Constantinople. Chroniclers describe the public rejoicing that took place in the streets on 17, 18, and 20 April 1422 with the introduction of the first galleys bound for Alexandria.[20] With hopes for divine approval of the enterprise, as well as financial success, the galleys were named after the patron saint of Florence, John the Baptist, and for Saint Anthony. For this portentous occasion all shops were closed while mass was celebrated and confraternity members and artisans marched in processions throughout the city.

The institution of a state galley system was aimed at two specific commodities, spice and silk, although many other items would find their way into the ships' holds.[21] In the fourteenth century, Florentines had depended on imported silk, *panni Tartarici*, from as far away as Mongol Asia; they also watched while their neighbors in Lucca developed a highly profitable silk industry. Although Florence already enjoyed the economic benefits of the wool trade, the ambitious oligarchs were determined to break into a new market.[22] The finest raw silk had to be obtained from the Levant but lower grades were also available from Spain, Greece, and from various Italian producers. In Florence the raw silk was processed, dyed, spun, and woven by increasingly specialized workers who learned to make brocade, velvet, and damask. By the 1420s silk manufacturing was sufficiently advanced to exceed domestic needs and to necessitate external outlets for Florentine products. In fact, in 1426 the Counselors of the Sea passed a regulation banning the importation of foreign silk cloth, thereby guaranteeing state protection of the silk industry against competition.

Recall that the central scene from the Bargello *cassone* (figure 1) features Saladin contemplating Adalieta's gift of silk garments. Here market strategy and state protection take the form of hospitable gift giving. Whereas Florentines once had been dependent on foreign silk, they now become the providers. In fact, they flooded Levantine markets not only with luxury goods but also with cheaper, coarse cloth that replaced local production.[23] Contemporaries in Alexandria might lament the

---

[20] Described by Armando Sapori, "I primi viaggi di Levante e di Ponente delle Galere Fiorentine," *Archivio storico italiano* 114 (1956): 69–91.

[21] For an analysis of profits and balance of trade, see Eliyahu Ashtor, *Studies on the Levantine Trade in the Middle Ages* (London: Variorum, 1978), especially sections 9 and 10.

[22] See the informative case study by Florence Edler de Roover, "Andrea Banchi, Florentine Silk Manufacturer and Merchant in the Fifteenth Century," *Studies in Medieval and Renaissance History* 3 (1966): 223–85; see also Fanny Podreider, *Storia dei Tessuti d'Arte in Italia* (Bergamo: Istituto Italiano d'Arti Grafiche, 1928), 93–164.

[23] Eliyahu Ashtor, "L'exportation de textiles occidentaux dans le Proche-Orient musulman au bas Moyen-Age (1370–1517)," in *East-West Trade in the Medieval Mediterranean*, ed. B. Z. Kedar (London: Variorium, 1986), 305 and 369–75.

introduction of cheap European goods, but the picture represents Saladin looking with rapt attention at Adalieta's gift, and Boccaccio confirms that the Saracens could not believe their eyes when they gazed at the sumptuous textiles. In the context of a growing trade imbalance, Saladin's vow to show Torello the "quality of his merchandise" implies not only chivalric courtesy but also potential commercial competition over Levantine markets.

Merchants and artists also looked closely at silk, with particular visual acuity and calculation. Cennino Cennini's *Libro dell'Arte* or *Craftsman's Handbook*, dated circa 1400, with its attention to visual characteristics and reference to techniques, is a corollary to the skills of those merchants who traveled to market fairs and were able to assess quality merchandise, calculate freight, and realize a profit on resale. In the course of offering detailed instructions for the imitation of various kinds of fabric in panel painting or in fresco, Cennino singles out gold and silver brocade, velvet, wool, and silk.[24] The imitation of silk fabrics on the Saladin and Torello *cassone* panels corresponds to Cennino's instructions: the artist applies gold leaf, covers it with paint, then scrapes or scratches out fold lines, contours, and internal patterns. Afterwards the gold leaf can be stamped in order to vary the texture and to produce even more scintillation, more reflections of light. Cennino also carefully explains how to imitate the cut pile of velvet, a relatively novel textile. Viewing the Saladin and Torello *cassoni* was an education in how to appreciate and to value the silks or luxury textiles represented on their painted surfaces as well as those actual fabrics contained within. While viewers took in the painter's artifice, they were also affirming the value of domestic production over imported goods.

Visualizing the Saracen consumption of Italian silks in terms of gift giving rather than commerce leaves out a host of risks and dangers inherent in international trade. The lure of profits to be made in Levantine markets was countered by over-regulation and administrative inconsistency, by bribery, and by corruption. Constant threats of plague and pirates accompanied merchant galleys, while the ports they visited were not infrequently subject to civil unrest. Once they arrived

[24] For the "period eye," see Michael Baxandall, *Painting and Experience in Fifteenth-Century Italy* (Oxford: Oxford University Press, 1972), 29–108. Cennino d'Andrea Cennini, *The Craftsman's Handbook: The Italian "Il Libro dell'Arte,"* trans. Daniel V. Thompson, Jr. (New York: Dover, 1960), 86–91. See also Brigitte Klesse, *Seidenstoffe in der italienischen Malerei des 14. Jahrhunderts* (Bern: Stämpfli, 1967). See the recent studies by Lisa Monnas, "The Artists and the Weavers: The Design of Woven Silks in Italy 1350–1550," *Apollo* 125 (June 1987): 416–24; eadem, "Silk Textiles in the Paintings of Bernardo Daddi, Andrea di Cione and their Followers," *Zeitschrift für Kunstgeschichte* 1 (1990): 39–58; and Rembrandt Duits, "Figured Riches: The Value of Gold Brocades in Fifteenth-Century Florentine Painting," *Journal of the Warburg and Courtauld Institutes* 62 (1999): 60–92.

in the Levant, Florentine merchants faced a bewildering number of port charges, duties, and taxes. Further complicating trading relations was the fact that units of measure varied from city to city and sometimes from product to product. And the preferred currency in the region remained the Venetian ducat rather than the Florentine florin. The smooth exchange of goods ran into very real and substantial snags at home and abroad. The state galley system, heralded with so much optimism in 1422, made slow progress and represented only a qualified success.

A preserved treaty of 1497, specifying commercial privileges granted to Florence by the Mamlukes of Cairo, describes the kinds of problems experienced by merchants throughout the fifteenth century.[25] The Sultan decrees that sales are to be recorded by notary so that neither party can break faith on an agreement. He promises to punish Turcoman thieves and others who might attempt to seize the property of Florentine merchants. He prohibits the taking of bribes and gratuities and condemns those who steal or interrupt foreign correspondence. But one of the most interesting provisions for an analysis of the Saladin and Torello *cassone* panels is the privilege granted to merchants to disguise themselves as Muslims:

> It has been mentioned that it is among the privileges of the Venetians that a number of their nation has business in the land of Syria, going from village to village for the purchase of cotton and Ba'albaki cloth, and that they fear for their persons and property from tribesman and robbers. And they have asked that they be permitted to wear the clothes of Muslims, Mamluk, and bedouin on their journeys, so that there be no temptation to rob them. So let his honorable Excellency promulgate his command permitting the aforesaid Florentine nation that, according to what is customary in conformity with the earlier privileges.[26]

In Boccaccio's tale and in the pictures that illustrate it, Saladin starts out in disguise as a Cypriot merchant only to be given a change of clothes by Adalieta. Torello, in Alexandria, exchanges his European dress for Saracen clothing when Saladin releases him from captivity and names him co-ruler. Throughout the story those disguises that appear to conceal identity in fact function to reveal a deeper, essential identity, one that transcends ethnic difference or national borders. But

---

[25] See John Wansbrough, "Venice and Florence in the Mamluk Commercial Privileges," *Bulletin of the School of Oriental and African Studies* 28 (1965): 483–523; and M. Amari, *I diplomi arabi del R. Archivio di Stato Fiorentino* (Florence: Le Monnier, 1863). For another approach to the alterity of merchants in the Levant, see Kathryn L. Reyerson, "The Merchants of the Mediterranean," in *The Stranger in Medieval Society*, ed. F. R. P. Akehurst and Stephanie Cain Van D'Elden (Minneapolis: University of Minnesota Press, 1998), 1–13; and Kubiski, "Orientalizing Costume," 176.

[26] Wansbrough, "Mamluk Commercial Privleges," 518.

against the kinship displayed by Boccaccio's aptly disguised chivalric protagonists, Florentine merchants travelling in the Levant adopted alien clothing primarily to protect themselves and their goods. The performance of alterity that they may have enjoyed in battles with mock Saracens and when tilting at the *Saraceno*, or quintain, played to a different audience in Cairo or Damascus than it did at home. Merchants who took refuge in Muslim apparel while travelling on business may have had additional reason to appreciate Torello making strategic use of his Saracen costume to spy on his wife and test her fidelity since they, too, spent months or years away from home. If the adoption of Muslim disguise seems to expose the vulnerability of Florentine merchants, Torello's appearance as a Saracen allows him instead to exert control. From his assumed perspective as an "outsider," Torello interrupts his wife's unwelcome second wedding and restores his position "inside" the family. But despite being granted the privilege to dress as Muslims, Mamlukes, or bedouins, Florentine merchants remained outsiders with limited autonomy in the Levant.

Conclusion

A close reading of the Saladin and Torello *cassone* panels suggests two interrelated points. First, marriage was considered so important to late medieval Florentines that it warranted all kinds of gift exchanges, including wedding chests decorated with stories, like Boccaccio's tale, that relate to international trade and politics. Marriage in late medieval Florence does not function primarily as a bond between individuals nor even between families, but rather as a microcosm of the state. Second, the pictures reveal a desire to see foreign relationships in terms of the familiar, to domesticate the Saracen Other. In so doing, Florentine audiences could imagine exerting control and discipline in alien environments as they were accustomed to doing at home. The reunion of Torello and Adalieta in the final scene of the Cini panel (figure 2) presents a phantom marriage between Christian and Muslim, a fantasy of diplomatic ties between Europe and the Levant, and an ideal relationship between producer and consumer in a nascent capitalist economy.

Figure 1: Anonymous, *Saladin and Torello I*, Florence, Museo Nazionale del Bargello (photo courtesy of Alinari/Art Resource, NY)

Figure 2: Anonymous, *Saladin and Torello II*, Venice, Collection Vittorio Cini (photo courtesy of the Giorgio Cini Foundation, Venice)

Figure 3: Anonymous, *Tilting at the Quintain*, Previously Paris, Musée du Louvre. Location unknown; author's photo

Figure 4: Gherardo di Jacopo, il Starnina, *Saracen Battle*, Altenburg, Lindenau Museum (photo courtesy of SLUB/Abt. Deutsche Fotothek)

Women Talking about Marriage in William Dunbar and Hans Sachs

Priscilla Bawcutt

The origins of this paper may be traced to a picture: a copy of an early sixteenth-century woodcut, sent to me some years ago, when I was completing an edition of the poems of William Dunbar.[1] Fascinated by certain parallels with one of Dunbar's most famous poems, *The Tretis of the Tua Mariit Wemen and the Wedo*, I investigated further, and discovered that the accompanying text was a poem written by Hans Sachs: *Wie Siben Weyber vber ire vngeratene Menner klagen* (*How Seven Wives Complain about their Undutiful Husbands*), and that it had a pendant: *Ein Gesprech zwischen Siben Mennern darinn sie ire Weyber beklagen* (*A Conversation between Seven Husbands, in which they Complain of their Wives*).[2]

It is not usual, of course, to link Dunbar and Sachs. They spent their lives far apart from each other — in Edinburgh and Nuremberg — and there is little likelihood that they came into contact, or knew each other's writings. Dunbar (c. 1460–c. 1513) was a court poet in the household of James IV of Scotland, and is famous for the variety of his poems and their brilliant craftsmanship. Sachs (1494–1576) was literally a craftsman, a master shoemaker, who composed songs, hymns, and prose dialogues, and is probably best known for his *Fastnachtspiele*, or Carnival Plays. Only a small number of Dunbar's poems survive, whereas the copious works of Sachs fill twenty-six volumes. Although their lifetimes overlapped, their religious beliefs were different: Dunbar was an orthodox Catholic, and in later life a priest; Sachs became a committed Lutheran in the early 1520s. It may seem surprising to yoke together two poets who (superficially, at least) have little in common. Nonetheless the two works mentioned earlier are interestingly inter-related, and it is fruitful to compare them.

The precise date of Dunbar's *Tretis* is unknown, but it was one of the first works to be printed in Scotland (c. 1507–8), and seems to have been popular with contemporary audiences. By the nineteenth century, however, it was considered so "gross . . . as to place it outside the pale of all respectable homes." Needless to

---

[1] *The Poems of William Dunbar*, ed. Priscilla Bawcutt, 2 vols. (Glasgow: ASLS, 1998). Quotations are taken from this edition.

[2] Quotations are from *Hans Sachs Werke*, ed. Adelbert von Keller and Edmund Goetze, 26 vols. (Tübingen, 1870–1909; repr. by Hildesheim: Olms, 1964). The two poems here discussed are printed in vol. 5:237–46. Their texts, which derive from the Nuremberg edition of Sachs (1558–1579), differ only in spelling from the broadsheet versions. On the texts and editing of Hans Sachs, see Mary Beare, "Some Hans Sachs Editions: A Critical Evaluation," *Modern Language Review* 55 (1960): 51–65.

say, scores of respectable men (and women, too) today read, edit, and avidly discuss it. The poem provokes powerful and varied responses: some have praised its "Rabelaisian gusto" and "comic zest"; others termed it "a scarification of women," and "a vicious indictment of marriage."[3] Nowadays it rouses the wrath of some, but by no means all, feminists; A. C. Spearing regards it as "more an uncovering of male sexual fantasies than a revelation of any truth about women."[4]

The story-line is deceptively simple. On Midsummer's Eve a weary male reveller chances to hear a conversation in a garden among three women, two of whom are married, one a widow; all are young, beautiful, and wealthy. The poem's substance is talk, three rhetorical monologues, diversified with anecdotes and set-pieces of landscape description. The women, who are nameless, have sometimes been criticized for being overly similar. But the absence of individuation seems deliberate. First introduced as "ladeis," they purport to speak on behalf of all women (in the Widow's phrase, "we wemen"), and represent archetypes of femininity. Yet they are by no means clones. The first wife is married to an old man, who is even more repulsive than January in "The Merchant's Tale":

> I haue ane wallidrag, ane worme, ane auld wobat carle,
> A waistit wolroun na worth bot wourdis to clatter,
> Ane bumbart, ane dronbee, ane bag full of flewme,
> Ane scabbit skarth, ane scorpioun, ane scutarde behind.
> To se him scart his awin skyn grit scunner I think.
> Quhen kissis me that carybald, than kyndillis all my sorow. (89–94)

The second has a young husband, but he is a "hurmaster," or lecher. Both are unhappy and mutinous: they complain of being forced into marriage "by wekit kyn," of the unkindness of their husbands, and of their lack of sexual satisfaction. The Widow, however, is experienced and more wily; she instructs them not to rebel publicly against their husbands, but to accept — and to manipulate — the status quo.

The poem's structure is modelled, in part, on a medieval courtly pastime of questions and answers, known as the *demandes d'amour*.[5] The Widow initiates the

[3] See *The Life and Poems of William Dunbar*, ed. James Paterson (Edinburgh: W. P. Nimmo, 1860), 5; Louis Cazamian, *The Development of English Humor* (1930; repr. New York: AMS Press, 1965), 92; J. Speirs, "William Dunbar," *Scrutiny* 7 (1938): 59; J. Leyerle, "The Two Voices of William Dunbar," *University of Toronto Quarterly* 31 (1962): 334. For a useful survey, see E. Roth, "Criticism and Taste: Readings of Dunbar's *Tretis*," *Scottish Literary Journal*, Supplement 15 (1981): 57–90.

[4] A. C. Spearing, *The Medieval Poet as Voyeur: Looking and Listening in Medieval Love-Narratives* (Cambridge: Cambridge University Press, 1993), 262.

[5] For fuller discussion, see Priscilla Bawcutt, *Dunbar the Makar* (Oxford: Clarendon Press, 1992), esp. 327–28, 344.

discussion by a series of questions to the Wives concerning the *divinum vinculum* of marriage:

> Think ye it nocht ane blist band that bindis so fast,
> That none undo it a deill may bot the deith ane? (47–48)

At the end the poet himself puts a question to his "auditouris":

> Of thir thre wanton wiffis that I haif writtin heir,
> Quhilk wald ye waill to your wif, gif ye suld wed one?

There is a clear parallelism between the core story and its frame: instead of a woman interrogating women, the poet now addresses male listeners, and singles out one of the Widow's most explosive topics — choice of marriage partners — for further consideration. It was not uncommon to end a poem with a question that invited the audience to consider some ethical problem. But the question is equivocal. Dunbar explicitly asks: which of these women would you marry?; implicitly, he asks: what do you think of them? Dunbar is playing an authorial game: concluding, yet in a most inconclusive way; implying that his audience was solely male, when it may well have been mixed; and playfully blurring the barrier between fictional "wiffis" and actual "auditouris." The poem was intended, from the outset, to be controversial. It raises the topic of what women desire from marriage — sexual satisfaction, property, power — but also lays bare what men fear in women.

The Widow is a brilliant example of an ancient comic type, the dominant woman or husband-tamer. Her long speech, which occupies nearly half the poem, deliberately disturbs the symmetry of its structure. Her elderly first husband was cajoled into leaving most of his property to a son, who was his only in name: "the churll wes gane chaist or the child wes gottin" (293). Striking animal imagery reveals her ascendancy over her second husband, once he too was stripped of much of his wealth. He is a beast to be "broddit," or goaded, into menial activity. One of her leading images is that of the horse and rider: the tamed horse was an archetype of domination. In its common sexual application, men were the riders and women were ridden. When women rode men, it violated social norms and implied a profound reversal of their usual roles. Other powerful medieval wives boasted of taking the bit between the teeth, and so does the Widow. She speaks both of rebellion against male authority — "I wald na langer beir on bridill" (348) — and also the husband's subjugation — "I wald haif riddin him to Rome, with raip in his heid" (331). The reversal of sex-roles is explicit in such as line as: "I maid that wif carll to werk all womenis werkis" (351).

There is similar role-reversal in the richly contemptuous "I crew abone that craudone, as cok that wer wictour" (326). The Widow here depicts marriage as a cockfight, and herself as a male bird. Elsewhere she envisages the husband's humiliation as a kind of castration, proclaiming that she had "geldit" him "of gudis and of natur" (392). This figure links with other brutal metaphors for the husbands as mutilated animals.[6]

The Widow boasts of success in marriage, but what she most enjoys is widowhood:

> Now done is my dolly nyght, my day is vpsprungin.
> Adew, dolour, adew, my daynte now begynis.
> Now am I a wedow, iwise, and weill am at ese
> I weip as I wer woful, bot wel is me for euer. (412–15)

The social reality was that remarriage was common. Nonetheless preachers and idealistic love poets praised the wife, symbolized by the turtle-dove, who remained faithful to her spouse forever. An actual Scottish example was Lady Seton, whose husband died at the battle of Flodden (1513). A widow for forty-five years, she was noted for her piety, and commended as a model of "honest conversatioun and chastite."[7]

Dunbar, however, plays with the antitype of the merry widow, who rejoices in her new-found liberty. In church she appears as devout as the real-life Lady Seton; tears for her dead husband are simulated by means of a "watter spunge" (437). (In a later English poem, dating from the mid-sixteenth century, a widow uses an onion for the same purpose.[8]) But her real delight is to preside over a gathering of "luffaris"; the word is ambiguous, and includes not only lovers, in the modern sense, but suitors.

> Bot yit me think the best bourd quhen baronis and knychtis,
> And othir bachilleris blith, blumyng in youth,
> And all my luffaris lele my luging persewis
> And fyllis me wyne wantonly with weilfair and ioy.
> Sum rownis and sum ralyeis and sum redis ballatis,
>
> . . .

[6] On the imagery in *The Tretis*, cf. P. Bawcutt, "Aspects of Dunbar's Imagery," in *Chaucer and Middle English Studies*, ed. Beryl Rowland (London: Allen & Unwin, 1974), 190–200; also eadem, *Dunbar the Makar*, 332–34.

[7] See Sir Richard Maitland, *History of the House of Seytoun*, ed. J. Fullarton (Glasgow: Maitland Club, 1829), 38–41.

[8] The poem is in Bodleian MS Ashmole 48, and printed in *Songs and Ballads, with Other Short Poems, Chiefly of the Reign of Philip and Mary*, ed. Thomas Wright (1860), no. xxxviii. See also Francis L. Utley, *The Crooked Rib* (Columbus: Ohio State University Press, 1944; repr. London: Heinemann, 1970), no. 78.

Bot with my fair calling I comfort thaim all:
For he that sittis me nixt I nip on his finger,
I serf him on the tothir syde on the samin fasson,
And he that behind me sittis I hard on him lene,
And him befor with my fut fast on his I stramp,
And to the bernis far but sweit blenkis I cast. (476 ff.)

Some critics have misinterpreted this scene as a sexual orgy.[9] But this coarsens Dunbar's subtle brushwork. The Widow indeed rewards her suitors, but part of the joke is how little she offers: sweet "blenkis" (495) are hardly orgiastic. Dunbar here plays a variation on a well-known comic topos: the lady who manages to flirt simultaneously with several men.[10] What is most novel is the hint of cruelty in Dunbar's Widow. Whereas other women squeeze their lovers' hands, she nips a finger, and "strampis" on a foot. She rejoices, above all, in the exercise of power, not just over a single man, but over a "thik thrang."

Critics often compare this work to Chaucer's "Wife of Bath's Prologue" and "The Merchant's Tale," poems with which Dunbar was certainly familiar. It is less common, however, to place the poem in a wider European context. To juxtapose it with the interlinked poems by Hans Sachs brings out some similarities — largely formal and generic — as well as striking differences.

Sachs's two poems were published in broadsheets in 1531, each containing a vivid woodcut. The woodcuts are not signed, but are usually attributed to Erhard Schoen (c. 1491–1542), a prolific artist who illustrated many works by Sachs.[11] These illustrations convey some striking aspects of the poems, particularly their narrative frame and setting.[12] As in *The Tretis*, *The Seven Wives* is narrated by a man (according to Sachs, he is "wunderstill"), who is concealed by a bush and separated by a fence from a group of women whom he is observing intently. Both

[9] Cf. Tom Scott, *Dunbar: A Critical Exposition of the Poems* (Edinburgh: Oliver & Boyd, 1966), 200: "an orgy of female lust . . . and wild fantasy."

[10] On this topos, see Bawcutt, *Dunbar the Makar*, 343–44. R. Pearcy noted similarities to a thirteenth-century Provençal poem in an untitled article in *Studies in Scottish Literature* 16 (1981): 235–39.

[11] See Ursula Mielke and R. Schoch, *Hollstein's German Engravings, Etchings and Woodcuts 1400–1700*, vol. xlvii (Rotterdam: Sound & Vision Interactive, 2000), 132–35; and Max Geisberg, *The German Single-leaf Woodcut: 1500–1550*, 5 vols. (New York: Hacker Art Books, 1974; first published as *Der Deutsche Einblatt Holzschnitt*, Munich, 1923–1930), III, nos. 1177 and 1178. The broadsheets are dated "1531." The texts in the collected edition are dated more precisely as "am 3 tag Martii" (*Seven Wives*), and "am 6 tag Martii" (*Seven Husbands*).

[12] Mary Beare stresses the importance of relating text and woodcut in "Observations on Some of the Illustrated Broadsheets of Hans Sachs," *German Life and Letters* n.s. 16 (1962–63): 174–85.

Dunbar and Sachs place the women within a flower-filled enclosure, but the fountain and small stream in Sachs are redolent of a hot, southern climate, and are absent from the northern poet's garden. The summer season is the same, but Sachs's "brachmon," or June, is less precise than Dunbar's Midsummer Eve, or St. John's Vigil (23 June), which connotes revelry and loosened inhibitions.[13] An art critic discussing these woodcuts says that "by showing the women outdoors, Schoen reinforces the association of women with nature."[14] This association, in fact, is far more explicit in Dunbar, where the women's beauty is compared to the flowers around them, and they desire to have the freedom of birds.

In Sachs the Seven Wives make their speeches in turn, each being allotted the same number of couplets (20 lines in all) — the deliberate assymmetry of *The Tretis* is absent. Wife 1 is an old woman with a young husband, who taunts her as an "old bear," frequents brothels, and forces her to look after his bastard. The second wife (in an obvious contrast with the first) is young; her old miserly husband spies on her surreptitiously — "like a mouse" — and keeps her locked up. (Sachs does not explain how she managed to escape on this occasion.) The third is impoverished (*arm*), married to a spendthrift, who is bone-idle and has no idea how to run his business. Only occasional hints of this appear in the woodcut. The rakish hat of Wife 2 makes one think of a young Cranach beauty; and the bare feet and tattered clothing of Wife 3 recall that she has the spendthrift husband. The views of the fourth wife are particularly trenchant: her husband is a sot, a drunkard, a *weinschlauch* or bag of wine. He comes home only to sleep off his excesses, and when he awakes he switches to brandy. A sow gobbles up his vomit — this is a repellent stock motif, which appears in another Schoen woodcut, dated 1528, depicting "Four Properties of Wine" (Geisberg, *Woodcut*, no. 1175). The fifth wife is married to a gambler, who, when he loses, beats her up.

There is implicitly a competition among the wives as to which of them has the worst husband. It is won, not by the seventh (as one might expect), but by the sixth, who proclaims:

> Was ir all funff klagt inn gemein
> Das hat mein man an im alleyn.
> Er bult, er eyffert, trinckt und spielt,
> Er leugt und treugt, ist faul und stielt.

---

[13] On the setting and season, cf. Bawcutt, *Dunbar the Makar*, 75–76.

[14] See D. Wolfthal, "Women's Community and Male Spies: Erhard Schoen's *How Seven Women Complain about their Worthless Husbands*," in *Attending to Early Modern Women*, ed. Susan D. Amussen and A. Seeff (Newark, DE: University of Delaware Press, 1998), 117–54, here 140.

(All the vices that you five bemoan,
My husband has them all, in himself alone.
He flirts, he is jealous, he drinks, he gambles,
He lies and cheats, he is lazy and steals.)

For her the only way out seems to be his death, whereas the earlier wives had turned to the others for advice. Sachs's Wives, however, are highly respectable; there is no hint that they have lovers. Schoen's woodcut depicts them as matronly figures: their hair decently covered, they sit talking soberly (in every sense). Dunbar's Wives are rather different; their "gilt" tresses stream over their shoulders, garlanded with flowers, and in the intervals between talking they feast and drink heartily from "ryalle cowppis apon rawis full of ryche wynis"(35). The revealing use of the plural in "cowppis," "rawis," and "wynis" should be noted.

There are other differences also between the two works, most obviously in the number of wives (to which I shall return), but also in the fact that Sachs provides a companion piece, in which seven husbands complain of their wives. The setting for this differs, however: it is evening, and the men are talking and drinking in a tavern. Significantly, although he sits slightly apart, no barrier separates the poet from this group. With a half measure of beer, he sits in a corner by the stove. There is a slight attempt to make the speeches of the husbands answer or correspond to those of the wives in the other series. Husband 1, for instance, when listing the faults of his old wife, says that she grumbles like an old bear. The old second husband laments that his pretty young wife spends too much time looking out of the window. The fourth implies it is the nagging of his wife that has driven him to the tavern — Wife 4 had indeed complained of having a drunkard husband. He makes the counter-charge that she herself spends as much on clothes as he does on drink ("Skirts, mantles, wraps and hats"). But such attempts at dramatization are slight and not very successful.

A more important difference between Sachs and Dunbar lies in their tone and degree of seriousness. Sachs, although humorous, is more sympathetic to his speakers, and their various complaints are taken seriously. It is characteristic that each of his poems ends with an explicitly moral conclusion, voiced respectively by the seventh wife and the seventh husband. The seventh wife thus says to the others: "Ir frawen, so nembt bey mir lehr" (You ladies, be instructed by me). Her advice, in effect, is that to complain publicly about one's husband is of little use and only brings shame upon both of them. It is better to use one's reason or common sense (*Verstand*) to punish him benevolently, so that he refrains from his bad habits. *Perhaps* he will so refrain.

The seventh husband proclaims, a little too easily, that he himself lives in an ideal state of harmony with his wife:

Yedes thut, was das ander will,
Und sind freundlich, friedlich und still.

(Each of us does what the other wishes,
And we are friendly, peaceful and calm.)

He asserts that it is the responsibility of a husband to guide, teach, and train his wife well, and that he himself therefore must be virtuous. Sachs concludes with a maxim, or proverb, that seems to have been a favorite of his; he uses it elsewhere in a similar context at the end of a *Fastnachtspiel* on marital strife (*der Bos Rauch*):[15]

Wie man dann spricht: Ein fromer man
Ein frommes weib im ziehen kan.

(As the saying goes: A godly man
can bring up a godly wife.)

Such teaching, of course, was not peculiar to Lutherans, but inherent in medieval thinking about marriage (cf. 1 Cor. 7:14).

This should be contrasted with Dunbar's conclusion, whose tone, like that of the whole poem, is ironic and playful, even amoral. *The Tretis* is punctuated by feminine laughter; but the wives in Sachs are distinctly lugubrious: *traurig* and *weinend*. The Widow, like Sachs's seventh wife, also instructs her hearers to learn from her words: "Ladyis, leir thir lessonis" (503). But her speech is both a mock sermon and a comical travesty of the didactic "Good Wife" treatises and other kinds of improving literature directed at women.[16] The lessons she inculcates are subversive and threaten the dominance of men.

Both Dunbar and Sachs were obviously acquainted with some of the multifarious traditions of medieval anti-feminism. But their poems may also be traced ultimately to a specific type of lyric, or song: this is a sub-branch of the *chanson de femme*, sometimes termed the *chanson de mal mariée*.[17] In such poems, found in French from the twelfth century onwards, the poet overhears a young wife's complaint about married life. Typically her husband is old, jealous, and a "vilain";

---

[15] Cf. *Der Bos Rausch*, in *Hans Sachs: Selections*, ed. Mary Beare (Durham: University of Durham Press, 1983), 70.

[16] Cf. Bawcutt, *Dunbar the Makar*, 138, 336–37.

[17] For criticism, see Pierre Bec, *La Lyrique française au moyen âge (XIIe–XIIIe siècles*, 2 vols. (Paris: A. & J. Picard, 1977–78), 1:69–90. For texts composed in the later middle ages, cf. A. Parducci, "La Canzone di 'Mal Maritata' in Francia nei secoli XV–XVI," *Romania* 38 (1909): 286–325.

usually she has an "ami," or lover. At other times, as with Dunbar's First Wife, it is the irrevocable nature of the marriage bond against which she rebels, calling it "un lien quy trop serre, que l'on ne peut deslier."[18] Commonly the season is spring, often May, and there is a natural setting, sometimes in or near an orchard, or "verger." A well-known example is "Je chevauchoie l'autrier," attributed to Moniot de Paris (end of the thirteenth century). It begins:

> I was out riding the other day
> along the banks of the Seine.
> Beside an orchard I noticed
> a lady whiter than wool . . .
> Very softly I heard her singing these words:
> 'Shame to the one who wed me to a boor' . . . [19]

At least one late medieval Scottish poem follows this pattern. It is a true lyric, with a refrain, although no musical setting is known. The poet overhears the sighs of a wife, who is bound to a "churle," and rejects the marital state, not just her husband. Desiring the freedom of young girls "at play," and to let down her "yallow hair," she exclaims: "Wa worth mariage for euirmare." Immediately following this in the manuscript is a rarer type of lyric — clearly selected by the compiler as a riposte to the first — the complaint of a *mal marié*, or battered husband.[20]

The poems of Dunbar and Sachs, however, are not in any sense lyrics, and, what is more, the single unhappy wife has multiplied into three and seven. There seems indeed to have been a fashion at this time — one might call it a topos — for such group complaints. In another German piece attributed to "Jorg Schiller" and printed in Nuremberg in 1501, the poet is an unseen observer who overhears five wives complaining in turn of their husbands: *Ein hubsch Lied von funff Frawen / wy sie einander clagten vber jre man* (A nice song of five wives, how they complained to one another of their husbands).[21] The setting is not developed, and the work is remarkable chiefly for its bawdy metaphors, designed for male

[18] For the text of this song, see Parducci, "Canzone," no. 6; the line furnishes the refrain.

[19] For text, music, and translation, see *Songs of the Troubadours and Trouvères: An Anthology of Poems and Melodies*, ed. Samuel N. Rosenberg, M. Switten, and Gerard le Vot (New York: Garland, 1998), 348–49. For other examples of these songs, see *Chansons des trouvères*, ed. S. N. Rosenberg and H. Tischler (Paris: Librairie générale française, 1995).

[20] The first piece is attributed to "Clappertoun"; the second is anonymous. See *The Maitland Folio Manuscript*, ed. W. A. Craigie, 2 vols. (Edinburgh: Scottish Text Society, 1919–1927; repr. New York: Johnson Reprint, 1972), 1:243–44.

[21] This work is printed in *Epochen der Deutschen Lyrik: Gedichte 1500–1600*, ed. Klaus Duwel (Munich: Deutscher Taschenbuch Verlag, 1978), 16–19.

titillation. This is the case also with a late fifteenth-century English poem, entitled by its editor *A Talk of Ten Wives on their Husbands' Ware.*[22] Here, as in most of these poems, the wives are identified only by number, not name. Interestingly, just as in Dunbar's *Tretis*, the wives speak more openly, of both their sexual desires and their husbands' shortcomings, because they are drinking deep and because they think themselves quite alone, "no man hem amonge."

Perhaps the best and funniest illustration of this theme occurs in its transposition into the world of beast fable by Dunbar's great predecessor, Robert Henryson. In his fable of "The Cock and the Fox," Chauntecleir has just been seized by the fox. Presuming him dead, three hens fall into discussion of their shared husband. Pertok, the first, delivers a moving lament for a lost lover: "yone wes our drowrie and our dayis darling." But her courtly eloquence is undercut by that plural "our," richly comic in its polygamous implications. Sprutok, the second hen, anticipates Dunbar's Widow in her cheerful acceptance of bereavement, chanting what sounds like a snatch of popular song: "Wes never wedow sa gay." Coppok, the last, speaks "lyk ane curat," and attributes Chauntecleir's death to divine vengeance for his many iniquities.[23]

It is not wholly clear why this type of female group complaint became popular in the late fifteenth and early sixteenth centuries. One factor might have been the medieval taste for lists and numerical structures, which seems to have increased, as the centuries passed, rather than diminished. One small example out of many is the addition to the Nine Worthies of the Nine Female Worthies.[24] Another factor might have been a trend towards greater realism and a preference for dialogue rather than monologue. Some authors perhaps felt that to increase the number of speakers would increase the comic effect. Yet this does not seem to be the case in practice: the works with larger numbers of speakers seem more mechanical (in structure) and repetitive (in terms of material). Dunbar and Henryson — with only three speakers — are the most artistically successful.

One exception to this generalization may be briefly mentioned, however, although I know it only from the description of Pierre Bec.[25] This is the so-called

---

[22] See Utley, *Crooked Rib*, no. 172: "Leve, lystynes to me"; the text is printed in *Jyl of Breyntfords Testament*, ed. F. J. Furnivall (London: Printed for Private Circulation, 1871), 29.

[23] See *The Poems of Robert Henryson*, ed. Denton Fox (Oxford: Clarendon Press, 1981); *Fables*, 483–543.

[24] For an English example, see Utley, *Crooked Rib*, no. 247: "Prefulgent in pretyousness, O Synope the queen," a work sometimes called "The ix Ladies worthie." For similar group debates in Sachs, ed. Keller and Goetze, see 5:188: three "arme hausmayd klagen auch"; 5:191: three wives complain about their "haus magd"; also 5:215: "Gesprech" of 5 persons; and 5:219.

[25] Cf. Bec, *Lyrique française*, 79–80.

chanson de neuf, apparently specific to Gascony: a round dance of *mal mariées*, from which, one by one, a wife emerges to sing and say what she would like to do to her husband: "Neuf commères que nous sommes, / Si mal mariées nous sommes! / Si mal mariées! / Une des neuf dit — Si mon mari était un taurillon, / Nous le mangerions bien toutes les neuf, / Nous le mangerions bien toutes." (. . . If my husband were a bull-calf, All nine of us would eat him up, We would eat him up!). Eventually the ninth and last sings: "Seule en fait de commeres je suis . . ."

(If my husband were a hen,
All alone I'd eat him up,
I'd eat him up entirely!)

The comedy springs largely from rhyme and imagery: the viewing of each new husband as a different "objet comestible."

Possibly most important of all was the influence of another satiric theme, sometimes termed the "gossips' meeting."[26] This concerns small, convivial groups of women who gather for talk, criticism of their husbands, and, above all, carousing. Such a party figures as the third "joy" in *Les Quinze Joies de Mariage*, where the wife and her "commeres" meet and drink copiously.[27] It is the basis also of *Les Evangiles des Quenouilles*, in which six women meet "es longues nuis entre le Noel et la Chandeleur" to exchange stories and popular folk-beliefs. One striking feature of *Les Evangiles des Quenouilles* is that its male author is not depicted as a hidden observer; the women are said to have commanded him to act as their secretary.[28] These works were popular in England as well as France. Around the time that Dunbar's *Tretis* was printed, English versions of both were circulating: *The Fyftene Joyes of Maryage* (Wynken de Worde, 1507 and 1509), and *Gospelles of Dystaues* (Wynken de Worde, c. 1507–9). There are also native English examples of the theme: one is a popular carol, which has as its burden:

Hoow, gossip myne, gossip myn,
Whan will we go to the wyne?[29]

---

[26] On this, cf. R. H. Robbins, "John Crophil's Ale Pots," *Review of English Studies* 20 (1969): 182–88.

[27] *Les Quinze Joies de Mariage*, ed. J. Rychner (Geneva: Librairie Droz, 1963).

[28] See *Les Evangiles des Quenouilles*, ed. Madeleine Jeay (Paris and Montréal: J. Vrin; Presses de l'Université de Montréal, 1985); and Madeleine Jeay, *Savoir Faire: Une analyse des croyances des "Evangiles des Quenouilles" (XVe siècle)* (Montréal: Editions Ceres, 1982).

[29] *Early English Carols*, ed. R. L. Greene (Oxford: Clarendon Press, 1935; 2nd ed. 1977), no. 419.

The most famous is probably Skelton's *Tunning of Elinor Rumming*.[30] Dunbar himself drew on this tradition in another poem, sometimes known as "The Twa Cummeris"; *cummer*, the Scots version of "commère," means godmother, gossip, and, more generally, female intimate. In this poem two boozy women flout the abstinence traditionally practised on Ash Wednesday, and sit drinking wine, "twa quartis, sowp and sowp."[31] Even as late as 1570 there is a distant memory of the theme in a Scottish prose pamphlet debating the crisis caused by the fall of Mary Queen of Scots. It opens: "As I lay resting in a chalmer thair come in twa wyfeis and sat doun to the drink . . . Thai spak at large, thinking na man hard thame."[32] It is possible from this perspective to view *The Tretis* (though not the poems by Sachs) as a richly elaborated gossips' meeting. The Widow speaks of her friends as "cummaris," and the ladies' enjoyment of wine is a persistent minor motif — we are told that they "carpit full cummerlik, with cop going round" (510). Dunbar implies that all women, whatever their rank, enjoy such small intimate gatherings from which men are excluded.

It hardly needs stressing that the works discussed in this paper are not transcripts of real life, but literary artefacts, and ones composed by men, not women. Yet whatever the authorial tone, which varies considerably, genuine grievances and injustices are aired, of undoubted relevance to contemporary audiences — disparity in the age of spouses, forced marriages, jealousy, and other forms of marital cruelty. Many widows were impoverished, but some were wealthy, and wielded considerable social and economic power. Few ordinary women would have had the leisure of the wives depicted by Dunbar and Sachs, or had access to such charming gardens. But most would have participated in some sociable group or other; like the "wyvis . . . spynnand on rokkis (distaffs)" mentioned in another Dunbar poem, they certainly worked together. Women, in the words of P. J. Goldberg, "turned to their peers for companionship, mutual support, exchange of information and spiritual and material succour."[33] Whatever the spin given to it by poets, the literary form of the group female complaint was no empty convention.[34]

[30] *Skelton: The Complete English Poems*, ed. J. Scattergood (New Haven: Yale University Press, 1983), no. xxx.

[31] Dunbar, *Poems*, no. 57.

[32] Cf. M. Loughlin, "'The Dialogue of the Twa Wyfeis': Maitland, Machiavelli and the Propaganda of the Scottish Civil War," in *The Renaissance in Scotland: Studies in Literature, Religion, History and Culture*, ed. A. A. MacDonald, M. Lynch, and I. B. Cowan (Leiden: E. J. Brill, 1994), 226–45.

[33] Dunbar, *Poems*, no. 27; P. J. Goldberg, *Women, Work and Life Cycle in a Medieval Economy* (Oxford: Clarendon Press, 1992), 318.

[34] I am grateful to Dr A. M. Stewart, of Aberdeen University, for assisting my comprehension and enjoyment of Hans Sachs.

Figure 1: Erhard Schoen, "How Seven Wives Complain about their Undutiful Husbands." Woodcut, 1531.

Figure 2: Erhard Schoen, "A Conversation between Seven Husbands in which they Complain of their Wives." Woodcut, 1531.

The Old and the Feckless: Fabliau Husbands[1]

Elizabeth W. Poe

Dissatisfied, or perhaps merely bored, the married woman will, more often than not, take a lover.[2] She realizes that there are certain risks involved in carrying on an affair right under her husband's nose, but she figures that they are minimal. She is confident that as long as she keeps a cool head, she can manipulate her sluggish spouse into either not noticing or, better yet, disbelieving her blatant infidelity. This is the stuff of Old French fabliaux.[3] Indeed, fully one quarter of the approximately 150 fabliaux treat the ups and downs, ins and outs of adultery. The basic plot is simple. The wife arranges for her lover to pay her a visit while her husband is out of the house; the husband returns a little sooner than expected; and the wife spontaneously concocts a scheme enabling the lover to leave the premises undetected, thus preserving the marriage and presumably also the affair. The ploy works every time, partly because the wife is so ingenious, but mostly because the husband is so stupid.[4]

Some fabliau husbands are so naive that they do not know a vagina when they see one. One man, who does not want his wife to find out what a coward he is, has been going out into the forest, hanging his armor on a tree, banging it up, and then boasting to his spouse in the evening that he has spent the whole day in heroic combat. Eventually, the wife discovers his lie, disguises herself as a

---

[1] I would like to acknowledge here my gratitude to John W. Baldwin, who tactfully drew my attention to his own work on the fabliaux, *The Language of Sex: Five Voices from Northern France Around 1200* (Chicago: University of Chicago Press, 1994), an excellent study of which I had been, embarrassingly, unaware. In preparing this essay for publication, I have indicated places where Baldwin's observations and mine, though arrived at independently, overlap.

[2] Per Nykrog, *Les Fabliaux* (Geneva: Droz, 1973), 187, remarks, "Une femme n'a pas besoin d'un motif bien précis pour tromper son mari."

[3] Philippe Ménard, *Les Fabliaux: Contes à rire du Moyen Age* (Paris: Presses Universitaires de France, 1983), 133, points out that "c'était toujours la femme qui trompait son mari dans les fabliaux," and not the other way around.

[4] According to E. Jane Burns, "This Prick Which is Not One: How Women Talk Back in Old French Fabliaux," in *Feminist Approaches to the Body in Medieval Literature*, ed. Linda Lomperis and Sarah Stanbury (Philadelphia: University of Pennsylvania Press, 1993), 188, women in the fabliaux are "not very smart." If one is judging them according to absolute or even feminist standards, Burns's assessment is indisputable, but viewed, as here, in relative terms, this woman is always the brains behind the operation.

knight, confronts the dastard, and gives him the choice of either fighting against her or kissing her ass, literally. He opts for the anal kiss. What is amusing in all of this is that even in this face-to-face, or perhaps more accurately cheek-to-cheek, encounter, the husband not only does not realize that these genitals belong to his own wife, but does not even recognize them as being female.

> Et cil esgarde la crevace
> Do cul et del con: ce li sanble
> Que trestot se tienent ensanble.
> A lui meïsmes panse et dit
> Onques mais si grant cul ne vit.
> Don l'a baisé de l'orde pais
> A guise de coart mauvais,
> Mout pres del tro iloc endroit.[5]

Another young man believes his bride when she tells him on their wedding night that she has left her vagina at home in a basket of hemp at the foot of her mother's bed. While he heads for his in-laws' house to retrieve the missing organ, she receives her boyfriend, the priest. On his way back to the nuptial chamber, the groom decides that he should do a test-run to be sure that he knows what goes where, so he sticks his virgin member into the hemp, whereupon a little mouse (which the young man — not illogically — assumes to be his wife's vagina) pops out from its hiding place in the basket and scurries off. When the crestfallen groom returns to the bedroom and confesses to his bride that he accidentally let her vagina get away from him, she reassures him that, evidently frightened by the unexpected intrusion, it has made its way back to where it belongs, between her legs. Still operating under the illusion that vaginas are mice, the solicitous husband vows never to let the cat get anywhere near his wife's crotch.[6]

But the stupidest of stupid husbands is the knight who lives with his wife for over a year without figuring out how to consummate the marriage, in spite of the fact that he possesses the requisite equipment.

---

[5] *Nouveau recueil complet des fabliaux*, ed. Willem Noomen and Nico Van Den Boogaard, 10 vols. (Assen: Van Gorcum, 1983–1998), which henceforth I refer to as NRCF. I shall cite individual fabliaux by the number assigned to them in the NRCF as well as by the volume of the NRCF in which they occur, in this case *Berenger au lonc cul*, NRCF 4:34, vv. 242–248.

[6] *La Sorisete des estopes*, NRCF 4:66. Brian Levy, *The Comic Text: Patterns and Images in the Old French Fabliaux* (Amsterdam: Rodopi, 2000), 61, draws our attention to the implicit identification here of the priest with the cat, analogous to that found in Les Perdris, NRCF 4:21.

Car sotie l'ot si deciut
C'onques n'avoit a feme giut,
Ne ne savoit que cons estoit:
Non por uec li vis li estoit!
(*Le Sot chevalier*, NRCF 5:53, vv. 31–34)

Even after his mother-in-law shows him on her own body what female genitalia look like and explains exactly where he should and should not stick his penis, the unimaginative young man still does not entirely understand. Seeing now what to do with his wienie ("andolle"), as he calls it, he asks, "So, what do I do with my balls?" ("Et que ferai je de me colle?" NRCF 5:53, v. 92).

Husbands in the fabliaux are easily made to doubt their own perceptions. In one notable instance a peasant coming home from his labors announces that he is starving to death. Pretending to take his metaphorical statement literally, his wife, Irma, convinces him that he is not long for this world.

—Erme, j'ai tel fain que je muir,
Fet il, sont boilli li maton?
—Morez, certes ce fetes mon!
Jamés plus voir dire n'orrez:
Couchiez vous tost, quar vous morez!
(*Le Vilain de Bailluel*, NRCF 5:49, vv. 32–36)

She wraps him in a shroud, closes his mouth and his eyes, and tells him that he has departed this life. The priest arrives as scheduled and, after pronouncing last rites over the husband, proceeds to engage in sexual intercourse with the wife. Every time the poor husband tries to protest their activity, one or the other of the lovers reminds him that he is dead. Accepting his fate, he shuts his eyes, and the lovemaking continues.

Gisiez vous cois, cloez voz ieus,
Nes devez mes tenir ouvers!
Dont a cil ses ieus recouvers,
Si se recommence a tesir.
Et li prestres fist son plesir
Sanz paor et sanz resoingnier.
(NRCF 5:49, vv. 106–11)

In another fabliau, a husband and his wife are sitting at the dinner table when the priest shows up at the door. Peeking in, he asks what they are doing. The husband answers, "We're eating." The priest says, "No you're not. It looks to me like you are screwing."

> "Que faites vous la, boine gent?"
> Li vilains respondi briefment:
> "Par ma foi, sire, nous mengons!
> Venés ens, si vous en dourons."
> —"Mengiés? Faites? Vous i mentés:
> Il m'est avis que vous foutés!"
> (*Le Prestre qui abevete*, NRCF 8:98, vv. 33–38)

Seizing the opportunity, the priest proposes, "You come out here while I go sit in there and then you can tell me whether what I have said is true or whether I lied."

> "O moi venés cha fors ester,
> Et je m'en irai la seoir:
> Lors pores bien appercevoir
> Se j'ai voir dit ou j'ai menti."
> (NRCF 8:98, vv. 44–47)

The gullible husband trades places with the priest and peers through the keyhole. Seeing his wife's derriere exposed and the priest on top of her, he screams, "Hey, what the hell's going on?" "What does it look like is going on?" says the priest. "Can't you see? I am sitting here at the table eating." The husband says, "If I hadn't heard you say it, I would never have believed that you were not screwing my wife!" "Well, I'm not," says the priest. "That's exactly what I thought a little while ago when you were in here with her." The husband accepts this explanation.

> — "Par le cuer, Dieu, ce samble fable,"
> Dist li vilains, "ja nel creïse,
> S'anchois dire nel vous oïsce,
> Que vous ne foutissiés ma femme!"
> — "Non fach, sire, taisiés, par m'ame!
> Autrestel sambloit ore a moi!"
> Dist li vilains: "Bien vous en croi!"
> (NRCF 8:98, vv. 72–78)

Fabliau husbands are cooperative to a fault. On occasion, they serve as unwitting accomplices to the escape of their wife's lover. One husband agrees to hold his thumb in the wine cask in the cellar while his wife goes off, supposedly in search of the stopper. She stays away long enough to entertain her lover in bed and send him safely on his way. Then she relieves her husband of his duty, telling him that she has just found the plug, without, of course, admitting that it had been tucked in her bosom all along.[7] Another husband comes home while his

[7] *La Feme qui cunquie son baron*, NRCF 9:104.

wife is lying in bed with her lover. The lover takes refuge under the covers without being noticed, as the wife accuses her spouse of spying on her. "You don't trust me," she pouts, whereupon he innocently apologizes for getting her upset. Having thus allayed the suspicions of her husband, the wife must now dispose of the lover. She asks her husband the ostensibly hypothetical question: "So what would you have done if you had found me and my lover in bed together?" Without hesitation, the husband replies, "I would have killed you both." She persists, "Do you want to know what I would have done in that same situation? I would have put my housecoat over your head" (which she does as she is speaking); "and I would have held it there until my lover had sneaked out of the room" (which he does as she is speaking). She then removes the garment, announcing that by that time the lover would have been gone, which he was. Her husband, none the wiser, is perfectly content, thinking that her little charade was nothing but a joke.

> Ses mari aussi s'esleaice,
> Qui tenoit tout a mokerie.
> (*Le Pliçon*, NRCF 10:116, vv. 112–13)

When fabliau husbands take active measures to prevent being cuckolded, they never succeed. They merely bring more humiliation on themselves. A husband posing as his wife's lover hopes to catch her in the act of adultery. But she, seeing through the guise, pretends to think that the imposter is her lover and orders him to be locked up and beaten. Battered and bruised, the husband is nonetheless delighted with his wife's apparent fidelity.[8]

> Onques puis en tot son aage
> De nule rien ne la mescrut!
> Einsi la bourjoise deçut
> Son mari, qui la vot deçoivre:
> Il meïmes brasça son boivre!"
> (*La Borgoise d'Orliens*, NRCF 3:19, vv. 321–25)

What he does not know is that while he was being held captive, she was cavorting with her lover elsewhere in the house. In a convoluted variation on this same theme, a miller contrives to commit adultery with a pretty young woman and agrees to let his apprentice have a share in the action. Learning of the plan, the miller's wife stands, or rather lies, in for the would-be mistress, and each of the two men makes love to her five times. Neither recognizes the substitute until

---

[8] Joseph Bédier, *Les Fabliaux: Études de littérature populaire et d'histoire littéraire du moyen âge* (Paris: 1894; Bouillon, 6th ed., Paris: Champion, 1964), 298; Ménard, *Fabliaux*, 219. Both Bédier and Ménard cite this fabliau as an example of the cuckold "battu et content."

the next day when the wife upbraids her husband, complaining that in fourteen years of marriage, he has never had intercourse with her more than twice a night (!) but that last night, when he thought that she was somebody else, he managed to get it up ten times. Suddenly the truth hits home: not only has he failed in his intended adultery; he has made himself a cuckold.[9]

All in all, husbands, as they are portrayed in the fabliaux, are losers. One man makes the mistake of boasting to his wife that she could never deceive him without his finding out about it. Rising to the bait, she invites a male friend of hers, who is impersonating a female nurse, to accompany her to an upstairs room, where they engage in vigorous sexual activity, as the unsuspecting husband waits downstairs. Still red in the face and short of breath, the wife rejoins her husband and gives him a blow-by-blow account of what has just transpired. The husband listens sympathetically, thinking all the while that she is describing an unusually draining blood-letting. He is not tipped off even by her mention of the soothing ointment that the nurse produced from a tube and injected into her gaping wound at the very moment when she could not have borne the pain another minute.

> "Et si ne vous en quier mentir:
> L'oingnement issoit d'un tuiel,
> Et si descendoit d'un forel
> D'une pel mout noire et hideuse,
> Mas mout par estoit savoreuse."
> Dist li borgois, "Ma bele amie,
> A poi ne fustes mal baillie:
> Bon oingnement avez eü!"
> Cil ne s'est pas aperceü
> De la borde qu'ele conta.
> (*La Saineresse*, NRCF 4:36, vv. 94–103)

In another fabliau, a priest bets a husband that he can lift three people piled one on top of another. The husband wagers a goose that he cannot. First, the priest makes the husband lie face-down on the floor; next, he tells the servant girl to stretch out, also face-down, on top of the husband. Then he puts the wife on her back on top of the servant girl; finally, the priest climbs on top of the wife and, according to the story, lets his "little ferret explore her rabbit hole" (*Le Prestre et la*

[9] *Le Meunier d'Arleux*, NRCF 9:110. This story suggests an amusing inversion of an unlikely situation debated by the canonists, as summarized in James A. Brundage, *Law, Sex, and Christian Society in Medieval Europe* (Chicago: University of Chicago Press, 1987), 381–82: "Circumstances, however, could sometimes make fornication no sin at all: a man who mistakenly slept with a woman thinking that she was his wife, for example, was held blameless."

dame, NRCF 8:95, vv. 134–36). Feeling a lot of pushing and shoving, the husband, who, from his vantage point at the bottom of the heap, cannot see what is going on above him, assumes that the priest is making a good-faith effort to perform the feat of which he claimed to be capable. Having worn himself out, the priest admits to the husband that he has lost the bet and that he will gladly pay him the goose. Technically speaking, the husband here is the winner, but, under the circumstances, winning makes him all the more a loser.

This character that I am calling the fabliau husband shows up in other genres as well. If we look to the south, for example, we find little stories called *razos*, some of which, except for being in prose rather than narrative verse, read very much like fabliaux. The poet Raimon de Miraval falls in love with a woman who refuses to have sex with him unless he agrees to marry her. When Raimon hears that she wants him as her husband, he is delighted but realizes that he must dream up some excuse to get rid of his present wife, who is, as it happens, a poet like him. He kicks her out, on the creative rationale that two troubadours in a single household are one too many and that she will have to go. Feeling more liberated than rejected, she sends for her lover, who whisks her away with him. Raimon's mistress, perhaps dismayed by how easily Raimon could be persuaded to divest himself of his first wife, decides to marry someone else. So Raimon loses both mistress and wife. In another of the *razos*, the troubadour Gaucelm Faidit is enamored of a lady named Marguerite, but she is in love, not with Gaucelm, but with Gaucelm's close friend Hugh. Married, of course, and frustrated that she has so little opportunity to be with the man whom she fancies, Marguerite feigns a life-threatening illness for which the only cure is a pilgrimage. With the permission of her husband, who is genuinely worried about her health, she plans a rendezvous with her boyfriend Hugh at the home of her admirer Gaucelm, who she knows will be away at that time. Although Gaucelm is absent, Gaucelm's wife is very much present; indeed, it is she who suggests that it might be amusing for the visitors to use the bed normally occupied by her and her husband. When Gaucelm later learns of all of this, he is beside himself with grief because not only has his lady been unfaithful to him, she has done so in his own bed. With one fell swoop, this husband has been betrayed by his mistress, his wife, and the man he thought was his best buddy.[10]

Within the lyric domain, we find the fabliau husband in the *chansons de mal-mariée* or songs of the Unhappy Wife. In poems of this type, a feisty young lady, who has been given in marriage to a jealous old man, at once laments her fate and flaunts her disdain of her spouse. "May God give me the heart to love my husband as long as I have a lover of my own choosing on the side." "It's not fair

[10] Jean Boutière and Alexander Herman Schutz, *Biographies des troubadours*, Édition refondue par Jean Boutière avec la collaboration d'Irénée-Marcel Cluzel (Paris: Nizet, 1964), 379–83, 392–403; 180–84.

when a young woman is given in marriage to a boor. But I will compensate for this injustice by taking a lover, and if my husband gets upset about it, let him find a mistress because, whether he likes it or not, I shall love!" "Put up with it, hubby, and don't let it annoy you. You can have me again tomorrow; my lover has got me tonight. The night is short; you'll get me back as soon as he has had his fill." "Let our husbands spy on us if they want to; we will make them cuckolds up to their necks."[11]

And it is not just wives who articulate their domestic woes in song. In a genre known as the *jeu-parti*, we hear henpecked husbands engaging in a game of one-upmanship about the hardships that they must endure. They ask each other questions like: "Which husband suffers more: the one who suspects his wife of carrying on an affair but is unable to prove it or the one who knows for a fact that his wife used to have a lover, but that she has been abandoned by him and that she will never deceive him again?" "Who is to be pitied more, the man who is constantly jealous of his wife or the one who knows that his mistress is deceiving him?" "Would you prefer for your wife to know that you are unfaithful to her or for her to be unfaithful to you without your knowing anything about it?" "Is it better for me to be beaten by my wife on account of my mistress or for my mistress to be beaten by her husband on account of me?"[12]

The truth of the matter is that fabliau husbands are to be found in all medieval French literature dealing with adulterous love, even in courtly romance.[13] Tristan loves Iseut, who is married to Marc, and Lancelot loves Guenivere, who is married to Arthur, to cite only the most famous of love triangles. But we do not laugh at Marc and Arthur, or at least not much. Mostly we forget about them, for we are too busy following the adventures of Tristan and Iseut, Lancelot and Guenivere, heroic characters whom we cannot help admiring.[14]

---

[11] Pierre Bec, *La Lyrique française au Moyen-Age (XIIe–XIIIe siècles)* (Paris: Picard, 1977), 2:13, 14, 16, 15.

[12] Arthur Långfors, ed., *Recueil général des jeux-partis français* (Paris: Champion, 1926): I, XXXVIII, 140–43; I, LXXVII, 286–88; II, CXXXIII, 130–33; II, CXXXIV, 134–37.

[13] Nykrog, *Les Fabliaux*, 187, writes, "Dans les deux branches de la littérature, le mari est le vilain, le jaloux, car c'est un personnage odieux et gênant par sa jalousie et par la contrainte physique qu'il exerce sur la femme, au grand détriment des désirs secrets de celle-ci." Thomas D. Cooke, *The Old French and Chaucerian Fabliaux: A Study of Their Comic Climax* (Columbia: University of Missouri Press, 1978), 68, notes that the jealous husband (and other stock characters) can be found in non-comic genres as well in the fabliaux.

[14] Sidney E. Berger, "Sex in the Literature of the Middle Ages: The Fabliaux," in *Sexual Practices and the Medieval Church*, ed. Vern L. Bullough and James A. Brundage (Buffalo: Prometheus Books, 1982), 163, explains that while the fabliaux and courtly love literature share a common set of presuppositions about love, "in true courtly love the striving of the man must fall short of consummation. When the striving goes beyond the pristine and ennobling relationship of pure courtly love, it takes two different paths:

Both by what it says and by what it leaves unsaid, the fabliau, however, ensures that we not set its adulterous lovers on a pedestal. In contrast to courtly romance, the fabliau does not try to explain how an adulterous relationship has come into being. It does not trace the stages of courtship nor does it analyze complex emotions.[15] The fabliau takes adultery for granted. It neither condemns nor glorifies it. The fabliau does not conceal what is essentially sinful behavior by clothing it in evasive or delicate language. In describing sexual relations, it does not resort to euphemism, opting instead for almost clinical terms (he inserts his penis into her vagina) or for metaphors, which are in their own way even more graphic: squirrels looking for nuts, horses grazing in meadows, ferrets poking around in holes, salve squirting from a tube.[16] The fabliau features a lover who is no Lancelot or Tristan, but a nameless, faceless, mindless man, preferably a priest, who proves his prowess, not with his sword, but with its anatomical counterpart. Most importantly perhaps, the fabliau brings the husband to the foreground, without, however, turning him into a sympathetic character.[17] Through these devices and others, the fabliau rejects the strenuous idealism of courtly romance.

1) it could turn to romance, in which the characters are motivated by genuine and deep affection (as in Tristan and Iseult); or 2) it could turn into fabliau, in which the love is more accurately depicted as lust, and this lust is consummated in any of a variety of bizarre or acrobatic ways in order to amuse us." Per Nykrog, "Courtliness and the Townspeople: The Fabliaux as a Courtly Burlesque," in *The Humor of the Fabliaux*, ed. Thomas D. Cooke and Benjamin L. Honeycutt (Columbia: University of Missouri Press, 1974), 69, sums it up neatly with an assertion which leads to a rhetorical question: "A lover is a sublime character, and a husband is an uninspiring bully, but how does marriage transform a sublime young lover into the tedious tyrant depicted by courtly doctrine?"

[15] Ingrid Strasser, "Mariage, amour et adultère dans les fabliaux," in *Amour, mariage et transgression au moyen âge*, ed. Danielle Buschinger and André Crépin (Göppingen: Kümmerle, 1984), 427; Ménard, *Fabliaux*, 17; Nykrog, *Les Fabliaux*, 187; Baldwin, *Language of Sex*, 159.

[16] To cite only two of the most succinct and most matter-of-fact accounts: "Le vit li a ou con bouté" (*Le Prestre qui abevete*, NRCF 8:88, v. 58.1); "A tant li met el con lo vit" (*La Damoisele qui ne pooit oïr parler de foutre*, NRCF 4:26, v. 204). R. Howard Bloch, "Modest Maids and Modified Nouns: Obscenity in the Fabliaux," in *Obscenity: Social Control and Artistic Creation in the European Middle Ages*, ed. Jan M. Ziolkowski (Leiden: Brill, 1998), 284, states, "There is in the fabliaux very little portrayal of the act itself." One wonders how much more portrayal Bloch or anybody else could want.

[17] Nykrog, *Les Fabliaux*, 111, describes the husband as "le personnage de premier plan dans le fabliau," while Ménard, *Fabliaux*, 139, rather misleadingly characterizes his role thus: "Ce pauvre diable peut rester dans l'ombre; il n'intéresse pas grand monde." The wife and the lover may wish that the husband would "remain in the shadows," but then there would be no adventure for them and no story for us. Cooke, *The Old French and Chaucerian Fabliaux*, 17, comments on the importance of keeping the audience from identifying with the husband.

In asserting that the fabliau is not idealistic, are we implying that it is realistic? In other words, do the outlandish escapades recounted in the fabliaux correspond to what was actually going on in thirteenth-century France? Did real people act like the husbands and wives of the fabliaux?[18] We may never know what was going on in non-aristocratic households at that time, but what we do know is that marriage in those days was a topic that was being hotly debated at the universities and in ecclesiastical circles. Theologians, canonists, preachers, and popes: all felt compelled to put in their two cents' worth.

Even the most basic question, namely, what constitutes marriage, remained unresolved throughout the period that interests us. Does marriage come into existence through the exchange of consent between the parties concerned, through their carnal union, or through a combination of the two acts?[19] And if a couple had to have had sex at least once before they were officially married, does that mean that Mary and Joseph lived together in sin all those years?[20] Moreover, if the only thing that a man had to do to transform his concubine into his wife was to declare that at some point, privately, in the past, he and she had exchanged vows, how could anybody know for sure who was married and who was not?[21] And then there was the thorny issue whether marriage is a sacrament. If it is, does that put it on a par with, say, Ordination and the Eucharist, or is there a hierarchy according to which some holy sacraments are holier than others? And if one concedes that marriage is good, does that make marital sex good? If so, what is it good for? Merely for producing children? Or might it also be valued for the pleasure that it affords or for the physical and emotional health that it promotes?

---

[18] Baldwin, *Language of Sex*, 235, raises these same questions: "Beyond the verbal interplay, however, what does all this talk tell us about social behavior? About what people actually did in northern France around 1200? How can we pass from the text to the contextual realm of sexual behavior?" He continues, "These questions need not concern the literary critic, but they stubbornly refuse to decamp from the center of the historian's task." Although no historian, I, like Baldwin, find these questions pertinent. Ménard, *Fabliaux*, 105, on the other hand, warns against any attempt to read these stories as realistic: "Il ne faut pas demander aux fabliaux une peinture fidèle de la vie conjugale ou de la sexualité médiévale. Les contes à rire cherchent à grossir, amplifier. Ils inventent sans scrupules."

[19] J. Brundage, "Implied Consent to Intercourse," in *Consent and Coercion to Sex and Marriage in Ancient and Medieval Societies*, ed. Angeliki E. Laiou (Washington, DC: Dumbarton Oaks, 1993), 246–48; idem, "Sexual Equality in Medieval Canon Law," in *Sex, Law, and Marriage in the Middle Ages*, ed. idem, (Brookfield, VT: Ashgate Publishing, 1993), 68.

[20] Brundage, *Law, Sex, and Christian Society*, 354–55; idem, "Sexual Equality," 68.

[21] Brundage, *Medieval Canon Law* (New York: Longman, 1995), 73; Brundage, *Law, Sex, and Christian Society*, 341.

And if sex is good only when it is procreative, does it become sinful when one of the participating parties fails to reach orgasm, which, according to the medieval understanding of human physiology, was essential for conception?[22]

In elaborating their abstract arguments, canonists adduced concrete instances, some of which were undoubtedly hypothetical, but others of which were real. Whether fictional or true, these examples sound for all the world like little fabliaux. Here are two taken from the *Summa Confessorum* of Thomas of Chobham, written in the year 1216.[23] The first relates how a bishop breaks up the love affair between a woman and a priest by tricking the latter into appearing publicly with another woman. As soon as woman number one sees her lover in the company of woman number two, she is consumed with hatred and resolves never to have anything to do with him again. The second tells of an archbishop who cures a priest and his mistress of their seemingly insatiable passion for each other by shutting them up in a small room, just the two of them, and not letting either of them leave. It is only a few days before the priest begs for release, his ardor, for that lady at least, having been permanently quenched.

Unlike Thomas of Chobham, the writers of fabliaux are reluctant to reprimand wanton priests. We see this most clearly perhaps in the fabliau in which a husband, not realizing that the priest is in the bed with him and his wife, gets up and accidentally puts on the wrong pants. He discovers the mix-up several hours later when he tries to make a purchase at the market and finds the priest's official seal in the pocket where he assumed his money to be. Word of the incident soon reaches the bishop, who reacts, not as we might expect, by admonishing this priest to keep his pants on, but rather by ordering all priests, for God's sake, to leave their seal of identification at home when they go visiting their mistresses.

> La nouvielle s'en espandi;
> Et li evesques l'entendy,
> Si vot a tous priestres deffendre
> Des saiaus a leur braies pendre.
> (*Les Braies le priestre*, NRCF 10:115, vv. 107–10)

If the writers of fabliaux appear unperturbed by the promiscuity of parish priests, it may be that they considered reformation of the clergy to be a hopeless task. Or they may simply have reckoned that it was not their responsibility to

[22] Brundage, *Law, Sex, and Christian Society*, 415, 425–33; Brundage, "Sexual Equality," 68. Charles Muscatine, *The Old French Fabliaux* (New Haven: Yale University Press, 1986), 131; J. Brundage, "Let Me Count the Ways: Canonists and Theologians Contemplate Coital Positions," in *Sex, Law, and Marriage in the Middle Ages*, 81–85.

[23] I took both of these examples from Brundage, *Law, Sex, and Christian Society*, 349. Baldwin, *Language of Sex*, 42, also cites two examples from Thomas of Chobham.

teach priests how to behave. But that is not to say that they were not intrigued by sexuality and its potential to shore up or to undermine a marriage.[24] There were two marital issues in particular that apparently titillated fabliau writers as much as they did canon lawyers.

The first was the so-called conjugal debt. Once a man and woman had ratified their marriage with carnal union, then each of them had the right to demand sex from the other whenever he or she felt like it. The partner was morally, indeed legally, bound to comply.[25] An early thirteenth-century canonist writes of a serf whose wife asked him to make love to her at the same hour that his feudal lord expected him to be working in the field. What was he to do? He was to fulfill his obligation to his lord first, but only if his spouse granted her permission. Moreover, if he had reason to think that by refusing to comply with her request he was putting her in "imminent danger of committing fornication," then he was obliged to set down everything else and give her what she wanted right then and there. One anonymous Anglo-Norman glossator endorses the conjugal debt as an effective safeguard against polygyny, since, as he reminds his reader, "no man can hope to satisfy more than one woman."[26]

The impossibility of keeping up with the conjugal debt was grist for the mill of several writers of fabliaux.[27] In one story, a cocky young man brags to his father that one wife will never be enough for him. He will need at least ten or twelve. His father, a man of experience, advises his son to try living with one woman for a year and then, if he still thinks he can handle more than that, he can have two, three, four, five, six, seven, eight, nine, ten, however many he wants.

> Et s'une ne vos puet durer,
> Je vos en feré deus doner
> Ou trois ou quatre ou cinc ou sis
> Ou set ou uit ou neuf ou dis,
> Ou tant com vos onques vodrez:
> Ja mar de ce en douterez!
> (*Le Vallet aus douze fames*, NRCF 4:29, vv. 19–24)

---

[24] Cooke, *The Old French and Chaucerian Fabliaux*, 155, observes correctly that there is never any dissolution of marriage bonds in the fabliaux. There are "no separations, no annulments." He is, however, somewhat less accurate when he claims, "Nor are there any attempts or even spoken desires to break up a marriage." As we shall see, both *Le Pescheor de Pont sur Saine* and *La Coille noire* contradict his generally true statement.

[25] Brundage, "Implied Consent," 249, 255; idem, "Sexual Equality," 67; idem, *Law, Sex, and Christian Society*, 447.

[26] Brundage, *Law, Sex, and Christian Society*, 359; Muscatine, *Old French Fabliaux*, 122.

[27] Baldwin, *Language of Sex*, 194.

The woman selected as his first wife gets wind of her husband's boast and secretly resolves to put him to the test. She demands sex so often that within six months he is but a shadow of his former self: skinny, sallow, listless, lustless, and limp. At the end of the year, when his father offers to furnish the eleven additional wives that he had promised him, the son declines, confessing that it has taken only one to sap him of his precious life-giving juices. In another fabliau about the conjugal debt, a wife persuades her husband to let her assign nicknames to their genitals: she calls hers Piglet; his Wheat. But Piglet wants to eat so much that in the end the poor husband can come up with nothing more than a little fart, which is, as he explains to her, all that remains of the original whole grain. He begs, "Have mercy on me, leave me in peace, for I have done your will so frequently that I am completely de-floured. That pig of yours is a real pain in the butt. Cover it up. It has made its last breakfast on my Wheaties."

> Vostre merci, laissiez m'an paiz,
> Que tant ai fait voz volantez
> Que toz me sui desfromantez:
> Trop est vostre pors engoisseus!
> Car recovrez vostre perteus
> Et vostre con, qui est punais!
> Ja par moi ne manjera mais:
> (*Porcelet*, NRCF 6:67, vv. 54–60)[28]

Intimately related to the first, the second issue that captured the imagination of both canonists and the writers of fabliaux was impotence as grounds for separation or divorce. As every student of canon law was well aware, there was impotence and there was impotence: on the one hand, that which was inborn, absolute, permanent, and, on the other, that which was circumstantial, relative, and temporary.[29] Two canonists debated with prurient pleasure the case of a woman who succeeded in getting her marriage annulled on the grounds that she was incapable of consummating it. Upon remarrying, the same woman had no difficulty having sex with her new husband. The questions, then, is, "Should she be obliged to go back to her first husband and try again?" Both of the canonists agreed that she should, but disagreed on how many times. One of them suggested that, after three failed attempts at intercourse with the first husband, she should be allowed to remain in the second marriage. The other, however, insisted that she should give the first husband as many chances as he wanted. As far as that unsympathetic canonist was concerned, this woman, whose passions ran alternately

---

[28] *La Dame qui aveine demandoit pour Morel sa provende avoir* (NRCF 9:108) recounts a longer, more complex version of the same story.

[29] Brundage, *Law, Sex, and Christian Society*, 339, 415, 457.

hot and cold, depending on her partner, could spend the rest of her life in a state of matrimonial limbo.[30]

Obviously, it was hard to verify that a man was impotent if he denied the charge. The three conventional modes of proof were sworn testimony of neighbors, evidence of three years of cohabitation, and physical examination of the man's genitalia to determine whether there were any conspicuous abnormalities. Sometimes professional stripteases hired by ecclesiastical authorities, euphemistically called "honest women," were brought into the courtroom to assess the defendant's virility. In their aggressive efforts to arouse him sexually, these expert examiners would uncover their breasts, kiss and fondle him all over, and play with his penis and testicles. Any man who failed to have an erection in response to these erotic gestures was deemed incurably impotent.[31]

The writers of fabliaux shared the canonists' fascination with impotence and its impact on marriage. One fabliau writer makes it plain that he understands and suggests that every married woman of his day understands that tangible proof of inability to fulfill the conjugal debt is sufficient cause for separation. In the story that I have in mind a husband comes home one day and throws a tumescent penis on the floor, claiming that it is his own. The wife immediately insists on a divorce. "Now we can get divorced! I refuse to stay with you any longer. I will remarry: a young, sexually active man this time, for you are totally worthless."

> Certes, or departiron nos!
> Ja mes avec vos ne seré:
> Un autre home respouseré,
> Qui sera jane et remuant,
> Car vos ne valez pas un gant!
> (*Le Pescheor de Pont sur Saine*, NRCF 4:28, vv. 134–38)[32]

[30] Brundage, *Law, Sex, and Christian Society*, 378.

[31] Brundage, *Law, Sex, and Christian Society*, 413, 457.

[32] It is hard for me to understand why Bédier, *Fabliaux*, 380, found this fabliau singularly disgusting. He asks his reader, "Est-il possible d'imaginer un conte plus répugnant que *le Pécheur de Pont-sur-Seine*?" Personally, I find *La Dame escoillee* (NRCF 8:83) much more offensive. Muscatine, *Old French Fabliaux*, 116, 121, lists *Le Pescheor* as one of several fabliaux illustrating that, ultimately, marital stability depends on a healthy sex life. Per Nykrog, "Obscene or Not Obscene: Lady Reason, Jean de Meun, and the 'Fisherman from Pont-sur-Seine'," in *Obscenity, Social Control and Artistic Creation*, 330, also reads *Le Pescheor* as a demonstration that "genital sexuality is the foundation of true happiness and love in marriage." R. Howard Bloch, *The Scandal of the Fabliaux* (Chicago: University of Chicago Press, 1986), 61, seems to think that the wife "sues for divorce." Fortunately, she never has to take such drastic measures.

The second fabliau dealing with marital impotence is *La Coille noire* ("Black Balls"), which, as one of only four fabliaux to be preserved in as many as seven manuscripts, appears to have been a favorite with medieval audiences. Although generally discredited by recent scholars who regard it as "silly," and "decidedly unengaging for modern tastes,"[33] this text merits our attention in the present discussion. Noticing for the first time after more than twelve months of marriage that her husband's genitals are black, the wife, disgusted, declares forthwith her intention to entreat the bishop to grant her a legal separation. Her husband warns her that if she lodges a complaint against him, he will register one against her. The woman reminds him that in threatening her this way he is only aggravating the situation. Appearing at the ecclesiastical court, the woman makes the following statement: "My husband and I have been married for over a year without my having carnal knowledge of him. But yesterday evening for the first time I perceived the thing that is causing his impotence, and I could produce many a witness who would testify to this truth: My husband has a prick blacker than iron and balls that are blacker than a monk's hood and as furry as the coat of a she-bear and as bulgy as a usurer's purse. I have told you the truth, the whole truth and nothing but the truth."

A l'evesque dit, n'a pas ris:
"Ci sui devant vostre presance,
Si dirai tot en audience
Por quoi je sui a vos venue.
Plus a d'un an que m'a tenue
Mes vilains c'onques nel quenui;
Mais arsoir primes l'aperçui,
La chose par quoi il remaint,
Et tesmoing en avroie maint
Qui tesmoigneroit a voir:
Mes mariz a lo vit plus noir
De fer et la coille plus noire
Que chape a moine ne prevoire,
S'est velue comme pel d'orse;
N'onques encor nule viez borse
D'usurrier ne fu si enflee!
La verité vos ai contee:
Lo voir reconeü vos ai
Au miauz que dire lo vos sai."
(*La Coille noire*, NRCF 5:46, vv. 50–68)

[33] Norris J. Lacy, *Reading Fabliaux* (New York: Garland, 1993), 2, 42.

The defendant responds by accusing his wife of wasting his hay by using it as toilet paper. Hearing this, the woman blurts out, "You're lying through your teeth! I haven't wiped my ass with anything for more than a year now!" "You hear that, Sir?! I knew it! So that's why my balls are so black!"

> Et cil sa parole li tranche
> Et dist: "Biaus sire, a vos me claim
> De ma fame, qui tot mon fain
> M'a gasté a faire torchons.
> — Vos mantez parmi les grenons,
> Fait ele, dan vilains despers!
> Plus a d'un an que ne fu ters
> Mes cus de fain ne d'autre rien.
> — Oez sire, lo savoie bien:
> Por c'est ma coille si nercie!"
> (NRCF 5:46, vv. 98–107)

Amid loud laughter in the courtroom, the bishop dismisses the case and sends the couple home to pick up the pieces of their marriage, or at least to clean up their act.[34]

If this fabliau was as popular as it was in its day, it is not because it is so silly but rather because it is so sophisticated. The writer of this fabliau wants us to believe that this uneducated woman, who is no genius, knows exactly what it takes to get a divorce.[35] We are to believe that she knows that, according to church law, a woman can initiate separation and divorce actions, even though civil law denies her this right.[36]

> Jel laisserai, et orandroit.
> J'irai a l'evesque tot droit,
> Si li mosterai cest afaire!"
> (NRCF 5:46, vv. 27–29)

[34] Burns analyzes this fabliau in some detail, but it would appear that she and I do not agree on its basic plot. I see no hint in the text that this woman had been neglecting her conjugal duty to her husband because "she was so busy soliciting sex from others" ("Women Talk Back," 204). According to my reading of the narrative, even her husband does not accuse her of promiscuity.

[35] Frederik Pedersen, *Marriage Disputes in Medieval England* (London: Hambledon Press, 2000), 62, 83, demonstrates that, at least in England in the fourteenth century, lay knowledge of canon law on divorce was quite advanced. Ordinary people would have received such information primarily through sermons.

[36] Pedersen, *Marriage Disputes*, 207; Brundage, *Law, Sex, and Christian Society*, 411.

We are to believe that she knows that black genitals, repulsive as she may find them, are not sufficient cause for dissolution of the marriage unless she can prove that the excessive pigmentation in her husband's genitalia renders him impotent (vv. 54–57).[37] We are to believe that she knows that evidence of cruelty can be admitted in divorce hearings.[38]

> "Or est vostre plaiz empiriez,
> Por ce que m'avez menaciee!"
> (NRCF 5:46, vv. 46–47)

We are to believe that she knows that her husband can delay the proceedings by interposing an exception to her charge, which holds up the judge's ruling on the separation issue, since the counter-charge, according to church law, must be resolved first. We are to believe that she knows that if her husband's exception is proved, her case will automatically be dropped. Thus, we are to believe that she knows that she has no choice but to deny his allegation.[39] Unfortunately for her, however, she cannot disprove his charge against her without simultaneously disproving her charge against him. That this ignorant woman should be so well informed of the intricacies of marriage law is patently absurd, and that is precisely the point. The purpose of this fabliau as I read it is to expose the ever-widening rift in thirteenth-century France between the academic debates of canonists and theologians and the experiences of ordinary people.[40]

Many scholars believe that the fabliaux serve little or no social function. They regard these stories as amoral and believe that their sole reason for existence is to

---

[37] Brundage, "Implied Consent," 252–53. We are further to believe that this woman knows that she can call in witnesses (vv. 58–59) to substantiate her allegation that her husband is impotent. Moreover, we are to believe that she and her husband are conversant with legal jargon. They appear to be perfectly familiar with the basic vocabulary needed to state their cases: *clamor* (vv. 33, 111), *departir* (v. 38), *plaiz* (v. 46), *tesmoing* (v. 58), *reconaistre* (v. 67), *oposer* (vv. 94, 95), *se clamer* (v. 99).

[38] Brundage, Law, Sex, and Christian Society, 455.

[39] Brundage, Law, Sex, and Christian Society, 410.

[40] Erik Kooper, "Loving the Unequal Equal: Medieval Theologians and Marital Affection," in *The Olde Daunce: Love, Friendship, Sex, and Marriage in the Medieval World*, ed. Robert R. Edwards and Stephen Spector (Albany: State University of New York Press, 1991), 46. Pedersen, *Marriage Disputes,* 62, might offer a different interpretation. If what he has documented for peasants in late fourteenth-century England was already true for ordinary men and women in thirteenth-century France, then such a woman as we have in *La Coille noire* really may have been aware of the fine points of canon law concerning marriage.

entertain.[41] They assert that once the ruse is introduced into the plot, Christian, or even courtly, morality flies out the window, to be replaced by an ethics of expediency.[42] As they see it, the fabliau projects a topsy-turvy world in which false values prevail.[43] There are, however, at least two recent scholars who have challenged the received wisdom on the function of the fabliau: Mary Jane Schenck and Norris Lacy.[44] Schenck maintains that the fabliaux reflect the desire for an orderly world where events do not occur randomly. She perceives in these texts a pervasive concern with human justice.[45] Similarly, Lacy considers the fabliaux to be "profoundly conservative," inasmuch as they "show us the 'proper' relations of wife to husband, in accordance with certain medieval notions about 'God's plan'." [46] Lacy's point is illustrated most strikingly perhaps in *Le Pescheor de Pont sur Saine*, when the fisherman answers his wife's question about how his detached penis has come to be restored to the place where it belongs. He describes its reinstatement as a miracle performed by God Himself, who wants to see this marriage sustained.[47]

— Comment vos est il revenu?
— Ja l'a Dieu fet par sa vertu,

---

[41] Jürgen Beyer, "The Morality of the Amoral," in *The Humor of the Fabliaux*, 41, for instance, regards the fabliau as "a genre that is permeated by the conviction of the inability of man to learn and the unimprovable creature qualities of the human being, man or woman."

[42] Ménard, *Fabliaux*, 116–17. Muscatine, *Old French Fabliaux*, 153, maintains that fabliaux do have a "consistent value system," which he labels "hedonistic materialism."

[43] Ménard, *Fabliaux*, 133.

[44] See also Berger, "Sex," 175, who asserts that the fabliaux aim to teach as well as entertain. "We can learn (if only by negative example) from these tales as much as we can be entertained by them." Conceding that "the fabliaux were primarily written to make us laugh," Berger "cannot help feeling, however, that —considering when these pieces were written — the audience did learn something from them, regardless of what the authors' intentions were."

[45] Mary Jane Stearns Schenck, *The Fabliaux: Tales of Wit and Deception* (Amsterdam: John Benjamins, 1987), 32–33.

[46] Lacy, *Reading Fabliaux*, 37–38, 40.

[47] Cooke, *The Old French and Chaucerian Fabliaux*, 154, holds that it is characteristic of the fabliau as a genre that, in it, "the institution of marriage remains intact, even though it may have been a bit jarred." Referring specifically to *Le Pescheor de Pont sur Saine*, Thomas D. Cooke, "Pornography, the Comic Spirit and the Fabliaux," in *The Humor of the Fabliaux*, 148, is troubled by "a sense of uneasiness at the conclusion of this tale because the climax does not come from the needs the story embodies. It is closer to tragi-comedy." But do we need to take this story so seriously?

Qui ne voleit mie, ce croi,
Que tu departises de moi!"
(NRCF 4:28, vv. 179–82)

To summarize, the husband as he is portrayed in the fabliau is stupid, but he is no stupider than the husband found in other genres, including courtly romance. It is simply that in the fabliau we are not allowed to ignore him. The fabliaux are less subversive than courtly romances that unabashedly idealize adulterous lovers, leaving us with the impression that we would somehow be happier, nobler, wiser, or more enviable if we were having an extramarital affair. The corrupt world of the fabliau is only a slightly exaggerated representation of the world in which we live. Its values are our values. Irreverent but nonetheless Christian, the fabliau probes some of the same hard and not-so-hard questions addressed by thirteenth-century scholars and preachers.[48]

[48] Roy J. Pearcy, "Investigations into the Principles of Fabliau Structure," in *Versions of Medieval Comedy*, ed. Paul L. Ruggiers (Norman: University of Oklahoma Press, 1977), 99–100, detects a sophistic structure in many of the fabliaux. "All those who attended the universities of the area for however brief a period, and there is good reason to suppose that numerous authors of fabliaux may have been included in this group, could hardly have escaped some exposure to the influence of sophistic. Any of the various treatments of fallacies might in certain respects be regarded as a kind of blueprint for the fabliaux." In the view of both Berger and Schenck, the form of the fabliau is modeled on that of the exemplum. As Berger, "Sex," 172, explains, "Fabliau audiences would have been thoroughly familiar with the sermon structure, for they were preached to at least once a week, the sermons normally having as part of their structure an exemplum; many of the fabliaux are written in just this format." According to Schenck, *The Fabliaux*, 28, the fabliau borrowed the exemplum structure in order to "create its own world of meaning." Michael M. Sheehan, "Maritalis Affectio Revisited," in *The Olde Daunce*, 41–42, emphasizes the crucial role that liturgy and, more specifically, sermons played in the lives of uneducated people in the Middle Ages. He believes that the surviving medieval sermons reveal "what sorts of ideas about marriage ordinary men and women were regularly exposed to." Rüdiger Schnell, "The Discourse on Marriage in the Middle Ages," *Speculum* 73 (1998): 773–75, explains that marriage sermons are concerned with situations "that oppose the ideal." They look for "a compromise." "The marriage sermon's special perspective is marked in the text by two distinctions: between norms and deviations and between theory (what everybody should do) and practice (what many do)." "We are in a space that lies between absolute good and absolute evil. Here it is a matter, not of realizing an ideal, but of adapting to actual events. A marriage can succeed even when both spouses do not fulfill all the required norms and ideals. Relativity and pragmatism are the focus, not absolute standards and theoretical ideals." From these highly suggestive summary remarks, we see just what close cousins the fabliau and the medieval marriage sermon could be. The common structural and ethical foundations undergirding these two genres warrant further analysis.

In his classic study of the fabliau, Per Nykrog has observed that every married couple is "either ridiculous or boring,"[49] a statement whose truth I do not deny. I would fault Nykrog only for not being more precise. It is the couples featured in the fabliaux who are ridiculous, and it is boring couples like us who read about them with a vague sense of relief that our own lives are comparatively dull.

---

[49] *Les Fabliaux*, 189–90.

The Dilemma of the Widow of Property for Late Medieval London

Barbara A. Hanawalt

The property that came to widows upon their husband's death posed a dilemma for medieval Londoners and for a modern historian of property rights, remarriage, and the structure of London society. London widows of the merchant and artisan classes had considerable real property acquired either as dower or as inheritance. London dower laws gave widows a third of their former husband's estate for their life use if the couple had children and half it they did not. No restrictions barred them from taking this property into a second or third marriage. Other widows had inherited property in their own names, as well as their dower, and, upon their husband's death, they regained control over the administration of the property.

The society pondered the problems these wealthy widows posed. Their potential to cause disruption was great. While a maiden, the woman's father had legal charge of her, and while a wife she was legally covered by her husband. But a widow could enter into contracts alone, sue for debt, run her business, and marry off her children. Having gained this economic and legal freedom of action, moralists worried, would widows also exercise sexual freedom? Remarriage seemed a convenient solution to curb a widow's freedoms and distribute her wealth to another male. For the men in London who were striving to make their way in a commercial world, the presence of these widows with their real estate and their social standing, acquired from their former husbands, made them an irresistible market commodity. I will argue in this paper that the endowment of women with real property made them valuable conduits of wealth for the capital formation in late medieval London. Remarriage of widows created horizontal, non-kin ties in London that encouraged gild and class solidarity among the propertied, but also permitted the development of a merchant elite in the later Middle Ages.

If prospective husbands saw the widows as cash cows, we must also investigate the motivations of the widows themselves. What factors might influence a widow in her decision-making, and what options did she have? As we shall see, various factors such as the wishes of the former husband about remarriage, the needs of children, and the age of the widows influenced their choices. A widow in a period of plague might have little time to consider remarriage, and if she were already over forty, she might also not consider another marriage. Widows who were left a business to run might find it more convenient to have a husband to carry it on. The Church allowed for the semi-regular life of the vowess, the woman who lived in the world but registered with the bishop to remain in chaste widowhood. Regardless of their individual preferences and needs, all widows would face external pressures, such as suitors' designs on their property and moral standards imposed by the Church, the community, and folk wisdom. Freedom in the Middle Ages always came with a price, and for widows, the price could determine the limits of their freedom of choice.

Widows' Material Resources

Any medievalists who study social history would be most grateful for some source that permitted a reconstruction of population, including the number of children, adults, widows, ages of marriage, remarriages, servants, occupations, and so on. We have to reconcile ourselves to the fact that there are no censuses before the late eighteenth century. I have been telling graduate students, who are just confronting the problem of lack of records, that they can either reconcile themselves to analyzing the holes in Swiss cheese or to study the twentieth century, which is more like Cheddar cheese. Looking at the Swiss cheese factors, what can we say about medieval London widows?

We must begin with the formation of marriage. Medieval marriage was formed on the basis of an economic and social relationship rather than love. In many ways marriage was a "contractual partnership." That is, real property and chattels were exchanged in the form of dowry given by the wife at the time of marriage and dower promised by the husband to his wife as provision for her widowhood. The "partnership" also included cultural assumptions about the work that men and women would contribute to the household. Women's and men's work were more clearly defined then than now.[1] Nor were the partnerships equal, and certainly medieval marriages were not, for the husband had more control over resources than did the wife. But the presumption of a contract and distribution of labor made these marriages a partnership from their inception. First marriages were, for the most part, arranged by the parents of the bride and groom or by their next of kin or friends. Although no written contract might exist, family and friends regarded their negotiations as binding. The usual arrangement was for the husband to contribute real property and perhaps a trade or business, while the wife contributed money, goods, and perhaps real property. The wife's contribution, the dowry, was to provide capital for establishing the family and it would usually go to the children of the marriage. Because the wife was likely to outlive the husband and might well have young children to raise, the husband's dower provision insured that his partner would receive a portion of his property for her use during her lifetime and to raise the children.

[1] Barbara A. Hanawalt, *The Ties That Bound: Peasant Families in Medieval England* (New York: Oxford University Press, 1986), 205–19. These pages cover the partnership marriage in terms of work and dower.

London law provided that the widow would have one third of the husband's property for life use and the children would have an additional third by way of inheritance. Failing children, the wife would have life use of half the property. Children would receive the mother's dower portion on her death. The final third was left for settling the testator's debts and for the good of the husband's soul. The dower was generous because the widow could take it into another marriage and was often also able to take control over her children's portions until they came of age.[2]

In London law the minimum the widow would receive was her freebench. That is to say that

> after the death of her husband the wife shall have of the tenement in the said city, whereof her husband died seized in fee, and in which tenement the said husband and wife dwelt together at the time of the husband's death, the hall, the principal private chamber, the cellar wholly, and her use of the kitchen, stable, privy, and curtilage in common with the other necessaries appurtenant thereto, for the term of her life. And when she marries again, she shall lose the free bench and her dower therein, saving to her dower of the other tenements as the law requires.[3]

Thus Alice, widow of John de Harwe, applied to the city for the "widow's chamber": a portion of the tenement in which she and her husband dwelt and in which he died seized including the hall, principal chamber, and cellar along with the use of kitchen, stable, garden, and privy. The mayor awarded these to her even though her husband died intestate.[4]

The real advantages of dower for women and the core of the wealth it provided lay in the last part: "saving to her [the widow's] dower of the other tenements as the law requires." The husband had two ways of going about meeting the obligations of the dower in exchange for the dowry. The most secure way, it would seem, was to make a contract binding upon the parties before the marriage. Properties that the groom already owned or rented would be promised to the bride at the time of the marriage. After the parties agreed to the contract,

---

[2] Barbara A. Hanawalt, *Growing Up in Medieval London: The Experience of Childhood in History* (New York: Oxford University Press, 1993), 91–96 provides information of wardship arrangements in London and the percentage of mothers who took control over the wardships.

[3] Mary Bateson, ed. *Borough Customs*, Selden Society 21 (London: Bernard Quaritch, 1904), 2:126.

[4] Reginald Sharpe, ed., *Calendar of Letter Books Preserved among the Archives of the Corporation of the City of London: Letter Book E* (London: John Edward Francis, 1903), 33.

they came together at the parish church door where they were married [*ad ostium ecclesiae*] and announced the terms of dowry and dower before witnesses.[5] When a dispute arose later over the terms, witnesses would often refer to the exchange at the church door and recite the terms of the agreement made there. The advantage of this arrangement for dower was that the husband could not alienate the land assigned to dower and the wife's portion was secure.

The other way of giving dower was to promise to give one-third of the husband's estate at the time of his death. If the husband's fortunes increased over the period of marriage, this arrangement was a very good one and the wife got more real estate than she would have at the time of the marriage. But such an agreement was risky, because the husband's business could fail and the widow would lose the portion she might have had. One thing the husband could not do was to make his wife his heir in real estate. When husbands tried this in wills the court always disallowed it.

In the enrollment of wills in the Husting Court, 1,743 out of 3,300 non-clerical men's wills contain provisions for dower. Husbands sometimes added to the original dower by giving valuable chattels, and sometimes the husband gave his surviving widow the choice of taking the dower agreed in the marriage contract or taking London's customary right to one-third of the property. But whatever the provision, the predominate form that dower took in the Husting Court wills was real estate: eighty-six percent, compared to only thirteen percent dower in goods and money alone and one percent dower in an annuity. The wills recorded in the Archdeaconry Court are less detailed and more concerned with provisions for the testator's soul than the transfer of property. They also represented the poorer elements of the population and ordinary craftsmen of London.[6] Of the 116 men who made provisions for their widows, only eighteen percent mention real estate, while sixty-five percent simply refer to the residue of their estate. Seventeen percent specify the dower, usually adding to it with specific sums of money or a portion of the residue. The practice of dowering in real estate was, as one would expect, more common among the wealthy.

---

[5] Reginald Sharpe, ed., *Calendar of Wills Proved and Enrolled in the Court of Husting, London* (London: John C. Francis, 1889), 1:xli.

[6] Guildhall Library, Archdeacon's Court, MS. 9051/1 and 9051/2 (hereafter referred to as Archdeacon's Court and ms. number). The wills start in 1393 but are largely from the fifteenth century. The Archdeacon's Court and the Consistory Court of London recorded wills in addition to the Husting Court. These two ecclesiastical courts were more concerned with provisions for the soul of the deceased. It is often the case that people had two wills; one for the Husting Court and another for the ecclesiastical court. The Church also made efforts to extend the testamentary privilege to the poor and more ordinary people.

The widow was thus compensated for her contributions to the marriage. The dower's advantage in terms of perpetuating the family unit was that it guaranteed that the widow would be able to support and rear the children of the union because she had at least a third of her former husband's estate to provide for them as well as their inheritance. Only the very wealthy, the very poor, or the very foolish would enter into such an important obligation as marriage without an agreement either written or with witnesses. One of our questions, therefore, must be whether or not widows, given their relative freedom of choice and their wealth, were so foolish.

In assessing widows' potential access to wealth, we want to know how successful they were in realizing their dower rights. In London the widow's ability to claim dower might be tenuous because dower arrangements were often oral. On the Continent, which had a strong tradition of notaries being paid by both parties to draw up a written contract, misunderstandings could often be settled by appealing to a written record. In England the record might be written, but the oral tradition was still valid for legal record. Relatives and parishioners remembered the reading of the contract at the church door at the betrothal. But tenements set aside for the widow might change hands frequently. Thus, on the death of her husband, the widow might find herself in a legal battle with others, usually tenants, who claimed a prior right over the property. In a separate paper that I wrote on widows and the recovery of dower, I found that, while it is impossible to know what percentage of widows in London had a difficult time recovering their dower, fifty-three percent of those widows bringing suit for dower recovery were successful in retrieving the promised real property. The legal process took about eleven to twelve months to accomplish.[7] We may assume, therefore, that for the most part London widows did receive their dowers and even those who had to sue for a portion of their dower had success.

The generous provisions that London law made for widows was coupled with another law that protected the orphans of London citizens and served to funnel even more real estate and wealth through women. The law stipulated that no one who could profit from the death of the orphan could become guardian of the child. Those who would profit, of course, would be those who would inherit if the child was dead. Since most of the wealth in London was in the hands of men, the guardianship of the children was most often granted to the widow if she were alive. The law gave maximum protection to minor children by allowing them to remain with their mothers. The real estate and property that the children inherited could be administered by the mother, but usually a second husband or

[7] Barbara A. Hanawalt, "The Widow's Mite: Provisions for Medieval London Widows," in *Upon My Husband's Death: Widows in the Literature and Histories of Medieval Europe*, ed. Louise Mirrer (Ann Arbor: University of Michigan Press, 1992), 21–45.

men whom the father chose were designated to care for the inheritance and the mother would care for the child or children. Anyone undertaking to oversee the wealth had to make a fair return on the proceeds and had to have sureties to guarantee that the inheritance would be turned over intact and with a fair profit when the child either married or reached the age of majority (twenty-one years old).[8]

In the late medieval Husting wills, only 210 men designated guardians for their children. Their overwhelming preference (fifty-five percent) was for the mother to assume the role. After her, the testator looked to friends (twenty-seven percent), kin (eight percent), executors (six percent), and, finally, apprentices, servants, and churchmen.[9] When the London mayor's court of orphans determined the guardianship, a similar pattern emerged. The mother was favored as guardian in over half the cases that came into the court. She acted either alone or with a new husband. The father alone as guardian does not appear until the end of the fourteenth century, suggesting that the number of female heiresses had increased.[10]

While we cannot know the number or age of the widows, various cases from among those involving the marriage of orphans give some information about the ages of first marriage. Men of the merchant class seem to have entered into their first marriage in their mid-twenties or later and women in their mid- to late teens. Sixteen was the age at which a woman could inherit her portion of her father's estate if she married.[11]

In spite of the dangers associated with childbirth, women in the Middle Ages seemed to have outlived their husbands on the average. In the London Husting Court wills, 1,743 out of 3,300 men's wills (fifty-three percent) mention a surviving wife.[12] We may assume, then, that the widow was a common occurrence in late medieval England.

How wealthy were the widows who received a third of their husband's real estate in addition to personal and household goods? Needless to say, the material well-being of the new widow depended on a number of circumstances. Dower might have dwindled if the couple's fortune had been bad. On the other hand, the couple's economic partnership might have prospered in which case the husband might enrich the initial dower with further bequests of money or household items in the will. If the widow had been an heiress in her own right, or had

---

[8] Hanawalt, *Growing Up in Medieval London*, chap. 6.

[9] Data compiled from the *Husting Court Wills*, vols. 1 and 2.

[10] Hanawalt, *Growing Up in Medieval London*, chap. 6.

[11] Silvia Thrupp, *The Merchant Class of Medieval London* (Ann Arbor: University of Michigan Press, 1948), 192–93, 196, 213.

[12] *Husting Court Wills*, vols. 1 and 2. These are medieval wills from the late thirteenth century to 1500.

her own business, then she would have those assets in addition to the dower. Then, too, her status depended directly on her social class or status in society. A wealthy grocer's widow in London would have far more resources available than the widow of an artisan or day laborer. Age was also a factor. An old woman, left a widow, might simply have a retirement contract, either one that the couple had negotiated together or one provided in a will.[13]

Widows of prosperous merchants and artisans were very well off. Since real estate is not listed by its value, the best hint we have is the value of orphaned children's inheritance. The value was given only for chattels and money, but it indicates fabulous wealth. In 1309–1348 the average wealth per family was £80. Following the Black Death from 1349 to 1388 it rose to £416 and continued rising to reach £810 in 1389–1428 and £901 in 1429–1468. Wealth obviously became more concentrated following the visitations of the plague starting in 1348. Assuming that these values represent an approximation of the widow's third for dower, a man who married a widow had a very nice infusion of capital. If the widow had no children, he had the use of half of the former husband's property for the life of his wife. If the widow had minor children, he would most likely be awarded the use of their property until they came of age. For instance, a fifteenth-century grocer married a widow with a dower of £764 and was appointed guardian of her six children with permission to trade with their patrimony (an equal amount) until they came of age. In addition, he could expect to receive some goods in the form of a dowry from his new wife. He had, therefore, an excess of £1,528.[14]

Remarriage of Widows

Moralists lamented that men sought widows for remarriage because they were wealthy.[15] But with the opportunities for an infusion of capital of these proportions, who could resist? As we shall see, the competition for widows was great. But we must look at the broader factors that influenced widows to choose remarriage. Also important was the attitude of the women themselves toward entering into another marriage.

Medieval evidence does not permit a reconstruction of the percentage of widows who chose to remarry. Parish registers from the sixteenth century indicate

---

[13] See, for instance, Elaine Clark, "Some Aspects of Social Security in Medieval England," *Journal of Family History* 7 (1982): 307–20.

[14] Thrupp, *Merchant Class*, 107.

[15] G. R. Owst, *Literature and the Pulpit in Medieval England*, 3rd ed. (New York: Barnes & Noble, 1961), 119.

that twenty-five to thirty percent of the widows remarried, and for widowers it was higher. Remarriage was fairly rapid, with almost half of those remarrying within the year.[16] Canon law required no mourning period during which a widow or widower could not remarry.[17] In the London Hustings wills, only three percent of husbands specified that their wives not remarry.

The parish register figures are from villages and thus do not indicate urban patterns. Two London sources permit a reconstruction of at least two groups of the widows who remarried: women suing for recovery of dower and those coming to the London orphans' court with their children. Those women who came to the mayor's court to reclaim their dower could plead their cases alone or could enter their new husband as a co-claimant. These cases were initiated fairly quickly after the death of the former husband and the probate of the will, as can be seen by comparing wills with the initiation of the dower case. Thirty-four percent of the widows had remarried already and brought the suit with their new husband. The remarriage pattern followed the general crisis in the fourteenth and fifteenth centuries. The period of 1348 to 1374, the time of the worst devastation from the Black Death and plague, saw the remarriage rate move to fifty percent.[18] Widows suing to recover dower could be any age, but widows appearing with their orphaned children in the mayor's court of orphans were all of childbearing age, since they were claiming wardship of minor children. Fifty-seven percent of these widows remarried, in statistics derived from court records over the course of two centuries. Among these widows the bulge in remarriage was most noticeable in 1379 and remained high throughout the fifteenth century.[19]

Since women tended to survive plague better than men, the population of widows was greater following the continuing recurrence of plague, thus providing more widows for remarriage. Furthermore, the concentration of wealth, as we have seen from the orphans' portion, was greater following the initial visitation of plague. Intermarriage among Londoners, moreover, tended to concentrate wealth in the reduced post-plague population.

[16] R. S. Schofield and E. A. Wrigley, "Remarriage Intervals and the Effect of Marriage Order on Fertility," in *Marriage and Remarriage in Populations of the Past*, ed. J. Dupaquier, E. Helin, P. Laslett, M. Livi-Bacci, S. Sogner (London: Academic Press, 1981), 211–27, here 212, 214.

[17] Michael M. Sheehan, "The Influence of Canon Law on the Property Rights of Married Women in England," *Mediaeval Studies* 25 (1963): 109–24, here 121.

[18] Hanawalt, "The Widow's Mite," for the complete quantitative information.

[19] Barbara A. Hanawalt, "Remarriage as an Option for Urban and Rural Widows in Late Medieval England," in *Wife and Widow in Medieval England*, ed. Sue Sheridan Walker (Ann Arbor: University of Michigan Press, 1992), 141–64, here 150–51.

Changes in London society may have played the most significant role in the remarriage of city widows. Gilds became increasingly important in the regulation of London society and government following the Black Death. As these horizontal lines of trade and craft brotherhoods strengthened in the society, the selection of marriage partner tended to be within the gild. While most husbands may not have taken the precaution of one skinner, who required his wife to marry someone in the trade,[20] gild brothers might have had an implicit understanding about the matter. If one may judge from the numerous and valuable bequests that widows left to their husbands' gild, the loyalty must have extended to wives as well.

The recirculation of widows and their wealth within the gild was another type of protectionism in a period when gilds were becoming increasingly protectionist about their political and economic roles. Trade secrets would not leak out if the widow remained within the brotherhood. Thrupp found that the mayor and aldermen, who had control over the marriage as well as the wardship of orphans, arranged for eighty-four percent of merchants' daughters to marry merchants. When widows remarried, the proportion was even higher. In thirty-seven cases from the fifteenth century thirty-four widows chose husbands from the merchant class, twenty-two of these were from the same company as the former husband.[21] Goldsmiths' widows seemed to have preferred goldsmiths.[22] The same pattern may be observed for the craft gilds. Rappaport was able to demonstrate that by the sixteenth century gilds insisted that suitors for the hand of a gild widow join their gild as a condition of remarriage.[23]

In addition to loyalty to a former husband's gild in choosing to remarry, widows had their own motivations for remarriage. Perhaps the childless widow wished to have children, but the problems of managing the former husband's business was a strong motivator for remarriage. While women could, by law, take over their husband's business either when he was away or when widowed, the problems of doing so could loom large. Complaints from apprentices indicate

---

[20] Guild Hall Archives, Archdeacon's Court MS. 9051/1, fol. 105v.

[21] Thrupp, *Merchant Class*, 28.

[22] Thomas F. Reddaway, *The Early History of the Goldsmiths' Company, 1327–1509* (London: Edward Arnold, 1975), 275–321 has reconstructed biographies indicating marriages when known.

[23] Steve Rappaport, *Worlds Within Worlds: Structures of Life in Sixteenth-Century London* (Cambridge: Cambridge University Press, 1989), 400–41. In 1592 Mr. Wilks appealed to the Merchant Taylors because Hell Hudson, a Vintner's widow, would not marry him unless he transferred to her company. The Merchant Taylors responded by sending a delegation to widow Hudson to see if she would join them. But she declared that she "will by no means assent to leave her trade." Finally, Wilks was allowed to leave the Merchant Taylors and become a Vintner.

that the widows were not always capable of training them as their contracts specified.[24] Merchant widows could not travel to the international markets and had to rely on agents that they could only hope were honest. Some trades, such as tanners and butchers, were really men's trades in which women did retail but not processing.[25] And then there was the promise of a comfortable life, enriched by companionship, but also the prospect of yet another dower.

Thomasine Bonaventura was an intelligent and enterprising country woman who amassed considerable wealth through her marriages. She was born into a gentry family in Cornwall in the 1450s and had a brother who was a priest in Kent but with connections in London. She probably moved to London as a high class servant, most likely in a merchant tailor's household. She married Henry Galle and, when he died in 1467, she received not only a dower of half his property (she was a widow with no children), but also a bequest of £100 in cloth from his shop, the terms of his apprentices, and £100 in cash. It appears that she planned to take over the business. Soon, however, she married another tailor, Thomas Barnaby, and the business passed to him. Barnaby died in less than a year. Again Thomasine was left without children and an additional dower. She then married John Percyvale, another tailor. He eventually became mayor of London, and she acquired the title of "Dame." When he died in 1503, she apparently assumed his tailoring business, including the training of apprentices. She was so wealthy that she fell victim to one of Henry VII's money-raising schemes. He pardoned her for a trumped-up offense in exchange for a payment of £1000.[26]

The marriage market in London was fiercely competitive. As Hanham observed about the Cely family: "Matchmaking was an enormously serious business for the parties and their relations, a favorite sport for those less directly involved in the outcome."[27] George Cely, mercer and stapler, competed for the hand of Margery, widow of Edmund Rygon. She was a second wife, young and childless, and had been made chief executor of Edmund's estate with the bulk of his property at her disposal for the good of his soul. Like the Celys, he was a Stapler and had property in Calais. Here was the classic opportunity to keep Rygon's considerable wealth within the select group of Staplers. George had competition in his

[24] Hanawalt, *Growing Up in Medieval London*, 160–63.

[25] Derek Keene, "Tanners' Widows, 1300–1350," in *Medieval London Widows, 1300–1500*, ed. Caroline M. Barron and Anne F. Sutton (London: Hambledon Press, 1994), 1–28.

[26] Mathew Davies, "Dame Thomasyne Percyvale, 'the Maid of Week' (died. 1512)," in *Medieval London Widows, 1300–1500*, ed. Barron and Sutton, 185–207. A colorful version of her rags to riches story appears in Charles M. Clode, *The Early History of the Guild of Merchant Tailors*, pt. 2 (London: John Murray, 1874), 11–13, 20–21.

[27] Alison Hanham, *The Celys and Their World: An English Merchant Family of the Fifteenth Century* (Cambridge: Cambridge University Press, 1985), 309.

wooing. William Cely wrote in 1484 that a maternal relative of Margery's had arrived in Calais, apparently on a reconnaissance mission for the family, to find out what George's prospects were. William wrote that

> … it is said here by many persons here how that ye be sure ['contracted'] to her. With the which, sir, I am well content and right glad thereof. And sir, all those here that knoweth you, both merchants and soldiers, commend you greatly, saying 'if that gentlewoman should be worth double that she is ye are worthy to have her.' And as for making of search of your dealings here, I trow there is no man that maketh any. If they do, they need go no farther than the books in the treasury, where they may find that your sales made within less than this year amounts above 2,000 li. strg., where that all the people that laboured for to 'a be afore you, he and his brother had not in this town this twelve months the one half of that.

George not only had to prove his business success, but he also had to provide an attractive dower for widow Rygon and woo her with precious gifts. Dower, of course, was real estate, and he bought more than £485 worth in this period along with jewels, plate, and a costly ring. Later, his sister-in-law was to claim that he spent more than his proper share of the stock, which he had inherited with his brother, Richard, her husband. In addition, he bore the cost of the wedding feast.[28]

While George's wooing of a wealthy widow was successful, other suitors revealed the pitfalls of pursuing independent-minded widows. The market in the late fourteenth and fifteenth centuries favored the widow in London. A draper laid his case of investment in courting a widow before the mayor in the hopes of recovering something from her estate. He had, he claimed, made a contract of marriage before witnesses with the widow and had spent time and money on her business for three years because he assumed that it would all accrue to his profit when they married. He also spent some £20 on gifts for her and her friends and finally went off on a trading venture to Spain to buy merchandise for her worth £400. When he returned, she was favoring a rival and would not see him. She died unmarried, and he was trying to reclaim his investment against the £2,000 estate she left behind.[29]

The competition for widows appears in a petition brought by Nicholas Boylle, draper of London, who complained to the Lord Chancellor that John Walsale had run into Nicholas in Lombard Street and told him that he knew of a widow who was worth 200 marks and more and that he would undertake to try to persuade her to favor, love, and show good will to Nicholas if he would give him a bond for

[28] Hanham, *The Celys and Their World*, 309–15.

[29] Thrupp, *Merchant Class*, 106–107.

£20 to be paid if he succeeded in bringing about the union. John made the approach and reported to Nicholas that she wanted to know if young Nicholas had the good will of his father, and she also wanted to be assured in front of his father that he would leave all his goods and livelihood to her and his son. He delivered her gifts in earnest of his intent. She utterly refused him and married Richard Sebe, a mercer of London. Nicholas's complaint was not against the market-wise widow, who made her own matrimonial decisions, but against John who wanted to collect his commission even though no marriage resulted.[30]

Independent widows negotiating their own marriages caused a number of petitions and court cases. But the disappointed prospective husbands also appeared. Roger Radnore of Worcester, a chapman, complained that he had made a contract of marriage twelve months earlier with Alice George, a London widow, and she had sworn in church to the contract and had delivered goods to him. But a rival, William Whetehall, appeared and "subtly labored with Alice" and she made another contract and married him. When Roger came to London to buy goods according to his occupation, Alice and William had him arrested for the goods she had given to him when they were engaged.[31] On the other hand, Elizabeth Baxter, late wife of John Croke, says that John being "of his own free will and liberty lawfully contracted matrimony" with her and "at his own cost caused the matrimony to be solemnized in the book before the Archdeacon and before many people." They lived together for half a year after that "with love and charity as husband and wife." But another woman, Elizabeth Cotton, claimed prior contract and was upheld in the consistory court. Now John has retained goods she brought to the marriage as well as those he pledged to her, beat her, and had her and her mother arrested and put into prison.[32]

The competition for widows shows the value that aspiring capitalists and social climbers in late medieval London put on the capital which widows controlled. Marriage to a widow with property gave immediate access to moveable chattels and rents from real property that formed her dower. For a man like George Cely, who had spent his time in the English hinterland collecting wool or in the foreign market of Flanders, it was a way of establishing social credibility in London as well. The very value of the property widows held in dower interested gilds in keeping the wealth and trade secrets within their control, and so they encouraged remarriages with gild brothers. With the apparent compliance of the independent widows, London society created strong horizontal ties not only through gild brotherhoods, but also through marriage with widows of their gild brothers.

---

[30] London, The Public Record Office, Chancery Petitions (C1 classification). These are undated but come mostly from the fifteenth century. C1/43/65.

[31] Chancery Petitions, C1/46/111.

[32] Chancery Petitions, C1/61/485.

Counsel and Consent: Preparing for Marriage Litigation According to the Fourteenth-Century York Cause Papers

Frederik Pedersen

We now know a lot about the legal framework concerning marriage in the middle ages.[1] We know how the law developed, from the first unworkable definitions of the exact moment of the creation of the marriage bond contained in Gratian of Bologna's *Harmony of Discordant Canons* (also known as the *Decretum*) from c. 1140 to the sophisticated Parisian model in which consent was created solely by the spoken words of the couple, which was first espoused by Pope Alexander III some decades later. We know that the church insisted on the publication of the parties' intent to marry. Although legally this publication was desirable, it was not a necessary prerequisite for the creation of a binding union. We know about the procedures and institutions that the church developed in order to avoid uncertainty about the legality of alleged marriages. And we know that, at least by the fourteenth century, the laity had understood and mostly applied the canon law rules of marriage to their lives, and that they trusted the courts to provide an equitable and final solution to disputes about marriage, too. Finally, we know that lay couples usually followed the rules of canon law almost to the letter when they wanted to create the bonds of marriage, publishing banns on three consecutive Sundays, exchanging marriage vows in front of the church door, and standing before the congregation during a celebration of mass following the exchange of vows.

In contrast to this almost idyllic picture of the reception of *canon* law, it has been argued that, by the end of the fourteenth century, the laity in London, at least, had developed a system of *secular* tribunals and courts for dealing with conflicts outside the royal system of justice, which even claimed jurisdiction in preference to the ordinary legal system, and that, on the whole, this local administration of justice worked efficiently.[2] This prompts the question of whether a similar

[1] This article refines and extends the analysis of some of the York cases found F. Pedersen, *Marriage Disputes in Medieval England* (London: Hambledon Press, 2000). In the book I did not have an opportunity to describe and analyze what preparations litigants made before they reached the final stages of litigation. The York material has therefore been re-read and re-analyzed to highlight the participation of the litigants' family and local community in the early stages of litigation. As the subject matter of the cases does not change, readers may inevitably find that there is some repetition of descriptive material from the book. However, the analyses have not been published before, nor have the conclusions that have been reached here.

[2] Barbara A. Hanawalt, "The Power of Word and Symbol: Conflict Resolution in Late Medieval London," in *Of Good And Ill Repute: Gender and Social Control in Medieval England* (Oxford: Oxford University Press, 1998), 35–52.

development can be found when we turn to the laity's interaction with that other great monolith of judicial power — the church, specifically with its jurisdiction over marriage — or if the church had managed to have its claim to exclusive jurisdiction over marriage accepted by the fourteenth century.

In this essay will be presented detailed evidence from eight cases from the archbishop's court in fourteenth-century York giving examples of the different ways in which people tried either to safeguard against or prepare for marriage litigation. A particular focus will be on the different kinds of pre-court tribunals found in these written records.

The earliest record of the archbishop's court in York comes from the register of Walter Giffard (1266–1279), which records a session on the archbishop's porch at Bishopsthorpe. From around the year 1300, the previous *ad hoc* arrangement had been superseded by a more formal structure, which kept a regular written record of its proceedings. This court was given its own statutes in 1311 by Bishop William Greenfield.[3] A substantial number of case files produced by the court scribes have survived. Some 255 litigation files come from the fourteenth century, and eighty-eight of these deal with marriage. The quality of the York material is high: it preserves a wide variety of the documents produced by the court and the marriage cases alone contain around eight hundred documents of varying lengths, which provide evidence of all aspects of court business, from procedural documents — such as libels, positions, and interrogatories — to the sentences of the court.[4] The York cause paper files also include letters and transcripts of earlier cases from officers appointed by the court to investigate the facts of a case in the field. Although many cases survive from the fourteenth century, a comparison with the volume of cases recorded in surviving fifteenth-century act books, which record the daily transactions of the court, makes it clear that the cause paper material represents only a fraction of the business conducted. If the annual caseload was of the same magnitude in the fourteenth and fifteenth centuries, the courts would have investigated approximately 18,000 cases in the years from 1300 to 1400, and the surviving cases would represent less than one and a half percent of the total number of cases presented to the court. However, on the positive side, the surviving case files appear to be a representative sample of litigation in York, with no discernible overall principle behind their survival.[5]

---

[3] David Wilkins, ed. & comp. *Concilia Magnae Britanniae et Hiberniae a synodo Verulamiensi AD CCCCXLIV ad Londinensem AD MDC* (London: Gosling, 1737), 2:409–15.

[4] Norma Adams and Charles Donahue, Jr., "Introduction," in *Select Cases from the Ecclesiastical Courts of the Province of Canterbury, c. 1200–1301*, Selden Society 95 (London: Selden Society, 1981), 37–72.

[5] Charles Donahue, Jr., "Female Plaintiffs in Marriage Cases in the Later Middle Ages: What Can We Learn from the Numbers?" in *Wife and Widow in Medieval England*,

It is common sense to insist that pre-court preparations must have taken place to evaluate evidence and to establish whether litigants had a case in law. But so far little evidence has been forthcoming about how this took place. Although it is not the purpose of the cause papers to document these preparations in detail, they do contain fragmentary evidence of formal and informal meetings that demonstrate 1) that preparations did take place, 2) that the system of the church courts benefited from the work done by the laity in informal meetings and in more formally convened tribunals, and 3) that the York laity accepted and trusted the church courts to provide an equitable solution to their marriage disputes. These informal meetings and formal tribunals took a multitude of forms ranging from informal conversations to highly formalized meetings in the church (though not with an explicit mandate from the ecclesiastical hierarchy). It is also clear that although these pre-court meetings were common, they were not a prerequisite, and they appear to have affected only those cases that involved litigants who can be shown to have been (or arguably should have been) under some form of tutelage. There *is* thus evidence for an extra-curial system of justice in York, and this article concludes with some comments on the question of whether the laity developed out-of-court institutions like the ones identified by Hanawalt.[6] I argue that because these tribunals did not develop standardized rituals or powers like the lay courts identified in Hanawalt's article, they were never a part of a formal legal system. On the contrary, the fact that the York tribunals were so disparate in form indicates that the laity never seriously challenged the jurisdiction of the church in marriage cases.

Although Frederick Maitland famously exclaimed about Paul's letter to the Corinthians "few texts have done more harm than this," and that the canon law on marriage based on it was "not pleasant to read," he overstated his case.[7] Medieval canon law made it easy for people to contract marriage under informal circumstances, and it *was* difficult to say when a marriage had been contracted and the marriage bond established. But the situation was not as impossible as Maitland implied, especially since in practice the canon law depended on a large proportion of its work being performed outside the courtroom. Although the surviving court records are filled with instances of marriages contracted under the most

ed. Sue Sheridan Walker (Ann Arbor: University of Michigan Press, 1993), 183–213; Frederik Pedersen, "Demography in the Archives: Social and Geographical Variables in Fourteenth-Century York Cause Paper Marriage Litigation," *Continuity and Change* 10 (1995): 405–36.

[6] Hanawalt, "Word and Symbol."

[7] Frederick Pollock and Frederic William Maitland, *The History of English Law Before the Time of Edward I*, 2nd ed., rev. S. F. C. Milsom, (Cambridge: Cambridge University Press, 1968) 1:485.

unusual circumstances — in beds, taverns, fields, cowsheds, and outhouses or private rooms, with or without witnesses — the ease with which marriage could be established and the ample scope for unintended marriages to be created by parties using the wrong formulae made it desirable, but not necessary, for the parties to ensure that some sort of semi-legal circumstance surrounded the exchange of vows. The vast majority of marriages were probably surrounded by legal ceremonies that safeguarded the intent of the parties, but for that very reason they do not appear in the historical record. However, some traces of these legal ceremonies and safeguards do appear in the records of the medieval church.

One common way of safeguarding a marriage was to make sure that a representative of the church was present to supervise the exchange of vows. In the York material, seventy-one witnesses to marriages were related to the church in some capacity. Twenty-two of these were chaplains and twenty-one were unspecified *clerici*. It is likely that both the litigants and the court felt that such people were a kind of "expert witness." Their training sensitized them to the meanings of the vows that they witnessed, and in some cases they were even called by the parties or by their parents to recite the words of the vows that made a marriage legally binding so that the parties could contract their marriage with the intended force, either as a marriage *verba de futuro* (which we would now call an engagement) or as a marriage *verba de presenti* (which we would now call a legally binding marriage). Correspondingly, none of the preserved decisions of the court went against marriage if a priest or notary public claimed that he had been present at an exchange of vows that established marriage by *verba de presenti*. If a cleric testified to his knowledge of a celebration of marriage, that marriage was dissolved only if the marriage could be shown to be invalid for other reasons, such as force, fear, consanguinity, or legal incapacity. The existence of a marriage can thus be said to have been taken for granted by the court if attested by a cleric.

The participation of clerics in marriage cases safeguarded lay marriage negotiations and often saved the parties from prolonged involvement with the legal institutions of the church. Tribunals and informal meetings also appear in the York marriage cases with some regularity. Usually such tribunals convened to establish whether words sufficient to create a marriage bond had been exchanged, and thus they determined whether there was a case to be heard before an ecclesiastical court. Although the authority of these tribunals was rarely, if ever, defined, it is safe to say that it was never questioned by the laity or by the ecclesiastical courts. The written sources of these courts show that informal meetings and tribunals met *ad hoc*, and never settled into a fixed composition. Sometimes they consisted of lay people, sometimes of clerics, and sometimes of a mixture of the two. But presumably in an attempt to increase the reliability of the tribunals, they usually included at least one or two people with legal training. In most cases these tribunals did a good job, and although one might fear that they were open to manipulation by unscrupulous litigants and parents, they seem to have been remarkably efficient filters of marriage cases, saving the courts much of the initial work required for the assembly of a proper legal case.

Marrying with or without the Presence of a Cleric

A sensible precaution against a later legal challenge was to establish marriage with a certain measure of formality. This often meant that marriage negotiations were conducted in a semi-formal way with one or more priests or notaries public present. Although it may be argued that such a precaution shows nothing but the good sense of the intending parties, its frequency indicates that the cleric's presence was an integrated part of many marriages. One detailed example is the case of *Dowson* c. *Brathewell* (1391).

Dowson c. *Brathewell* was heard in York as a *causa matrimonialis et divortii* (a marriage and divorce case) because the defendant, Alice Brathewell, claimed to have contracted a legally binding marriage to a man called William Roger who lived in Pontefract, rather than to the plaintiff, William Dowson. For our purposes the important details are contained in the events that lead to her alleged marriage to William Dowson. William Dowson rode into Doncaster in 1391 and took lodgings at Alice Brathewell's hospice. We do not know why, but William decided that Alice might be the right woman to approach with a proposal of marriage. He therefore let his two servants, John Bukton and John Clerk of Grenhale, initiate marriage negotiations. Another John Clerk, John Clerk of Doncaster, who appeared as a witness for Alice Dowson, set the scene:

> after dinner the said John Bukton declared to the said Alice that the said William Dowson was a very rich and fitting husband for her, inducing and enticing the said Alice to contract marriage with the said William as well as he could, when she declared that it was not her intention to have a husband within a year from the time of her husband's death.[8]

William's witnesses did not allege that she agreed to marriage on this occasion. Instead, she wanted to have another meeting in which they would decide when and whether to get married. Her neighbors intervened at this point; they

[8] "Et post cenam dictus Johannes Bukton asseruit dicte Alicie quod Willelmus Dowson predictus fuit multum dives et potens ac competens maritus pro ipsa, inducendo et allitiendo dictam Aliciam quatenus potuit ad contrahendum matrimonium cum dicto Willelmo, ipsa Alicia respondente quod non fuit intentionis sue habere maritum infra annum a tempore mortis mariti sui": CP, E 188–6 (1391).

felt that having William stay with Alice while they were conducting marriage negotiations was not proper, so he was made to move to another house in Doncaster.[9]

Marriage negotiations resumed on the following day in a croft belonging to Alice Brathewell, and the question of whether these negotiations ended in a marriage *per verba de presenti* or *per verba de futuro* was crucial to the outcome of the case. In an attempt to provide evidence of circumstances to make it unlikely that Alice had consented to marriage, Alice's witness, John Clerk of Doncaster, explained that John Bukton tried "in every possible way and manner he could" to persuade Alice to marry William Dowson. Although he was present, William remained silent and let his servant present him in his most favorable light. Alice was concerned about her reputation in Doncaster and, seeming to break the unwritten rules of marriage negotiations, answered for herself,

> and after great fuss had been made of the said Alice, Alice herself answered that the matrons of the village of Doncaster and her other neighbors would reproach her if she were to contract marriage so thoughtlessly to a stranger whom she did not even know before, in the presence of the said William Dowson, Master John Maltby, a chaplain, John Clerk of Grenhale, and this witness.[10]

William Dowson's negotiator, John Clerk of Grenhale, who was also interrogated by the court, insisted that Alice and William had not only contracted a valid marriage on this occasion, but that they had accompanied the exchange of words with the exchange of kisses while holding hands and he claimed that the whole party had gone to Thomas Taverner's inn to drink ale. There John Clerk of Grenhale said that Alice had admitted the existence of a contract in front of witnesses.[11] Alice argued that she had only agreed to consider the offer of marriage

[9] "Et ideo propter vitandi [sic] scandalum dicte Alicie predicti burgenses ville de Doncaster fecerunt dictum Willelmum recedere de hospitio dicte Alicie et providederunt sibi in alia parte villa [sic] de hospicio aliunde, ut dicit iste juratus": CP, E 188–6 (1391).

[10] "Et post magnam instantiam dicte Alicie factam, ipsa Alicia respondit quod matrone ville de Doncaster et alii vicini sui multum de ea obloquerentur si ipsa contraheret matrimonium ita indeliberate cum uno extraneo cuius notitiam nuncquam prius habuit, presentibus Willelmo Dowson predicto, domino Johanne Maltby cappelano, Johanne Clerk de Grenhale et isto jurato": CP, E 188–6 (1391).

[11] "Ad primum articulum dicit quod . . . in quodam stabulo infra mansum dicte Alicie in villa de Doncaster, contraxerunt dicti Ricardus et Alicia stantes sub hac forma, viro tenente mulierem per manum dexteram et dicente, 'Hic accipio te, Aliciam, in uxorem meam et ad hoc do tibi fidem meam,' muliere econtrario respondente, 'Hic accipio te, Willelmum, in virum meum et ad hoc do tibi fidem meam,' et traxerunt manus et osculabantur adinvicem

and had told John and William that she would give her final answer six weeks hence.[12] She seems to have been telling the truth, for William and John returned later the same day to put further pressure on Alice to give an answer before the six weeks were up. Alice and her helpers agreed to answer within the next month:

> And after a small interval of time said William Dowson and John Bukton came back after they had left and with great persistence succeeded in reducing the said term of six weeks to one month by the consent of said Alice, in the presence of this witness, John Clerk of Grenhale [and] master John de Maltby, a chaplain, in the words of this witness.[13]

The commissary general's court in York held with Alice Brathewell and decided that a binding marriage had not been established at these negotiations. She lived in a neighborhood where there was ready access to a priest and had taken the sensible precaution of employing this priest to be present when she conducted her marriage negotiations. The court disregarded the depositions of William's two witnesses, possibly because Alice had countered with the argument that William's witnesses were unreliable since they were his servants. The court based its decision that there was no valid marriage between Alice and William Dowson on Alice's three witnesses, two of whom were clerics. In the end, her precautions, the semi-legal character of the marriage negotiations, and her insistence on having witnesses to the exchange saved her from a marriage she did not want.

Greystanes c. *Dale* (1394) is a more complex case. Like the *Dowson* case, this was a divorce and marriage case, though it was originally heard as an enforcement of marriage case in Durham and was appealed in York. While the appellant argued that a legally binding marriage superseded his marriage to the plaintiff, he introduced a new defense.

---

presentibus isto jurato, Johanne Bukton, conteste suo, et Henrico Herthom. Et tunc incontinentes accesserunt ad domum Thome Taverner, vicini sui, et biberunt cervesiam. Et ibi audivit dictam Aliciam recognoscere et fateri huiusmodi contractum matrimonialem in presentia dicti Willelmi, presentibus isto jurato, Johanne Bukton conteste suo, Henrico Herthom et aliis de quorum nominibus non recolit. Item requisitus dicit quod audivit dictum Willelmum et Aliciam tantum unica vice contrahere": CP, E 188–12 (1391).

[12] "predictus Johannes Bukton, Willelmus, et Alicia statuerunt terminum sex septimane proximo tunc sequente ad habendum finale [sic] responsum ipsius Alicie de matrimonio inter dictum Willelmum et Aliciam contrahendo": CP, E 188–6 (1391).

[13] "Et post modicum temporis intervallum dictus Willelmus Dowson et Johannes Bukton — post recessum ipsorum — redierunt et cum magna instantia dictum terminum sex septimanarum de consensu dicte Alicie usque ad unam mensem abreviari optinuerunt, presentibus isto jurato, Johanne Clerk de Grenhale, domino Johanne de Maltby, cappelano, ut dicit": CP, E 188–6 (1391).

John Helcott, a forty-year-old parishioner of Staindrop, explained that he and many others had been present with the bride and groom, the father of the bride, three of her uncles, the rector of a local church, and Adam Alwent, a chaplain and kinsman of the groom, on 20 March 1392 in a place called "Lonefield" where marriage negotiations had taken place. It was agreed that the bride should bring a dowry of twenty marks, and in return the groom swore that he had not contracted marriage with any other woman and that he did not want any other woman in marriage. Later, at an unspecified date, banns were to be read and the two married *in facie ecclesie*. Having reached an agreement, the parties called for a third priest to prompt the parties in the recitation of marriage vows *verba de futuro*. The priest successfully prompted the parties and a proper marriage was celebrated some weeks later. However, neither an impressive turnout nor the publicity surrounding the event prevented this marriage from becoming the subject of litigation when the groom's jilted girlfriend won a case of enforcement of marriage vows in Durham, a decision that was then challenged in York. There can be little doubt, however, that had the court in Durham enquired more deeply into the case it would have known about the marriage negotiations and doubtless decided against the plaintiff. The eventual outcome in York was that the second marriage, that between Thomas Dale and Emma Corry, was upheld — doubtless because they had taken the precaution of inviting clerics who thus became solemn witnesses at the occasion of the exchange of vows.

Thomas Dale and Emma Corry had three priests at their negotiations and subsequent exchange of vows. However, safeguarding a marriage took the presence of only one cleric, as can be seen from the case of *Lyremouth and Holm* c. *Stokton* (1381). In this case, we hear of a tribunal that met at the instigation of Roger Moreton in his house in York to establish the legality of vows before a case was officially heard in York by the court of the archbishop. The vows under investigation were a standard *verba de presenti* exchanged around Palm Sunday between William Stokton, a servant of Roger Moreton, and another servant of his, Isabel Holm.[14] However, unlike the vows, the case itself proved to be less than straightforward, for William Stokton admitted to contracting with another woman, Elena Lyremouth, two years previously. On that occasion, he refused to take up cohabitation because of his apprenticeship with Roger Moreton, who, it turned out, wanted William to marry his servant Isabel.

Not surprisingly, the proposed marriage to Isabel Holm caused some consternation in Elena's house, where the matter was discussed informally. In Elena's presence, the witness Cecilia Hessay asked William about his wedding plans with Isabel some time before the marriage between William and Isabel took place. Swearing on a scroll (and thus performing an act that was clearly intended to

[14] CP, E 126–5 (Galfridus del Cave).

give the occasion a legal importance), William confirmed that he intended to marry another woman. Cecilia added that she often heard William swear that he would rather have married Elena than Isabel at the end of his apprenticeship. A ceremony involving Isabel and William took place in a room in Roger de Moreton's house in St. Saviourgate in the presence of Geoffrey de Hebston, another of Roger Moreton's servants, and Master Geoffrey Cave, a notary public. The presence of a notary at this occasion proved a wise precaution, for around Christmas 1381, Roger Moreton convened a tribunal in his house, "Le Somerhall." The tribunal consisted of himself, one of his servants called John de Flayreburgh, Geoffrey Cave, and Master Thomas Rednesse, a chaplain. Together they interrogated William to find out more about his marriage to Isabel. On this occasion, William swore that he had married Isabel and that he therefore had no right to any other woman.[15] Despite the evidence of William's second oath, this tribunal came to the conclusion that there was a case to be answered, and the case was later heard by the court in York.

William Stokton had thus participated in three meetings to discuss his marital status: the two meetings in Roger Moreton's and in Elena Lyremouth's houses were very informal; the last meeting was very formal and convened under the auspices of his master. The meeting in "Le Somerhall" was a highly structured attempt at defining the nature of the two marriages. This tribunal may have been more elaborate than the one in Elena's house and have included members with a legal training, but it arrived at no firm conclusion about the two marriages and instead the case was sent for final sentencing at a proper legal institution, the archbishop's court in York.

Marriage as a Business Contract

Considering the ease with which one could contract marriage in the fourteenth century, it is not surprising that the church courts needed some preparatory meetings to prepare litigation before a case was heard before the public tribunal of the archbishop's court, and this was particularly the case when the parties were young and untutored in the ways of creating a marriage. It was therefore common for the marriage contracts of the youngest litigants in the cause papers to be safeguarded by a contract between the intending groom and the bride's parents or between the parents of the intending parties. An instance of this is CP E 89 (1364–65) where a contract was made when the bride was around the age of nine and the groom around fifteen years of age. Considering the fact that the girl was

---

[15] Johannes Flayreburgh heard him swear to the marriage and "quod nullam jus habuit ad habendum aliquam aliam in uxorem": CP, E 126–5.

to live in the household of the groom's sister, which also included the groom, it is not surprising that it included safeguards to the girl's honor.

Marrays c. *Roucliffe* (1365–1366) started sometime before 27 September 1365, when the court in York appointed Edward of Cornwall, one of the court's proctors, as a guardian for Alice, the teenage daughter of Gervase of Roucliff.[16] This was most likely done in response to the presentation of an oral libel by John Marrays, who claimed to be Alice's legal husband. John appointed a proctor on 4 October 1365. He chose to be represented by John de Stanton, an experienced proctor of the court in York.[17] The issue was joined in a written libel on 14 October. In his libel John claimed that he had married Alice in the presence of her parents and family and that he had married her with their express consent by the help of words of present consent. He further claimed that she had been of legal age when she later confirmed her intention to go through with the union in front of several people worthy of trust.[18] The case was thus a fairly simple case of nonage. But it also included a rather unusual instance of a condition to the marriage: John had promised Alice's mother that he would not have intercourse with her until her mother thought she was ready for sexual intercourse, and he had safeguarded this promise by agreeing to pay a fine in case he did not hold to a date agreed between him and Alice's mother.

The court interrogated John's first twenty-three witnesses from 16 November to mid-December 1365.[19] Their function was to establish the facts as John saw it: that John and Alice had celebrated marriage in front of witnesses around Christmas 1364; that they had spent a night together in the nuptial bed; that they behaved like a married couple; and that Alice had been of sufficient age to contract marriage. John's sister, Annabile, the wife of Stephen Wastelyn, gave the court a detailed summary of the events as John's side saw it. She told the court that John had introduced Alice, who at that time was a physically mature twelve-year-old, into her household three weeks before Christmas the previous year and that two weeks later Alice had married John.[20] The ceremony had taken place in a room called "the Steward's chamber" in the monastery of St. Mary in York and had been witnessed by a number of people. Most importantly, among these was Richard Bernard in whose room the exchange took place, but also Master Adam de Thornton (who was a notary public), Alice's mother Elena, the widow

[16] CP, E 89–13 (1365–66).

[17] CP, E 89–28.

[18] CP, E 89–25.

[19] The last recorded date for the interrogation of these witnesses is 8 December, but a further four witnesses were heard before January 1366.

[20] "Item dicit quod dicta Alicia toto tempore quo stetit in comitiva istius jurata . . . per aspectum corporis apparet quod sit etatis quattouordecim annorum": CP, E 89–27.

of Gervase of Roucliff, and Robert Roucliff, who was presumably her uncle.[21] Richard Bernard presided over the exchange and prompted the parties with the words to be used. He could therefore confidently assert that the marriage had been contracted by *verba de presenti*.

The issue whether Alice had been forced to contract against her will receive special attention. Richard Bernard informed the court that Alice had not been forced and had contracted freely and with a happy face.[22] Katherine, the wife of Robert Roucliff, had been especially concerned about whether Alice understood the implications of being married to John. Alice stayed with her on the night preceding the ceremony in St. Mary's, and Katherine had repeatedly asserted that she was happy with the arrangement. In fact, Katherine said:

> This witness then asked the same Alice if she was in good will to go to Karthorp to her mother and she responded that 'yes' because she wanted, as she said, to go to any place where John wanted to send her.[23]

As an affirmation of the contract the couple lay together in the same bed for at least one entire night on the night of the feast of the apostle Thomas (21 December 1364) to ratify the marriage.[24] After the contract, Alice stayed in Annabile's household from Christmas to the feast of St. James (25 July 1365).[25] During her stay at the Wastelyn estate, she was clearly regarded as John's wife and she continued to accept gifts from John "as if she were his wife."

There can be little doubt that the people at the Wastelyn estate regarded her as John's wife, but *how* they regarded her exact legal status is somewhat unclear.

---

[21] At least two more people were present: William Pottel, the estate carpenter, and Adam Porter, the janitor of the monastery of St. Mary in York, accompanied Alice home after the ceremony. See below.

[22] "fuerunt presentes in camera dicti jurati infra scepta monasterii beate Marie Eboracensis Johannes Marras, Alicia dudum filia Gervasii de Roucliff, dominus Adam de Thornton, Elena, mater carnalis dicte Alicie, Robertus de Roucliff et iste juratus, ubi et quum Johannes et Alicia matrimonium adinvicem per verba de presenti contraxerunt ... Et dicit in juramento suo quod dicta Alicia voluntarie et cum bona vultu ac nullius vi vel metu ducta contraxit ut supra deposuit": CP, E 89–27, Richard Bernard.

[23] "Et ipsa jurata interrogavit tunc eandem Aliciam an fuit in bona voluntate eundi apud Karthorp ad matre sua et illa respondit quod sic quia voluit ut dicit ire ad quemcumque locum ubi dictus Johannes voluit eam mitere": CP, E 87–27.

[24] CP, E 89–27, Annabile Wastelyn. The abbot of St. Mary's Monastery in York, William Marrays, told the court that this event took place on the night of the feast of the apostle Thomas (21 December 1364).

[25] She was abducted by force and with weapons (*vi et armis*), according to CP, E 89–27, Stephen Wastelyn.

Although the union created in the monastery of St. Mary was contracted with legally binding words (if we are to believe John's witnesses), it appears that the inhabitants of the estate were aware that she could not have full sexual relations with John. This may be the reason they sought out visible demonstrations of her consent to the union. Accepting his gifts (which were mundane) is clearly one such indicator.

We know virtually nothing about how the contract between John and Alice's parents came about. We may speculate that the ceremony in St. Mary's included negotiations about the terms of the contract. It is notable that the occasion was not the ostentatious, public occasion we might have expected given the wealth of the parties. Legal officers may have been present or the contract may have been witnessed by lay people. But clearly it was respected by John, who may or may not have been influenced by the prospect of having to pay what was undoubtedly a heavy fine for non-compliance with the stipulations of the contract.

Formal Ecclesiastical Tribunals

The tribunal that met on 7 February 1346 in the case of *Huntington* c. *Munkton* was convened as part of the ordinary work of the court of the dean of the Christianity in York and gives us an impression of how the court prepared for a case in which a teenage girl had decided to challenge her parents' authority.

It was common for the intending parties to allow an investigation into their previous affairs in response to objections to their current marriage arrangement. In cases of marriage and divorce, this was a necessity. An exchange of vows in the past had often been attended by what may be characterized as expert witnesses, in most cases clerics who could be expected to have a more detailed understanding of the canon law rules of marriage formation. In desperate circumstances, however, such as the case of *Huntington* c. *Munkton* (1345–1346), the meeting of a formal tribunal to establish the validity of vows could be used by those litigants who had not been so sensible as to take the precautions outlined above. Sometimes, though, such a tribunal could become the victim of a series of attempts to force the outcome of their investigations, not only by the intending parties but also by their parents. In *Huntington* c. *Munkton* is an example where the tribunal was first manipulated by the daughter Agnes, who wanted her marriage to John of Bristol upheld, then by her mother, who emphatically did not.

Agnes claimed to have already married John of Bristol, but her stepfather and mother disliked John, and they alerted the dean of the Christianity of York to the fact that there might be fornication or a possible clandestine marriage between John and Agnes. In preparation to the court meeting proper, the dean's court put together a tribunal of three clerics, who assembled in Agnes's parents' house on the morning of 7 February 1340 to discuss the matter with Agnes's parents, her uncle William Huntington, and John of Bristol's parents. Agnes's mother wanted the tribunal to find that there was no marriage, while John and Agnes tried to persuade Agnes's mother and stepfather to remove the obstacles they had put in the way of their marriage. John went so far as to state his willingness to marry Agnes, even if it meant losing the legacy left to her by her father, Richard Huntington. He even offered the money to Agnes's stepfather, Hamo Hessay, if only he would agree to the union. But Agnes's mother was adamantly opposed to the marriage. Gilbert Pocklington, one of the three clerks of the dean's court present at the meeting, said that:

> He heard the said Agnes's mother say threateningly that she [Agnes] would draw a maternal curse upon herself if she swore to any [marriage] contract unless it be a conditional one, namely [on condition that] her parents agreed.[26]

After the preliminary meeting in Mulberry Hall, one member of the tribunal, John Couthorp, a clerk of the court of the dean of the Christianity and a kinsman of Agnes, continued to investigate the case and became convinced that John and Agnes *had* exchanged unconditional marriage vows on several occasions. John, Agnes, and a servant called Margaret Foxholes confessed this privately to him, and John Couthorp finally decided to confront Agnes's mother with this information. Her reaction was prompt: if John Couthorp did not stop associating with John of Bristol, Agnes's mother would have his legs broken.[27] Thus, by a mixture of intimidation and persuasion, Agnes's mother and Hamo Hessay managed to keep evidence of an unconditional contract out of the court of the dean of the Christianity when it met a week later.

The meeting was an official affair. It convened by the authority of the dean of the Christianity in York and was presided over by three representatives of that court. The parties' parents were also present, as was the uncle of Agnes of Huntington, who was later to prove a staunch friend for her. The purpose of the meeting was also well defined: it was the intention to establish whether there was a case to answer before a fully convened meeting of the dean's court. In the end this court decided against the marriage of John and Agnes when Agnes gave up her case as a consequence of parental pressure.

---

[26] "Dicit etiam idem juratus quod audivit matrem eiusdem Agnete sibi dicere comminandem quod inferret sibi maledictionem maternam si aliquem contractum faceretur nisi conditionale, videlicet si parentes dicte Agnete consentirent": CP, E 248–23d.

[27] "Audivit etiam idem juratus matrem dicte Agnete cominare eidem jurato quod dimitteret societatem dicti Johannis vel frangi faceret crura eiusdem jurati": CP E 248–23d, John de Couthorp.

Formal Lay Tribunals

The tribunal in the case of *Huntington* c. *Munkton* was convened as part of the ordinary work of the court of the dean of the Christianity in York. But in another case, *Lovell* c. *Marton*, the tribunal appears to have been a purely secular affair.

Lovell c. *Marton* was brought before the *Curia Eboracensis* by Elizabeth Lovell, the daughter of Sir Simon Lovell, against Thomas Marton, the son of Robert Marton. In her positions Elizabeth claimed that she had conducted marriage negotiations with Thomas,[28] that they had contracted a legitimate marriage by exchanging vows *verba de presenti*, and that Thomas had sworn to the existence of a marriage at a meeting held in the church of Hovingham which brought together "many people worthy of trust," in particular Elizabeth's and Thomas's families. On the surface the case was fairly straightforward. The court needed to determine whether Elizabeth and Thomas had exchanged valid marriage vows. But additional complications soon arose. Since this exchange of vows, Thomas had solemnized his wedding to Elena, daughter of Jordan of Aneport from the diocese of Lichfield.[29] But this solemnization was not argued as an impediment to his marriage to Elizabeth. We know about it only from a memorandum published by the court granting Thomas the right to live separately from Elena until the case had been determined in York. Furthermore, in his responses in York, Thomas did not deny that he had exchanged marriage vows with Elizabeth, but he emphasized that he had made it clear at the meeting in the parish church of Hovingham that the vows had been conditional upon the consent of his friends.

Elizabeth brought nine witnesses who testified that she had contracted marriage with Thomas on two separate occasions. Two of these witnesses had been present at an exchange of vows on the Sunday before the Purification of the Virgin just past (2 February 1326). The exchange had taken place in Thomas's father's brewing house in Drokom in Rydale, where Thomas had said to Elizabeth, "behold my oath that I will take no one as my wife except you," and she replied, "behold my oath that never will I have anyone as my husband except

[28] "Tractatus habebatur inter eosdem de matrimonio inter eosdem ineundo": *Lovell* c. *Marton*, CP E 18–5 (1327–1328).

[29] "[Thomas Marton] confessus fuit . . . se solemnizasse matrimonium cum quadem Elena, filia Jordani de Aneport commorantis apud Ryngoy in episcopatu Cestr' pendente lite super matrimonio inter Elizabath' filiam domini Simonis Lovell' militis pendente indecisa; asseruit tamen se precontraxisse cum prefata Elena antel litem inchoatam." Printed in R. H. Helmholz, *Marriage Litigation in Medieval England*, Cambridge Studies in English Legal History (Cambridge: Cambridge University Press, 1974), 195. The diocese of Chester was not created until 1542. The phrase *in episcopatu Cestr'* therefore must refer to the diocese of Lichfield.

you."[30] In token of their marriage they held hands and kissed each other in the presence of Elizabeth's sister, Agnes, and a certain John Bartholomew.

Though Elizabeth and Thomas doubtless intended to contract marriage on this occasion, they had in fact only contracted a marriage *verba de futuro* by their words, and this flaw was pointed out to Thomas by his confessors, the Dominican friars. On the morning of 16 April 1326, Thomas — lying naked in his bed — and Elizabeth discussed the validity of their contract in the presence of Agnes and Euphemia, another of Elizabeth's sisters, who had come to visit Thomas in his father's manor:

> The said Thomas said then that it had been said to him by the friars, his confessors, that the previous contract was not valid; but that both [he and Elizabeth] could contract marriage with another wherever they wanted. And then by the free will of both of them they uttered the words written below, with said Thomas first speaking and holding said Elizabeth by the right hand: 'here I take you Elizabeth as my faithfully joined wife to have and to hold until the end of my life and I give you my word for this.' To which said Elizabeth replied: 'here I take you, Thomas, as my pledged husband, to have and to hold until the end of my life and I give you my word on this.'

This contract was witnessed by Agnes, Euphemia, and Richard Hyman, Thomas's servant. Thomas and Elizabeth contracted their marriage without the knowledge and consent of their parents.

For our purpose the important date was 7 November 1326, when a meeting took place in the parish church of Hovingham some twenty miles outside of York. By whose authority it was convened is unknown, but we know that it was presided over by Sir Simon Lovell, Elizabeth's father. Among those present in Hovingham were Elizabeth's father, her aunt, and Thomas's parents. Also present were Edmund Stanley, William de Easingby, and two men — William Appleton and William Thornton — whose role in the proceedings, as we shall see, remains ambiguous.[31] What is certain about the meeting in Hovingham is that those

---

[30] "'Ecce fides mea quod non ducam aliquam in uxorem nisi te.' Et ipsa statim respondebat: 'Ecce fides mea quod nullo tempore habebo aliquem in virum nisi te habeam'": CP, E 18–5.

[31] The documentation for this period of the court's existence is sparse, but a certain William Appleby was a proctor of the court some thirteen years later. Since the suffix -ton is the English version of the Scandinavian suffix -by it may be suggested that William Appleton could have been a member of the court in York at this time. William Appleton certainly seems to have been there to advise Thomas and Elizabeth in the canon law of marriage.

present met to discuss the evidence for or against the existence of a marriage between Elizabeth and Thomas. The evidence put forward is outlined above, but when Thomas had finished his evidence, something unusual happened. In his deposition, Thomas had confirmed every detail of Elizabeth's story, which should have been the end of the story. But when he had told his version of events and returned to the small group consisting of Elizabeth, William Appleton, and William Thornton, the four of them started whispering among themselves. Within a short while, Thomas returned to add a detail to his story: he might have consented to the marriage, he said, but in his mind he had expressed a reservation — he had not wanted to marry Elizabeth unless his *amici* consented to the marriage.[32] Legally, this was a poor excuse, and it would hardly have any impact in a normal trial. What possessed Thomas to express these reservations before the tribunal can only be guessed at, but it may be speculated that it was not unrelated to his parents' attempts to marry him off to Elena de Aneport outside the diocese. Thomas's statement may have been designed to sow just enough doubt about the validity of his marriage to Elizabeth to force the informal (and presumably, family-based) tribunal to send the case to be heard by another, professional, tribunal consisting of trained lawyers who would settle once and for all in a public forum whether a marriage existed between Thomas and Elizabeth. It may also have been part of his considerations that a professional tribunal would have the power to prevent his marriage to Elena of Aneport, as indeed it did. Whatever Thomas's motives were, in his mind and in the estimation of his advisers, his admission of mental reservations posed a threat to the legality of the vows between him and Elizabeth. Thomas's objections were disregarded by the court in York, and a sentence for Elizabeth upholding the marriage was passed on 27 October 1328.

The exact nature of the meeting in Hovingham church is unclear. Richard Helmholz called it "a meeting of the important men of the community in the parish church,"[33] but this is clearly wrong, given the composition of the tribunal and the fact that Elizabeth's aunt was one of the people interrogating Thomas and Elizabeth. It seems rather to have been a meeting of the parties concerned and their families, presided over by Sir Simon Lovell. The venue and the way

[32] "Et postmodum, dictus Thomas, post huiusmodi confessionem dicte Elizabet, parum deliberavit cum Willelmo de Thornton et Willelmo de Appilton. Et statim rediens ad dictum Simonem et alios superius nominatos, fatebatur se talia verba matrimonialia in forma per ipsam Elizabetem recitata eidem Elizabeti dixisse et protulisse. Adiecit tamen idem Thomas quod tempore quo talia verba matrimonialia fecit et protulit dicte Elizabete, in mente et voluntate cogitavit quod dictum contractum non adimpleret nisi adesset voluntas amicorum suorum. Et tunc dicta Elizabet eidem respondebat quod de cogitatione nescit, sed ille contractus fuerat simplex, sine conditione aliquali. Cui asssertioni dictus Thomas nichil in contrarium respondebat": CP, E 18–5.

[33] Helmholz, *Marriage Litigation*, 191.

in which two of the people present, William Appleton and William Thornton, acted as legal counsel to Thomas and Elizabeth make it clear that Thomas knew what he was doing and that he did so after consultations with his apparent opponent, Elizabeth.

This case appears among the cause papers as an instance case. In other words, Elizabeth Lovell appears to have sued to have the court enforce her marriage to a reluctant Thomas Marton. However, a closer examination suggests that neither Elizabeth nor Thomas was averse to the marriage. Instead, it seems that Thomas's father, Robert Marton — who in sharp contrast to Elizabeth's father, Sir Simon Lovell, was not referred to by title by the court scribe — had other plans for Thomas. Just how marrying Thomas to Elena of Aneport during the hearing of the case in York fitted into his plans is impossible to say. One would have thought that Thomas Marton's father would have been happy to have Elizabeth, a member of the aristocracy, as a member of his family. Whatever his reasons, Robert Marton's actions were an unambiguous attempt to circumvent the court in York. The marriage to Elena de Aneport took place in a diocese outside the jurisdiction of the northern province where the reading of the banns was unlikely to attract attention, and it took place after the beginning of the case in York. It was claimed for York only because a case had already been initiated there. However, despite initial appearances, the case is not simply one of a teenager who spoke too soon and later regretted it, but can be seen as a manifestation of teenage insistence on marrying against the wishes of parents. It has already been argued above that the laity had a good grasp of the basic church rules of marriage, but Thomas's surprising action at the meeting in Hovingham suggests two other things: that the laity had developed means, including pre-court hearings like the one above, to determine whether a case should be heard by a proper legal tribunal, and that people like Thomas Marton and Elizabeth Lovell were willing to use these hearings to force a decision in their case by formal court, rather than by a meeting of their families and friends.

Informal Lay Tribunals

The meetings in Hovingham and in York's Mulberry Hall carry a number of hallmarks of legal occasions. They included the parties and their advisers, and the parties' families were present. The parties also took advice and formally deposited their statements before the tribunal. And in both cases the litigants saw the case continue into a proper legal forum.

The formality of meeting in Hovingham is in marked contrast to a meeting in *Foston* c. *Lawless* (1393).[34] In this case we find a group of people gathered together in the room of a Sister Margaret Ely, a nun in St. Clement's monastery in

[34] CP, E 198 (1393).

Clementhorpe, who enquired under informal circumstances into an exchange of vows. The case proper was heard by the church courts from October 1393 to July 1394. The matter of the suit was the legality of the vows exchanged between the widow Alice de Foston and Robert Lofthouse, a draper of York, with whom she had two children. Present at the meeting in the monastery of St. Clement were the parties, Margaret Ely, Alice Foston's son William (who is the source of the information that follows), and Sister Beatrice Benyngton. William told the court in York that he had *not* been specifically called to be present on a certain day, but that he happened to overhear an exchange of words between the three while he was in the room. Margaret Ely asked Robert Lofthouse:

> 'Why did you refuse to swear with Alice who is present here' and he responded, 'the troth that I pledged there I shall keep and I shall make her as good a woman as I am a man and I want to have her as my wife.' And the said Alice responded, 'I hold myself content and I always held myself well content and you promised me this a long before this.'[35]

This meeting was informal and shows few of the characteristics of the Hovingham tribunal. William Foston was only present because his mother was there, and the occasion was not surrounded by any of the paraphenalia of a legal occasion. The parties did not have representation and they did not consult with advisers. Nor did they formally deposit their testimony. In fact, the only other witness to the occasion, Sister Beatrice Benyngton, said that she had to move closer to Alice and Thomas to hear what they were saying. Nevertheless, the occasion also seems to carry some special importance due to the presence of the two nuns. Though it is doubtful whether it can be characterized as a tribunal, properly speaking, it did manage to fulfill the same function, namely to establish whether there was a case to be answered before a more formal court under the auspices of the *Curia Eboracensis*.

An Impotence Case

The previous cases have illustrated that it was common for the litigants in York to explore the issues of their cases before they came before the court proper. These investigations took several forms, from the informal meeting in Sister Margaret Ely's chamber in Clementhorpe to what appears to be a very formalized tribunal

[35] "Dicta Margareta quesivit a dicto Roberto Lofthous, tunc presente, quomodo nitebat fateri cum Alicia de Foston, predicta ibidem presente. Et ipse respondebat: 'Fidem quam ipsam promisi, servabo et faciam eam bonam mulierem sicut ego sum vir et volo habere eam in uxorem meam.' Et dicta Alicia respondebat: 'Teneo me bene contenta et semper tenui me bene contenta, et ista promisistis mihi longe ante istud tempus' ": CP, E 198–1, William Foston.

at the parish church of Hovingham in the case of *Lovell* c. *Marton*. Mostly these meetings were convened, but the informal meeting in Clementhorpe seems more casual. What these meetings had in common, however, was that they explored the issues at hand and established whether there was a case to answer before a properly convened ecclesiastical tribunal.

But not all tribunals met solely to establish the facts of a case before submitting it to the church courts. They could also serve the additional function of trying to cure what was seen as a medical or magical condition in the impotence case of *Lambhird* c. *Sanderson* (1370).[36] The defendant in this case, John Sanderson of Wele, was cited before the court in York in June 1370 by his wife Tedia Lambhird, who petitioned to have their marriage dissolved alleging his impotence. They had previously cohabited for four years, after which time Tedia moved away from John. The couple was then summoned before the dean of Holderness, Thomas of St. Martin, who ordered them to resume their cohabitation. They did so for an unspecified length of time, but in the six months preceding the hearings in York they had lived in separate households. As in the *Lyremouth* case, John Sanderson was exposed to two tribunals with two different aims: one was an informal attempt by his family to discover if his impotence could be cured; the other was a formal physical examination by the court in York.

A somewhat messy attempt to solve the couple's marital problems was made sometime before the case was heard in York in the elder John Sanderson's barn. The witness Thomas Stephenson saw Tedia and John:

> In a barn in Wele belonging to John Sanderson, the father of John, the defendant, on a certain day around the feast of the Ascension of Our Lord three years ago, before the hour of nones of that day, trying to perform intercourse with due diligence for that work. And he says by his oath that he then saw the member of said John laying low and in no way rising or becoming erect. And at that time he saw the brother of said John stroke the said member of John. And he says that he often saw the said John and Tedia, concerned in this case, both before and after that time lying together in one bed, but he did not see them trying to perform intercourse.[37]

[36] CP, E 105 (1370).

[37] "In orreo Johannis Sanderson, patris carnalis Johannis, de quo agitur, apud Wele quodam die circa festum ascensionis domini, tribus annis elapsis, ut credit, ante horam nonam ipsius diei, carnali copule operam adhibentes cum diligentia debita in hac parte. Et dicit in juramento suo quod tunc vidit virgam ipsius Johannis submissam et nullo modo se erigentem vel erectam. Et tunc vidit fratrem carnalem ipsius Johannis, de quo agitur, palpare ibidem virgam Johannis predictam. Et dicit quod sepius tam post quam ante dictum tempus vidit ipsos Johannem et Tediam, de quibus agitur, uno lecto simul nudos jacentes, sed non vidit eos carnali copule operam adhibentes": CP, E 105 (1370).

It is impossible to tell from the evidence whether this attempt at intercourse occurred before or after Tedia's and John's first encounter with the church's legal system, the court of the dean of Holderness, but it is likely that it took place after Tedia had taken advice from the court or from her confessor. The incident is certainly not the kind of activity that one would expect the church to condone. Regardless of its good intentions, the attempt was to no avail, for the neighborhood rumor was that John and Tedia never consummated the marriage.

Considering the evidence contained in the results of the tribunal of "good and honest women" that the court in York assembled, it can be said with certainty that there was a good physical explanation as to why John and Tedia did not have intercourse. When the case was heard in York, the court decided to have John examined *per aspectum corporis*. This kind of investigation was performed by a group of women appointed by the court to attempt to arouse sexually the man in a case of alleged impotence.[38] The description of John's penis given by the three women who investigated him leaves no doubt that his impotence had a physical explanation:

> And she says that the member of said John is like an empty intestine of dead skin not having any flesh in it, or veins in the skin, and the middle of its front is totally black. And said witness stroked said member with her hands and put it in semen and having thus been stroked and deposited it neither expanded nor grew.[39] Asked if he has a scrotum with testicles she says that

[38] James A. Brundage, *Law, Sex, and Christian Society in Medieval Europe* (Chicago: University of Chicago Press, 1987), 163–64, 290–92, and 376–78, describes the canon law stance on impotence. The rather surprising way of establishing the fact of a man's impotence seems to have been unique to England: Helmholz, *Marriage Litigation*, 87–90. For a history of this kind of tribunal, see Jacqueline Murray, "Trial by Congress," *The Lawyers Weekly* 6.44 (20 March 1987): 20–21, 31; eadem, "On the Origins and Role of 'Wise Women' in Causes for Annulment on the Grounds of Male Impotence," *Journal of Medieval History* 16 (1990): 235–49; P. J. P. Goldberg, ed. and trans., *Women in England c. 1275–1525: Documentary Sources*, Manchester Medieval Sources (Manchester: Manchester University Press, 1995), 219–22, contains a translation of an impotence case from 1432 (CP, F 111, *Russel* c. *Skathelok*). By placing this transcript in the section on prostitution, Goldberg implies that the women who appeared before such tribunals were prostitutes. This seems unlikely given that the women were always married and described as having good standing in the community.

[39] This appears to be the only known instance of this nexus of words being used in English sources. My decision to translate *flore* as "semen" is based on the following reasoning: Charlton T. Lewis, *A Latin Dictionary Founded on Andrews' Edition of Freund's Latin Dictionary Revised, Enlarged, and in Great Part Rewritten*, in collaboration with Charles Short (Oxford: Clarendon Press, 1987), s.v. "flos" has the translation "the best

> there is in that place the skin of a scrotum, but the testicles do not hang in the scrotum but are connected with the skin in their extremities, as is the case among young infants.[40]

This description of John's penis given to the court makes it clear that John suffered from a relatively common malformation of his penis now known as hypospadias, and the court annulled the marriage, an unsurprising outcome given the evidence.

Conclusions

The cause paper evidence in York suggests that in contrast to the situation suggested by Hanawalt for secular courts in London, the church's monopoly on the settlement of matrimonial disputes was never seriously challenged in York. It also suggests that this monopoly was wholeheartedly embraced by the laity. The pre-court activities of litigants and their families outlined above shows that the laity cooperated with the church in preparation for litigation so that disputes over marriage could be presented to the courts in an orderly manner or, perhaps, settled without the involvement of the church. Our analysis shows that such preparation was always performed on an *ad hoc* basis, as evidenced by the fact that the meetings and informal attempts at dispute settlement took on a plethora of forms and never settled into one specific form or procedure. The existence of such a consensus about the proper forum for the dispensation of justice in marriage cases is the only way to explain the varying levels of formality and the multitude of structures that surrounded these tribunals. Although they existed and were very active, lay tribunals were not there to replace a meeting of a church court. Instead

---

part of something" or "the highest part, the top, crown, head of a thing, froth of wine"; R.E. Latham, exec. ed., *Revised Medieval Latin Word-List from British and Irish Sources*, The British Academy (London: Oxford University Press, 1965), s.v. "flos" has "menstruation." *Flos* thus refers to some sort of distillation or effluent. Its conjunction with the masculine *fratris* makes it impossible for it to refer to an effluent from the female body, such as menstrual blood, and it therefore refers to an effluent from the male body. I would like to express my gratitude to the neo-Latin discussion group on the Internet whose comments about the meaning of the phrase are condensed in this note.

[40] "Et dicit quod virga dicti Johannis est quasi quedam intestina vacua de mortua pelli, non habens carnem interius nec venas in cute et est medietas anterior eiusdem nigra totaliter. Et ista testis palpavit dictam virgam cum manibus suis et posuit eam in flore fratris et sic palpata et deposita nec dilatabat se nec crescebat. Interrogata si habet bursam cum testiculis dicit quod est ibi pellis bursalis sed testiculi non pendent in bursa sed sunt contigui cum carne in unguibus sicut est in juvenibus infantibus": CP, E 105 (1370).

they supplemented the church courts and weeded out those cases that the church tribunals did not need to hear. They were, in other words, intended to supplement rather than replace the church courts, and thus lend further credence to the assertion that the laity of medieval England accepted the right of the church to settle disputes over marriage.

Marriage Gifts and Fashion Mischief

Susan Mosher Stuard

Gifts awarded at marriage formed a major conduit for transfer of familial wealth in medieval times. Today our chief transfer of family-held wealth occurs with the death of the senior generation, and today's economists sometimes bewail the loss in opportunity costs from capital tied up in the estates of fiscally conservative elders. Medieval people relied on a distribution of wealth more advantageous to youth and growth in the economy since they were more conscious than we of the great difficulty and expense of establishing newlyweds in households; they supported that activity well. A household, staffed by newlyweds, served as a fundamental social, economic, and political building block for society, and elders acknowledged that by vesting their youth with assets. In Florence, "some new husbands [already] headed their own households, but most still lived as sons, younger brothers, or more distant relatives — under someone else's roof."[1] An impressive dowry could remedy that situation, and the groom, perhaps twice his bride's age, often set about creating his own *casa* upon marriage: thus lineages spread out new households all over town. Ideally, youthful energy and ambition augmented marital gifts so the great undertaking of creating a household prospered.

In early Lombard law a *quarta* of family wealth was given to a son when he married so that he could sustain his new household.[2] This, the so-called "male" dowry of early medieval society, was the chief marital assign of the era and propitious for the growth of a young, and expanding, society. Population expanded and trade prospered from this generous distribution of familial wealth to the young in the eleventh and early twelfth centuries.

But wedding gifts reversed in the direction in which they moved soon thereafter.[3] This was certainly the case for the Mediterranean region where traditional husbands' gifts to wives were replaced by a "Roman" dowry, a bride's inheritance or Falcidian quarter that would terminate her legal demands on her natal family for

---

[1] David Herlihy and Christiane Klapisch-Zuber, *Tuscans and their Families* (New Haven: Yale University Press, 1985), 228. For example, there were wealthy Albizzi and Alberti residences spread throughout the city as married sons established their own residences. This diversity of housing is characterized by the authors as "viri-local."

[2] Barbara Kreutz, "The Twilight of Morgengabe," in Samuel K. Cohn jr. and Steven A. Epstein, ed. *Portraits of Medieval and Renaissance Living* (Ann Arbor: University of Michigan Press, 1996), 131–48.

[3] Diane Owen Hughes, "From Brideprice to Dowry in Mediterranean Europe" *Journal of Family History* 3 (1978): 263–96.

support. In earlier times women had owned their gifts from husbands as outright possessions, whereas the new Roman dowry was more ambiguously assigned. Henceforth a husband supported his wife and her offspring with the insurance supplied by the Roman dowry that was wholly under his control. This momentous shift in the direction in which capital moved (wife's family to husband rather than husband or his family to wife) occurred over the twelfth and thirteenth centuries. As Pierre Bonnassie has argued, Roman dowry was likely to be the first instance of family wealth converted from property to cash. It answered a strongly felt need to preserve family land holdings intact, so daughters were endowed with cash and sons held property.[4] Manlio Bellomo has argued that Roman dowry was converted to cash in Italian towns so that husbands were assured capital sums for investment purposes.[5] In Italian towns it soon became law that while a woman owned her Roman dowry and would have it under her control if she became a widow, while her husband lived he had control of it. He could invest it and make profit from it, but the sum must remain intact. He must not alienate it or lose it, a tall order when commerce entailed economic risk.

This shift in marital assigns and the conversion of dowry to cash are some of the more momentous economic developments of the medieval era, yet they were barely recognized by historians until the last quarter of the twentieth century. Capital investment, the cash economy, and the very nature of urban households were refigured by this effort to live "in all things" according to Roman law, as lawmakers in Siena asserted.[6] Perhaps it is because economic historians seldom look at inheritance patterns to understand economic change that this important shift was ignored for so long. But, as Bellomo has argued, the ready cash that fell into the hands of men when they married underwrote European commercial expansion. Even if, as was dictated by law, new husbands invested dowry funds conservatively, their "cash flow" situation was enhanced considerably at marriage. Men were able to use whatever other cash they had on hand in high-risk ventures because their financial positions were sustained by dowry awards from brides' families.

This conversion to cash is an important theme to consider for the later medieval period as well. Just as Roman dowry, given in cash, transformed investment opportunities for men in the twelfth and thirteenth centuries, conversion of other

[4] Pierre Bonnassie, "A Family of the Barcelona Countryside and its Economic Activities around the Year 1000," in *Early Medieval Society*, ed. Sylvia Thrupp (New York: Appleton:Century-Crofts, 1967), 103–23, here 120–1.

[5] Manlio Bellomo, *Ricerche sui rapporti patrimoniali tra coniugi* (Milan: Giuffre, 1961), 825.

[6] Eleanor Riemer, "Women in the Medieval City: Sources and Uses of Wealth by Sienese Women in the Thirteenth Century" (Ph.D. diss., New York University, 1975), 71–73.

marital gifts to cash further enhanced husbands' economic position in later decades. Simply put, husbands liked gifts of cash; they preferred the liquidity of cash to wedding gifts of clothes, "plate," linens, hangings, *cassoni* (wedding chests), and other ornaments. The bride's wardrobe was a bone of contention for a newlywed couple, and husbands often gave ostentatious gifts to their brides but voiced complaints about this outlay of funds. In these years in Venice, a strong initiative was mounted to turn the husband's counter-gift to his bride into a cash award so that he could invest the gift as capital rather than see it expended on his bride's wardrobe.[7] Jane Fair Bestor argues that, according to late medieval legists, a man could not even alienate property by giving gifts to his wife because even when given the gift remained part of his patrimony. As such it could be recalled, or pawned, or sold, that is, turned into cash.[8]

Still, no urban Italian family of any standing was content with the simple award of cash at marriage, but augmented the *dos,* as it was called, with all sorts of counter-gifts, trousseaux, *corredi*, and wedding paraphernalia. In 1353 the Florentine Giovanni Niccolini arranged for his ward, Tommasa, wedding gifts including "one belt, mounted in silver with a purse with silver enamel, [worth] three gold florins." Tommasa also received two sets of silver buttons, an old green cloth for a gown, fine crimson cloth for another gown, new green cloth for a coat, three pairs of slippers, three pairs of shoes, twelve caps, one mirror, a comb, linen thread, wimples, miniver and samite for two hats, stockings, and veils, as well as linens and other household items. Cost added up, particularly for clothes and precious accessories, since they were paid for in gold florins, the currency of long-distance trade.[9]

Husbands continued to bring pressure to bear in many different ways to convert diverse marital gifts into cash, yet families liked to award presents and apparently wives were eager to receive gifts in kind. This set up tensions within marriages where the demands for display warred with a desire for investment funds. Not only did conflict arise between husband and wife, but husbands were often of two minds themselves, seeking gifts in cash yet constrained by the demands of honor and prestige to add their own rich presents to the array of the bride's gifts. In Venice in 1360 civic statutes solved men's quandaries by dictating

[7] Stanley Chojnacki, "From Trousseau to Groomgift in Late Medieval Venice" in *Medieval and Renaissance Venic*e, ed. Ellen Kittell and Thomas Madden (Urbana: University of Illinois Press, 1999), 141–65.

[8] Jane Fair Bestor, "Marriage Transactions in Renaissance Italy" *Past and Present* 164 (1999): 4–46.

[9] *The Chronicles of a Florentine Family, 1200.1470*, ed. Ginevra Niccolini di Camugliano (London: J. Cape, 1933), 65–68.

that no husband might give more than thirty *lire di grossi* in dress or jewels to his bride, and that extended through the first four years of marriage.[10]

Men's reactions to the conflicting demands made upon them are thoroughly recorded in the Venetian Senatorial debates that led to the passage of the sumptuary law of 1360, but we hear very little from women, who no longer controlled their dowries, and now saw their other wedding gifts and finery under attack for conversion to cash and further curtailed by sumptuary laws.

I spend some time sketching this context because, strange to say, the resulting pressures brought to bear in well-to-do households helped create the first age of European fashion that flourished in the streets of fourteenth-century Italian towns.[11] Urban fashion promoted the consumption of fine goods and began to stimulate demand. Indeed, it is possible that without opposing agendas for marital gifts, fashion — that is, one style replacing another in brisk succession — might never have taken hold as firmly as it did. But with conflicting agendas for marital wealth, and sumptuary laws that intervened in family decision-making, tensions played out between men and women in such a way that fashion emerged.

The fulcrum on which the highly gendered nature of response to urban sumptuary laws turned rested on the laws' proclivity to legislate restraints on women's, youths', and children's consumption, to limit festivities like wedding celebrations, and in general to treat women, especially brides, as persons in need of restraint. Meanwhile, adult men were exempt from most limits on dress and consumption. Husbands in particular profited from intervention of law while their own consumption remained largely free of restriction. Men could dress to the hilt, if they had the means to do so. Newly married women watched large capital sums change hands at their nuptials and they had no control over it; they faced growing restraints on their wedding finery and on their consumption generally. This set up conditions for envy to grow, and thus for men and women to play very different roles in establishing fashion as a feature of urban life.

It is, of course, a treacherous undertaking to interpret silence, particularly in a century like the fourteenth in Italy where records have gone missing. Still, brides and other married women in Italy's towns appear to have been adamantly silent in the face of sumptuary restraints that blamed them, their spending (*sumptus* actually means spending), and their public appearances, particularly at weddings, for disturbing the social order.

[10] Margaret Newett, "The Sumptuary Laws of Venice" in *Historical Essays*, ed. T. F. Tout and James Tait (London: Longmans Green, 1902), 262. See note 27 below for texts of Venetian sumptuary law.

[11] Trading cities, especially those that were capital cities or near courts, saw a growth of fashion, compared to other regions of fourteenth-century Europe, but the rich resources of social and economic life in northern Italy and Italian commercial expansion render fashion's emergence more visible in Italy.

In the same era, Aragonese women at court complained bitterly about the pain caused by the king's and pope's restrictions on their clothes. One woman's plaintive lament:

> . . . l sagramen,
> car nostres vestirs ricx
> an nafratz e aunitz;
> qi o tractet sia marritz,
> per que cascuna entenda
> que non port vel ni benda
> mais garlandas de flors
> en estieu per amors.
>
> (let the order be lifted; / they've harmed and dishonored / our rich clothing. / May the law's author suffer / to see every woman resolve / not to wear veil or wimple / but garlands of flowers / in the summer for love.)

The anonymous trobaritz who sang this lament regarded the king of Aragon's stewards as the source of her "dishonor." Would women in Florence or Venice be any less acute in identifying those responsible for writing the restrictive laws under which they chafed?

Christine de Pizan knew all about the meaning of clothes, but unfortunately commented on the clothes of the opulent French court, with not a word about her native Pisa. Later, in the fifteenth century, the Italian women accepted in humanist circles, Nicolosa Sanuti and Battista Petrucci, would devote learned treatises to the indignities imposed on Italy's women by sumptuary laws, but their earlier compatriots were mute in the face of sumptuary laws.[12] Lack of literacy may not be blamed. According to the chronicler Villani, girls attended grammar school in fourteenth-century Florence. In other cities private tutors educated the daughters of well-to-do families. Even if literacy were not achieved in childhood, a woman like Margherita Datini of Prato might study her letters in her adult years, becoming sufficiently literate to keep up a lively correspondence with her husband.[13]

---

[12] Catherine Kovesi Killerby, "Practical Problems in the Enforcement of Italian Sumptuary Law, 1200–1500" in *Crime, Society and the Law in Renaissance Italy*, ed. Trevor Dean and K. J. P. Lowe (Cambridge: Cambridge University Press, 1994), 99–120.

[13] Giovanni Villani, *Chroniche de Giovanni, Matteo e Filippo Villani,* ed. A. Racheli (Trieste: Austriaco, 1857) chap. xciv. See Charity Cannon Willard, *The Writings of Christine Pizan* (New York: Persea Books, 1994). On Nicolusa Sanuti and Battista Petrucci see Jane Bridgman, "'Pagare le pompe'" in *Women in Italian Renaissance Culture and Society* ed. Letizia Panizzza (Oxford: European Humanities Research Center, 2000), 209–26. For Margherita Datini see Francesco de Marco Datini, *Le lettere di Margherita Datini a Francesco di Marco Datini*, (Prato: Cassa di Risparmi e Depositi, 1977).

There are three rare surviving fourteenth-century letters from the widow Cataruza da Pesaro to her brother-in-law, composed to raise dowry for her daughter, and six more equally rare letters from the Florentine Dora del Bene, discussing family matters. Neither woman makes complaint about laws, nor how they discriminated against women.[14]

Despite her illiteracy, St. Catherine of Siena availed herself of a scribe, so her strong opinions reached her correspondents and have been preserved to this day. Angela of Foligno left a vast record of her spiritual life through the offices of her confessor, as did other beatified and sainted women. Holy women found a way to be heard or read, but more ordinary married laywomen did not. Even while shouldering the greater part of blame for excessive spending in well-to-do families, married women did not write down their thoughts. But they rebelled; men have recorded those acts. Villani stated unequivocally that women deeply resented Florentine sumptuary laws. Earlier in Genoa women had protested the laws restricting their wedding gifts, while in the Straits of Messina women rebelled openly when sumptuary laws imposed restraint on their consumption.[15] Clearly there was some spirited response to these laws from women, but there is almost no record of it available today.

Even if their voices were mute, married women's roles in both production and consumption were significant for fashion's ascendancy in fourteenth-century towns. Understanding the transformation in consumer markets may rest on respecting two very different sorts of evidence: clothing, the expressive power of which is connotative and affective, with a visual impact that is immediate and powerful, as great as but different from that of words, which are so useful in capturing just how, and how well, an urban audience grasped the meaning of clothes.[16]

---

[14] Linda Guzzetti, "Donne e scrittura a Venezia nel tardo Trecento" *Archivio Veneto* 152 (1999): 5–32. The texts of the three letters appear, 29–31. For Dora del Bene's six letters at Florence see *Alcune lettere familiari del secolo XIV*, ed. Pietro Dazzi (Bologna: G. Romagnoli, 1868), 46–55

[15] On Genoa see Diane Owen Hughes, "Urban Growth and Family Structure in Medieval Genoa" *Past and Present* 66 (1975): 3–28. On Messina see Giuseppe Giudici, "Una legge suntuaria inedita del 1290" *Atti dell'Accademia Pontaniana* 16 (1886): 100–22.

[16] Grant McCracken, *Culture and Consumption* (Bloomington: Indiana University Press, 1988). See also Richard Goldthwaite, *Wealth and the Demand for Art in Italy, 1300–1600* (Baltimore: Johns Hopkins University Press, 1993) and idem, "The Renaissance Economy: The Preconditions for Luxury Consumption," in *Aspetti della vita economica medievale.* Atti del convegno di studi nel X anniversario della morte de Federigo Melis (Firenze-Pisa-Prato, 10 Marzo, 1984) (Florence: Istituto di storia economica, Università degli Studi di Firenze, 1985), 659–72. Goldthwaite speaks of an aesthetic revolution in the fifteenth century that turned consumption away from the more garish effects favored in the fourteenth century.

Written records that survive from the century give the impression that authorities in towns were unable to keep up with the pace of change in women's dress, that is, fashion. Men in authority were disturbed by new fashions, and they blamed women for following them. This is slim documentary evidence for women's roles in determining taste, but it argues strongly for greater social consequence assigned to appearances than in earlier times. Women exerted much of their influence over taste through being seen, rather than being read or heard. They seem to have spoken little, but their fashions spoke loudly.

The words recorded in that age make it clear that fashion in women's apparel was transgressive, that women were interlopers in the world of fashion. Men were authorized to introduce fashions: the higher the standing in the community, the more a man's taste in clothes was slated for imitation. Leading citizens could afford to dress in the finest garments and accessories available in markets, and they viewed their primacy as leaders of fashion to be both proper and fitting. This became in time a convincing rationale for remaining largely unrestricted parties in the civic sumptuary laws that men wrote. To speculate for a moment, the pace of change might have continued at a more stately pace had men's roles as arbiters of fashion remained unchallenged, but with emphatic meaning attached to public dress, leading citizens encountered an unanticipated situation. Neither law nor custom could keep members of their own households, women chief among them, from finding ways to dress fashionably, as men themselves dressed fashionably. Apparently this disturbed men's notions of entitlement, but as the periodic bouts of sumptuary lawmaking indicate, it was difficult to control.

In the world of fashion, ironies abounded that pitted men and women, husband and wife, groom and bride, against each other. Giuseppe Giudici was probably correct in saying that, politically speaking, women tended to resist sumptuary restraints on conservative grounds. Women desired a return to their former condition when they had possessed unrestricted control over their wedding gifts and other possessions according to *antiche usanze* (ancient usage).[17] Roman dowry and the laws constructed around it cut into women's control over personal property. That their ingenuity in response to restrictions of their rights affected markets and demand by promoting radical new styles was no less consequential because it was an unplanned and perhaps, initially, an unintended consequence. Meanwhile men boldly assumed important new roles as models of fashion in the fourteenth century, yet expressed a strong collective desire to hold the line for others through writing complex sumptuary codes. Men grappled more directly and self-consciously with the implications of stylishness in a nascent consumer culture, but through legislating restraints they inadvertently created an environment in which women were inclined to experiment. With sumptuary laws, city-states intruded upon the

[17] Giudici, "Una legge suntuaria inedita del 1290," 122.

traditional prerogatives of households, usurping some of the authority belonging to heads of household, despite the laws' express purpose of buttressing a man's authority in his home. The ironies of unintended consequences within the new world of fashion resulted in cross purposes and unforeseen outcomes.

According to Ronald Rainey, there are 2,283 surviving volumes of the Florentine *Esecutore degli ordinamenti di giustizie* of which a number of folios were devoted to recording charges against women who broke sumptuary laws. These are records of the *Ufficiale delle donne* — an office devoted to trying offenses committed by women. The office consisted of a trained notary hired from outside Florence for a six-month term. He brought with him six expert assistants *(famuli)* to write up charges.[18] These men had responsibility to hang around church doors and street corners and check to see if *gabelle* (taxes) had been paid to wear finery controlled by the sumptuary code in force at the time. Notaries were to summon to court any woman wearing forbidden finery who failed to display a leaden seal stamped with a fleur-de-lis that proved the garment or accessory was legal, that is, attested to the paid *gabelle*. In court a charged woman, often represented by her lawyer, would have to plead the charge, and if she failed to convince, she would pay a stiff fine.

The novelist Franco Sacchetti could scarcely resist the absurdities in this effort at law-keeping in his *Trecentonovelle*.[19] In 1384 the officer in charge was a Messer Amerigo degli Amerighi of Pesaro. Sacchetti probably heard the incidents he would relate in *Novella* 137 with his own ears because he served in the Signoria to which Messer Amerigo reported. Messer Amerigo was being driven nearly wild in discharging his duty. The Signoria had the temerity to chastise him for lax enforcement, so Messer Amerigo vented his pent-up frustrations. His officers, he complained, had to confront women flouting the law, and they always came off badly. Women offenders argued more adroitly than they did; sometimes with clever fingers they transformed a forbidden headdress before a law-enforcer's very eyes, or at other times they scornfully renamed an ornament. Officials might insist "'You cannot wear those buttons,' to which the woman might answer, 'Yes, sir, I can, because they are not buttons but beads as they lack button holes.'"[20] Women knew their law: decorative buttons without a corresponding buttonhole had been forbidden to women in Florence by law since 1355.[21] Beads, on the other hand, could be construed as legal ornaments.

---

[18] Ronald E. Rainey, "Sumptuary Legislation in Renaissance Florence" (Ph.D. diss, Columbia University, 1985), 292–98.

[19] Franco Sacchetti, *Trecentonovelle* (Florence: Sansoni, 1946), 303–5.

[20] Sacchetti, *Trecentonovelle*, 303–5.

[21] Like trims on robes, buttons as decoration marching down a sleeve from shoulder to wrist were a style popular among men at Florence; see later discussion.

The Signoria was not entirely unsympathetic to the plight of their hired enforcer Messer Amerigo. One answered him: we are knocking our heads on walls here, while another chimed in that there were more important matters of state to attend to. A third found a proverb to offer, "Che vuole i malanno, si se l'abbia" (May whoever wishes pursue such difficulties), and a fourth noted that even the mighty ancient Romans had not prevailed against their women when it came to dress and consumption.[22] Sacchetti's empathy with Florentine women who had bested foreign law-enforcers stopped just short of collusion; however the Signoria's own efforts first to palm off enforcement on a foreign appointee, then take him to task, only to respond to his indignant reaction with a lax, "well, do your best and leave the rest," is more significant. Limiting consumption was a far different matter in practice from the exercise of debating and passing sumptuary laws.[23] Ambivalence in high places to enforcing these elaborate laws suggests that the wise Florentines who had drawn them up knew all along that such law was a somewhat futile attempt at curbing behavior, nor would it be particularly advantageous to them if Florentine women strictly complied.

The man who resoundingly supported the passage of sumptuary laws was very likely also the man who paid the *gabelle* so his wife or daughter could wear forbidden fashions, often the articles acquired as wedding gifts. He was often complicit in breaking the law and may have shown gallantry assisting a stylish Florentine matron to avoid the fashion police, as Rainey has noted.[24] It would not be lost on lawmakers that *gabelle* were an effective luxury tax imposed on an elite notorious for avoiding taxation. Imposed fines served as a useful soak-the-rich taxing scheme. Debate about sumptuary laws served as a means for confronting a new economic reality: fashion had become culturally consequential and was beginning to affect consumer behavior and demand.

Lawmakers did not necessarily expect strict compliance with the laws, as Sacchetti's story attests. Designers often favored exemptions; they even tolerated infractions of the law. What they seem to have been after was a seemly hierarchy of consumption rather than the swift-changing pageant of new fashions that had begun to sweep them along. What disturbed them most was that fashions obliterated distinctions. Lawmakers, the grave, wealthy, and wise leaders of cities, understood that clothes mattered. They themselves followed fashions and justified fine

---

[22] This refers to Roman women's revolt against the Oppian Law in 195 B. C. E., related in Livy, *Historia* ,trans. Evan T. Sage, Loeb Classical Library (London: W. Heinemann, 1935), 9:412–5 (34.1).

[23] " . . . fu detto per tuto l'officio a messer Amerigo, che guardasse di far quello che ben fosse e l'avanzo si stesse:" Sacchetti, *Trecentonovelle*, *Novella* 137, 305.

[24] Rainey, "Sumptuary Legislation in Renaissance Florence," 309; the young gallant in the case discussed was Pepino di Antonio Albizzi.

garb as dressing for success. If one sold luxuries to foreign princes, the least one could do was demonstrate how those luxuries like great medallions, silver buttons, gilded belts with ornamental daggers, fine borders, and silver spurs were worn with dash. Clothes marked a new social ascendancy for wealthy men in towns; fine clothes marked great merchants as social peers to nobly born men who claimed old titles and landed wealth. But a gorgeous new fashion in silver-enameled buttons or in silver-gilt belts lost some of its luster when every woman in town sported the same thing, along with a fair sampling of pimply-faced youth and even small children.

Rarely, very rarely, men ran afoul of the *Ufficiale delle donne.* In 1347 three men were arrested for wearing pleats, but the charge was not at all typical.[25] This case seems to have been a citizen's arrest of sorts, with a number of outraged witnesses affixing their names to the court record. Generally speaking, the court ignored what men wore, even if men's clothes, and particularly their accessories, consumed more in the way of precious materials like fine silks, jewels, silver, and gold, than did women's wear. Women's offenses were the concern of the court, augmented by occasional charges brought against youth and children. This is to argue that sumptuary law was effective — not in eliminating ostentation among wealthy women, youth, and children — but for the most part in dampening their ostentation to a seemly display of less luxury than that of their husbands and fathers.

Thus the record of the *Ufficiale delle donne* makes interesting reading. The cost of garments, rich brocades, cloth of gold, ermine, ponderous jewelry, and accessories of silver or silver gilt were of interest to the officers, as might be expected. But the court record appears to be as concerned about the messages embroidered on women's clothes as on the opulence of garments, at least from the 1320s when figural displays of all sorts were first forbidden by sumptuary law in Florence.[26]

This brings me to Laurence Gérard-Marchant's remarkable list of forbidden figural motifs on clothes for which women were required to appear in the Florentine court: stars, crescents, *styli,* chains, bands, crowns, crests, strings, coins, rings, dots, points, checks, ribbons, knots, Solomon's knots, clouds, shields, blades, arrows, pavilions, embrasures, battlements, castles, rocks, and mountains. There were flowers, thistles, roses, leaves, clovers, acorns, and palms. Embroidered bestiaries were recorded: birds, cocks, geese, dogs, foxes, lions, peacocks, stags, butterflies, and fantastical sirens, dragons, griffons, and exotic creatures like leopards. Hare, boar, bear, and swallows, as well as *homunculi,* appeared in the

---

[25] Florentine State Archives, *Esecutore degli ordinimenti dei Giustitie* 75, fols. 9r–13r, 30 May, 1346. See *Esecutore* 92, fol. 5r for July 17, 1347. The inquisition is quoted in Rainey, "Sumptuary Legislation in Renaissance Florence," 393, note 103.

[26] Rainey, "Sumptuary Legislation in Renaissance Florence," 86

records.[27] I do not do Gérard-Marchant's extensive list justice, since I mention less than half his examples in the interest of brevity. It makes one wonder: what woman walks the street with a *homunculus* on the bodice of a dress, or the sleeve of a cloak, and what does she intend by it? The *homunculus* was a phantasm that gave bodily manifestation to the Aristotelian belief in male seed as a perfect tiny creature. Life begins with the *homunculus* in the Aristotelian scheme, but such a *homunculus* is a component of an elaborate scholastic argument about procreation; he seems a strange embellishment for fourteenth-century women's clothes.[28]

With the Holy Family and the Virgin as exempla, the fourteenth-century Tuscan *Meditations on the Life of Christ* took leisured women to task for spending their time on such fancy needlework as decorating their clothes with strange and exotic symbols:

> If it was necessary for [the Virgin] to earn food by the work of her hands, what shall we say about clothes, . . . They had no extra or superfluous or frivolous things. (These are against poverty and even if she could have them, the lover of poverty would not. Did the Lady, whatever she worked on, make for love some fancywork: No!) These are done by people who do not mind losing time. But she was so poor that she could not and would not spend time in a vain occupation nor would she have done such work. This is a very dangerous vice, especially for such as you.[29]

But once married, women spent leisure time embroidering their wardrobes. The wardrobe of fine dresses and ornaments acquired at marriage (the number of dresses, two to four, was sometimes set in sumptuary law) should last a woman a lifetime, just as her dowry was to see her into widowhood and old age. Clothes with messages sewn on them freshened up that wardrobe of good clothes, and conveyed meanings that could be interpreted by the crowd in the streets. Today those affective meanings are lost to us because of women's silence. We must imagine the intention behind displaying the motifs, figural elements, designs, and signifiers that decorated their clothes. What is certain is that clothes spoke

---

[27] Laurence Gérard-Marchant, "Compter et nommer l'étoffe à Florence au trecento (1343)," *Médiévales* 29 (1995): 99–102.

[28] Charles Dempsey asserts that putti, the infant sprites that became popular in Renaissance art, were virtually unknown before they appeared on the tomb of Ilaria del Carretto, d. 1406. The tomb was designed by Jacopo della Quercia. *Homunculi* might be early renditions of putti, but there is no evidence in the literature to support this contention. See Charles Dempsey, *Inventing the Renaissance Putto* (Chapel Hill: University of North Carolina Press, 2001), 10–11.

[29] *Meditations on the Life of Christ,* trans. Isa Ragusa, ed. eadem and Rosalie B. Green (Princeton: Princeton University Press, 1961), 72–73.

loudly in women's silence. Curbing spending was the generally stated purpose for sumptuary restraints. Figural motifs were cheap by comparison to rich displays of jewels or silver or gold. Figural motifs required skill with a needle, colored threads, and leisure time for pulling out old designs of say, Solomon's knots, and replacing them with, say, peacocks and butterflies. An entire world for creating fashion and new eye-catching fashions opened up for women with needles and time on their hands; it was not cost-free fashion, but it was relatively cheap in comparison to the rich objects that men wore or that had been given in lesser quantity to women when they were brides.

By the 1380s when Sacchetti wrote, enforcers were as concerned with rooting out infringements involving explicit visual messages on clothes as they were with searching out rich materials in Florentine women's wardrobes. It is even possible that figural motifs were more distressing to authorities than wearing prohibited gear like jeweled headdresses, rows of silver-gilt buttons that reached beyond the elbow to the wrist, wide sleeves lined with fur or velvet, brooches, or any of the other expensive accessories that the laws forbade.[30] Yet women persisted in adding figural designs to their clothes.

Context is important here. Well-to-do young matrons appear to have been the persons most frequently taken to court, and while some belonged to leading families, some came from more modest backgrounds. None of these women were likely to purchase their own finery. Dowries and wedding paraphernalia were awarded women when they married — fine *cassoni* bear witness to the opulence of some of these gifts. Husbands gave their brides counter-gifts of clothes and jewels, and paid the *gabelle* so this finery might be worn in the streets. Such a wardrobe was to last a woman a lifetime, and, as scholars have argued, it was not entirely a bride's own but could be reclaimed by her husband. On occasion husbands' gifts were withdrawn and bestowed on a new bride entering the family.[31] Women may have owned, but they did not control, their dowries.

Some possible motives for personalizing a wardrobe with figural designs become clear in the face of the restraints on women's ownership. If a bride's fine clothes were to last a lifetime, fashion would be difficult to achieve. Embroidering and re-embroidering clothes with new figural elements introduced the possibility of being fashionable, of swift-paced change, and something new to flaunt in the streets. If geometrical shapes and astronomical signs appeared one month, foxes,

[30] Simona Slanika, "Male Markings: Uniforms and Gender in the Parisian Civil War," *The Medieval History Journal* 2 (1000): 209–59 argues that livery, especially sewn-on emblems became important over the course of the fourteenth century in northern realms.

[31] Christiane Klapisch-Zuber, "The Griselda Complex" in eadem *Women, Family and Ritual in Renaissance Italy*, trans. Lydia Cochrane (Chicago: University of Chicago Press, 1985), 213–46.

thistles, and roses might appear the next. The pace of fashion replacing fashion picked up. Women attracted attention as the public inspected their clothes for new symbols. Women became the focus of all eyes; thus they affected taste in towns. Women's clothes might be opulent, and this, of course, also riveted eyes, but what they did with those clothes represented the genuinely new and fashionable. Dogs, lions, and geese could just as well appear on the clothes of less well-to-do people in imitation of affluent women, and then decorum in the streets would be further disturbed.[32]

Venetian laws expressed less concern with figures than did Florentine laws, but there was a comparable interest in two labor-intensive fashions adopted by Venetian women: *frexatura perlarum* and *drezadori* or *drezatores perlarum*. The former were embroidered borders, which the Venetian sumptuary code of 1299 permitted to the bride only. The latter were strings of pearls (*margueritas,* sometimes imitation glass beads produced at Murano). These ornaments as well as *cavezatura,* a row of gold buttons, received much attention from the august chambers of government.[33] Prohibitions on them appear again in the sumptuary code of 1334; when that code was repealed at the end of the decade, both worked borders and beaded headdresses were exempted, that is, allowed to continue in force. Rows of buttons, embroidered (and possibly beaded) borders on gowns and cloaks, and beaded head ornaments could be redesigned by their possessors, or resewn as added adornment to fine garments that were originally wedding gifts. As in Florence, all that a Venetian woman needed was a supply of beads, ribbons, and silver-gilt buttons snipped off other garments, a needle, and the skill to use it, and the leisure time to adorn the fine dresses given originally as wedding gifts to create a new fashion.

So increasingly in big towns, what captured the attention of lawmakers was not just opulent and costly finery but what could be done to it. Prohibited styles were often home-designed fashion. Headdresses, a chronic concern of lawmakers, were constructed at home. Parti-colored garments (for example, green on the left

---

[32] See Diane Owen Hughes, "Sumptuary Laws and Social Relationships" in *Disputes and Settlements,* ed. John Bossy (Cambridge: Cambridge University Press, 1984), 69–100.

[33] Newett, "Sumptuary Laws of Venice," 262–4. For the text of the 1299 law see Cesare Foucard, ed., *Lo Statua inedito delle nozze veneziane nell'1299* (Venice: Tipografia del Commercio, 1858). For the law of 1344 see Roberto Cessi and Mario Brunetti, *Deliberationes del Consiglio dei Rogati (Senato), serie "mixtorum,"* Libri XV–XVI (Venice: A Spese della deputazione, 1960–2) vol. 2, 314, 323–4. For the repeal of this law and discussion see Venetian State Archives, Maggior Consiglio Deliberationes, Spiritus (copia), fols. 213v–214 (287v–288). To compare fashion in Bologna see Maria Giuseppina Muzzarelli, *Gli Inganni delle apparenze* (Turin: Trapni, 1996) and *Guardaroba medievale* (Bologna: Il Mulino, 1999).

side, red on the right) could be cut and sewn at home from old garments on hand. Sleeves could be re-cut or lined with a rich fabric. Gilt buttons could be arranged in a new decorative row.

This dimension of sumptuary display appears to be particular, if not unique, to the commercial centers of northern Italy. In landed realms, office, title, and station determined the right to display sewn-on emblems and badges in much the same way that ermine, gold, and jewels were regulated.[34] In royal or ducal courts and capitals, hierarchy was enforced through sumptuary law, and here the imaginative use of a repertoire of figural displays, borders, and the like was less likely to occur. In towns swiftly evolving fashion was fed by the swift adoption of new figural displays, and their equally swift discarding for the adoption of another.

Some Italian towns seem to have managed quite well without sumptuary laws at all. Ragusa, the present Dubrovnik, provides a case in point. In 1235 the Ragusan Great Council passed a law regulating dowries and display at weddings, a very early example of sumptuary legislation, but apparently one not repeated.[35] A plausible reason for this turnabout in policy was that Balkan silver flooded the town with newly mined ore and a lively goldsmithing trade grew up over the late thirteenth and fourteenth centuries. Ragusa exported fabricated silver to the Italian mainland and supplied the great Italian commercial markets like Venice with bangles, jewels, silver utensils, rings, crowns, and great gilded silver belts. Since the Venetian fleet put in at Ragusa, it was good advertising when townspeople paraded around in locally crafted silver accessories. So it comes as no surprise that by the 1280s a 750-*hyperpera* dowry for a noble daughter was augmented by further gifts in silver, gold, and jewels.[36] Generally the cash award of dowry was accompanied by fifty to 100 *exagia* of gold that a bride controlled herself and could turn into finery. Much later, in 1423, limits were reinstated with a new statute that limited awards of dowry in Ragusa to 1,600 *hyperpera* and set the worth of gold or silver jewelry and other finery that accompanied the cash gift to a value of 700 *hyperpera*.[37] At almost half the worth of the dowry, this was a generous allowance for a bride's personal display, and she owned it outright and might do with it as she pleased.

---

[34] Slanika, "Male Markings" 209–59 provides examples of this.

[35] V. Bogisic and C. Jirecek, ed. *Liber statutorum civitati Ragusii,* Monumenta Historico-juridica Slavorum Meridionalium, 10 (Zagreb: JAZU, 1904), xiv: Ordo de dotibus, 1235.

[36] Gregor Cremosnik, ed., *Spisi dubrovacke kancelarije,* Bk. 1*: Zapisi notara Thomazina de Savere 1278–1282,* Monumenta Historica Ragusina (Zagreb: JAZU, 1951), doc. 919. In the early fourteenth century the *hyperperon* as a money of account was equal to one-half a Venetian ducat. By the fifteenth century that ratio had reached 3 to 1.

[37] Dubrovnik State Archives. *Liber Viridis*, C. 180, fol. 140v. See reconfirmations, C. 371, fol. 234–235; C. 478, fol.296v.

So silver and gold were quite freely given and quite freely worn in Ragusa. With an endogamous elite in power, fear of display disturbing the social order appears to have been held to a minimum.[38] More importantly, perhaps, as Ragusa grew more prosperous over the fourteenth century, women grew richer along with men, at least in part because married women continued to control their personal property; they were not subject to discriminatory sumptuary laws like those in force in northern Italian city-states. No law specified women might wear silver buttons to the elbow, whereas men of their family might wear a full row of buttons on a sleeve reaching down to the wrist.[39] There were no laws aimed at controlling consumption by gender, nor did laws forbid specific fashions and figural displays to women. One might even conjecture that the entire fourteenth-century community conspired to show off local goldsmiths' artistry in the pursuit of increased exports of silver and gilded-silver wares to Italy, which, of course, enriched the community further.

In northern Italy urban laws and current arguments about woman's place in the scheme of things acted in concert in sidelining wealthy women from the marketplace and from formal participation as consumers because their fine clothes were purchased for them at marriage, and were designed to last a lifetime. In households that supported luxury purchases, deprivation was merely relative; it did not by any means imply doing without. Nonetheless, a sidelined position as consumer, when consumption had become a culturally consequential matter, created resentment, expressed at times through devising and wearing extreme fashions crafted at home. This is not to be wondered at, given the status of the households that women of fashion represented; wealthy women with social credentials did not enjoy being left out. As consumers, well-to-do women were marginalized even if their fashions made at home riveted all eyes in public.[40]

So women inhabited a problematic niche in the spectrum of urban consumers in northern Italy, and this in turn helped to stimulate successive rounds of experimentation in dress — a new cut of sleeve, a new headdress, or border, or trim,

---

[38] See Susan Mosher Stuard, *A State of Deference: Ragusa/Dubrovnik in the Medieval Centuries* (Philadelphia: Univeristy of Pennsylvania Press, 1992), 59–114.

[39] Rainey, "Sumptuary Legislation in Renaissance Florence," 218. The wife of a knight, doctor or physician was allowed to wear silver buttons on her sleeves which extended beyond the elbow but only if the total weight of those buttons did not exceed ten ounces. Men wore rows of silver buttons the full extent of the sleeve. See Master of the Urbino Coronation, *The Annunciation to Zacharias,* 1350–1400, Memorial Art Gallery, Rochester, New York. Buttons also appear as closures on cloaks worn by the three male witnesses and in a line to the wrist.

[40] Serving maids in Florence were restrained from wearing specific fashions, and heavy penalties were imposed. It is likely that maids wearing cast-offs from their mistresses, which were embellished by needlework, caused further confusion in the streets.

new embroidery of fantastical creatures on a bodice, new mesh or "tatting" over a garment. Affluent, well-provisioned households supported homemade innovations. Leisure time spent in the company of other women of the household and with women servants provided opportunity to invent. Incentive derived from the marginal condition itself. Social mores and sumptuary laws aimed to keep women retiring and modestly dressed, but with little success. All that the women of Florence or Venice seemed to need to add their own signatures to fashion were leisure time, materials at hand, and some opportunity to appear in public.

In response, the general pace of fashion replacing fashion picked up. Without spending significant sums in the marketplace, women became innovators worthy of attention. In Florence their inventive figural motifs were curbed in sumptuary legislation from the 1320s; in Venice homemade labor-intensive borders of glass beads earned censure from 1299. "Without [fashion] nothing would have changed so fast," Fernand Braudel asserted a half-century ago.[41] He pointed out the long-term consequences of a quickened pace for economic life brought on by the emergence of fashion in the fourteenth century, but he did not explain how acceleration, his key to capitalist development, was expressed in a society that had been quite content with traditional garb and a slow pace of change in apparel in former times. While well-supplied markets were necessary, without the non-market innovations that brides and married women introduced from the sidelines, it would be hard to imagine the pace of change picking up as briskly as it did. It appears that when visual signals gained consequence, some women insisted on their right to dress conspicuously, that is, to find a way to be fashionable, impress others, and so influence taste. Their wedding gifts might be converted to cash and their luxury apparel curbed by law, but they could create new fashions at home.

Braudel tended to view this consequential fourteenth-century turn to fashion as some new configuration of cultural, social, and economic behaviors, and he never assumed that markets alone created the accelerated pace of fashion replacing fashion that characterized the age. Clearly it lay outside the scope of his investigations, but it is no less the case, for that reason, that the pace of change accelerated at least in part owing to the nimble fingers of brides refashioning their wardrobes to remain fashionable for decades to come. The social pastime of dreaming up fashions, executing them, and wearing them in public bolstered urban people's already strong inclination to pay attention to visual signals. Women became innovators because, like the men of their households, they were firmly convinced that appearances were serious considerations, and that people had become what they appeared to be; so women improvised, and the public rewarded their efforts by

[41] Fernand Braudel, *The Structures of Everyday Life*, trans. Siân Reynolds (New York: Harper and Row, 1981), 324.

paying attention. Markets caught up with what fashionable women introduced by supplying the sets of buttons, glass beads, mother of pearl, gold and silver-shot ribbons or threads, and the endless list of other accessories that fed fashion. In towns the circle closed: women were sidelined by law and custom. They joined the fashion parade by inventing eye-catching new fashions at home. These in turn influenced the preferences of those who were customers in the marketplace, and retailers adapted their stock of goods to suit new consumer preferences.

Aesthetics figure into fashion as well. Unlike fifteenth-century consumption, which Goldthwaite characterizes as a transformation away from gilt and garish effects toward refined taste in books, art, and antiquities, the fourteenth-century aesthetic was, well, not very refined at all.[42] The more gilt, like the rather remarkable ninety-one inches of the gilded silver and enameled Cleveland belt, the more pleased the consumer appeared to be.[43] If excess length was lacking, width was emphasized, as with Guariento de Arpo's massed angel army, each fitted out in military uniform except for broad gilded belts with designs unique to each figure (*Heavenly Hierarchies*, Padua, Museo civico, c.1350). In towns fourteenth-century folk shimmered and twinkled, perhaps they even dazzled in direct sunlight, such was the glint of carbuncle-sized jewels and bright metal on their bodies. They were probably audible as well, tinkling and jingling as they walked along; they may even have clanked and jangled, such was the weight of their heavy metal accessories.

The lawmakers who devised sumptuary laws were urbane gentlemen. Well-educated, sardonic, and self-conscious about their motives, they were nobody's fools, even if today it appears to be extremely foolhardy to try to write laws about buttons to the elbow, wide sleeves, headdresses, borders, and geometrical figures on a garment. These men were more likely bemused by fashion than seriously distressed by its emergence as a new component of consumer demand. The challenge was to control fashion so that it served the economic and social interests of the persons who bore responsibility for encouraging trade in goods: that is, they themselves, the wise, grave leaders of Italy's great city-states. But fashion escaped controls; new fashions were loosed on city streets. As a result, some fashions derived from people who had motives other than theirs, who merely wished to attract attention and create sensation. Brides and newly married women figured importantly among those who wished to join, and stay, in the fashion parade. Fashion was process, and once unleashed, likely to live a life of its own.

---

[42] Goldthwaite, *Wealth and the Demand for Art in Italy, 1300–1600*. See also Michael Baxandall, *Painting and Experience in Fifteenth Century Italy: A Primer in the Social History of Pictorial Style* (Oxford: Clarendon Press, 1972).

[43] William Milliken, "Early Enamels in the Cleveland Museum of Art," *Connoisseur* 76 (October 1926): 67–72.

Tecla Servent and Her Two Husbands

Ronald E. Surtz

Is name destiny? Perhaps it was for Tecla Servent, who lived in eastern Spain, principally in Tarragona and Valencia, in the second half of the fifteenth century. The Cathedral of Tarragona, the town where Tecla Servent was born, was placed under the advocacy of Saint Thecla, a first-century female missionary and follower of Saint Paul. Saint Thecla was betrothed to a man named Thamyris, but inspired by Paul's teaching in praise of virginity, she refused to marry her fiancé. Lest other women follow her transgressive example, the governor of Iconium condemned Thecla to be burned, but the fire did not touch her. Saint Thecla then followed Paul to Antioch, where a certain Alexander fell in love with her, but she rejected him and made him a laughing-stock. For that, the governor condemned her to the wild beasts, but she baptized herself and the animals did not touch her. Saint Thecla continued to follow Paul, who told her to teach the word of God, which she did until her death.[1] It is difficult to imagine that any citizen of Tarragona would be unfamiliar with the life of Saint Thecla, and Tecla Servent must have grown up with the story of her city's holy patroness engraved in her memory.[2] Like her namesake, Tecla Servent endeavored to remain a virgin, rejected her husband to follow Christ, suffered persecution, and spread the word of God.

Tecla was born around 1455, the daughter of the farmer Antoni Jordà. From infancy she had visions of Christ, the Blessed Virgin, the archangel Michael, and several saints. At the age of fourteen she was married — against her will — to Guillem Servent, who for over twenty years beat her, owing to his hostility to her religious practices. Tecla sought refuge in the world of her visions, where

---

[1] One source even refers to Thecla as an "apostle." On the *Acts of Paul and Thecla*, see J. K. Elliott, *The Apocryphal New Testament* (Oxford: Clarendon Press, 1993), 374. For modern commentaries on St. Thecla's story, see Kerstin Aspegren, *The Male Woman: A Feminine Ideal in the Early Church,* ed. René Kieffer (Uppsala: Acta Universitatis Upsaliensis, 1990), 99–114; and J. L. Welch, "Cross-dressing and Cross-purposes: Gender Possibilities in the *Acts of Thecla*," in *Gender Reversals and Gender Cultures: Anthropological and Historical Perspectives,* ed. Sabrina Petra Ramet (London and New York: Routledge, 1996), 66–78.

[2] The predella of the principal altarpiece in the Cathedral of Tarragona depicts episodes from the life of Saint Thecla, emphasizing the attempts to martyr her. The altarpiece, sculpted by Pere Joan (1394/7–1458), was begun in 1429 and finished about ten years before Tecla's birth. See Emilia Altarriba and Josep Baluja, *La catedral de Tarragona* (Tarragona: Consell Comarcal del Tarragonès, [1990?]), 38–39.

she enjoyed a relationship with a more tolerant and understanding lover, namely Christ.[3]

At some point, perhaps in 1492,[4] Tecla abandoned her husband and moved to Valencia, where her revelations continued and resulted in her denunciation to the Inquisition, her arrest, and her trial, which began in 1495, when she was forty years old. Tecla's trial ended on 30 June 1496, with the sentence that she be reconciled with the Church in an *auto de fe*, that she not speak further of her visions to anyone, and that she return to Tarragona and be placed under house arrest in the care of her husband (fol. [55r]).

Tecla's special relation with Christ began in her earliest childhood with events that she herself would have forgotten, were it not for her mother; it was her mother who told her that, to everyone's astonishment, she began to receive visions and to talk about them at the age of one. When she was a year and a half or two years old, her mother would find her kneeling, and when asked what she was doing,

[3] The study of medieval female visionaries is a burgeoning field. Such ground-breaking studies as Caroline Walker Bynum's *Holy Feast and Holy Fast: The Religious Significance of Food to Medieval Women* (Berkeley and Los Angeles: University of California Press, 1987) offer many insights into various manifestations of medieval feminine spirituality. For Italy, see Elizabeth Petroff, *Consolation of the Blessed* (New York: Alta Gaia Society, 1979). For Spain, see R. E. Surtz, *The Guitar of God: Gender, Power, and Authority in the Visionary World of Mother Juana de la Cruz (1481–1534)* (Philadelphia: University of Pennsylvania Press, 1990), and idem, *Writing Women in Late Medieval and Early Modern Spain: The Mothers of Saint Teresa of Avila* (Philadelphia: University of Pennsylvania Press, 1995). Some of the same Castilian visionaries are also discussed Angel Muñoz Fernández, *Beatas y santas neocastellanas: Ambivalencias de la religión y políticas correctoras del poder (siglos XIV–XVI)* (Madrid: Comunidad de Madrid, 1994), and idem, *Acciones e intenciones de mujeres: Vida religiosa de las madrileñas (siglos XV–XVI)* (Madrid: Dirección General de la Mujer, 1995). Mother Juana de la Cruz is also the subject of a book by María Victoria Triviño Monrabal, OSC: *Mujer, predicadora y párroco: La Santa Juana (1481–1534)* (Madrid: Biblioteca de Autores Cristianos, 1999). Tecla Servent differs from the Castilian nuns and *beatas* (holy women) analyzed in the preceding studies because she was a married lay woman. For visions, especially Marian, received by lay people in late medieval and early modern Spain, see William A. Christian, Jr., *Apparitions in Late Medieval and Renaissance Spain* (Princeton: Princeton University Press, 1981).

[4] The widow Orfresina Conilleres, testifying in December 1495, declared that Tecla had stayed in her house when she arrived from Tarragona two and a half years previously. See Archivo Histórico Nacional (Madrid), Inquisición, Valencia, leg. 533 (10), fol. 6r. Future references to Tecla's trial will be indicated by the folio number in parentheses. Bracketed folio numbers refer to my own numbering of the part of the trial that corresponds to Tecla's account of her visions and to her sentence. Unbracketed folio numbers refer to the inquisitorial notary's numbering of the part of the trial that contains the examination of the defendant and the testimony of the witnesses.

Tecla answered that she saw a young child who wanted to play with her (fol. [1r]). The child, of course, was Christ, which means that Tecla's relation with her future spouse began when they were childhood companions and playmates. In another vision she received around the same time, the Virgin Mary appeared with the Child in her arms, and the Child asked Tecla if she wanted to be his. When Tecla answered that she would, the Christ Child responded that she would be his wife and that he would reveal important secrets to her (fol. [1v]). In the light of later events, perhaps this incident can be viewed as a sort of pre-betrothal, as well as a first articulation and divine authorization of Tecla's future role as a prophet.

Around 1469, when Tecla was fourteen years old, Christ appeared to her many times as he was at the age of thirty and demonstrated signs of love, such as those that a fiancé might manifest to his betrothed.[5] Meanwhile, her mother and other relatives were urging her to marry, but Tecla refused, preferring to enjoy the delights, pleasures, and plenitude she experienced in her visions of Christ. So great was that feeling of inner fullness that Tecla would go for days without eating, but her mother kept pressing her to marry, while Tecla kept insisting that she wanted to remain a virgin. Her mother beat her and kept up the pressure, so that Tecla finally relented, and her relatives married her off.[6]

At no point in her depositions does Tecla mention her husband by name. In fact, it is only in the inquisitorial notary's introduction to her testimony that we learn that her husband was called Guillem Servent. Tecla's failure to mention her husband by name may be a form of denial or, as we shall see later, it may be part of a strategy designed to reduce Guillem from a real person to a sort of conventional hagiographic blocking figure.

After her marriage, Tecla had less time for prayer and therefore experienced fewer visions. Nonetheless, her husband was displeased by her prayers and fasting, so displeased, in fact, that he often beat her (fol. [5r]). Before her marriage, demons would come to disturb her during her prayers and even vowed to kill her in order to prevent her from taking more souls away from them, but the archangel Saint Michael defended Tecla from the demons with sword and shield (fols. [3v–4v]).

[5] "li mostrava grandíssims senyals de amor, que esposat a esposada no podria mostrar tan grandíssims senyals de amor" (fols. [2v]–[3r]). Of course, the motif of the mystical marriage to Christ is a prominent feature in the lives of such female saints as Catherine of Alexandria and Catherine of Siena.

[6] Fol. [4v]. Tecla's consent to a forced marriage out of obedience to her parent is a hagiographic cliché. See Dyan Elliott, *Spiritual Marriage: Sexual Abstinence in Medieval Wedlock* (Princeton: Princeton University Press, 1993), 258. Tecla's age at the time (fourteen years) was the lowest legal limit for a girl to marry. See María del Carmen García Herrero, *Las mujeres en Zaragoza en el siglo XV*, 2 vols. (Zaragoza: Ayuntamiento de Zaragoza, 1990), 1:144.

However, now that she was married, the devils that had previously been vexing her ceased their torments. Her deposition is very explicit concerning the timing of this phenomenon: "And when her aforementioned husband beat her, the demons did not annoy her as they did before she got married."[7] Tecla's testimony thus suggests an equivalence between her husband and a demon. Whereas previously it was the devils who tried to keep her from praying and thereby from seeing Christ in her visions, now that antagonistic role is taken over by her demonized husband.

In her prayers Tecla asked the Lord to deliver her from such a cruel spouse so as better to engage in divine contemplation and the service of God, but the Lord refused and specified that Guillem would be cruel to her as long as he lived (fol. [5v]). Since part of Tecla's sentence was the stipulation that she return to Tarragona to live with her husband, it appears that the inquisitors disapproved of Tecla's abandonment of Guillem and deemed it more important for her to live under male authority than to be protected from further spousal abuse. After all, women independent of male control were apt to get into trouble, and this is probably what her judges believed had happened in Tecla's case.[8] Had she been a visionary nun, her supernatural experiences would still have received particular scrutiny due to her feminine gender,[9] but her virginal state and her religious lifestyle would have bolstered the credibility of her visions.[10] Tecla was neither a virgin nor a nun. Indeed, as a lay woman separated from her husband, Tecla had an ambiguous status, for her independent lifestyle did not conform to any of

[7] "Y que, en aquest que lo dit son marit li pegava, los demonis no la vexaven com feyan abans de casar-se" (fol. [5r]).

[8] Although testimonies concerning the need for wives to submit to their husbands are abundant in the Middle Ages, one particularly telling example comes from an inquisitor's manual, the *Repertorium inquisitorum*, printed at Valencia in 1494, that is, just a year before Tecla's trial began. Under the heading *femme*, the French translation reads: "Les femmes doivent être soumises à leurs maris. Telle est la loi. . . . L'homme est le chef (caput) de la femme. . . . Il faut que la femme se plie en tout et toujours à l'arbitre de l'homme" (*Le Dictionnaire des inquisiteurs*, trans. Louis Sala-Molins [Paris: Editions Galilée, 1981], 208).

[9] In his *De examinatione doctrinarum* (1423), Jean Gerson argues that "every teaching of women, especially that expressed in solemn word or writing, is to be held suspect, unless it has been diligently examined, and much more than the teaching of men" (quoted in D. Catherine Brown, *Pastor and Laity in the Theology of Jean Gerson* [Cambridge and London: Cambridge University Press, 1987], 223).

[10] For the relation between the virginal state and prophecy in the Fathers of the Church and in medieval monastic writers, see Peter Brown, *The Body and Society: Men, Women, and Sexual Renunciation in Early Christianity* (New York: Columbia University Press, 1988), 66–69; and John Bugge, *Virginitas: An Essay in the History of a Medieval Ideal* (The Hague: Martinus Nijhoff, 1975), 44–47.

the roles — maiden, wife, or widow — deemed suitable for women in the Middle Ages. Demonizing her husband was perhaps a strategy Tecla used to justify her abandoning him and thereby to excuse her failure to fulfill her proper spousal role.

In a later vision an angel took Tecla to the gate of hell, where she could see the torments of the souls who passed through there. She was so moved by the sufferings of the damned that she prayed God to turn her into the gate of hell so that no more souls could enter that place. We can see a dramatic reversal here, for such Fathers of the Church as Tertullian had labeled Eve and thereby her daughters as the "gate of the devil" — and by extension, the gate of hell — because it was through the female sex that evil had entered the world.[11] Tecla reinterprets the gate image, giving it a positive cast, for, despite her dubious theology, she, a woman, intends to prevent souls from suffering infernal torments.

Meanwhile, the angel who had brought Tecla to hell disappeared, and the demons began to torment her and to mock her saying: "Now we will take vengeance on you for all the insults you do us."[12] When Tecla cried out to Christ, asking him why he had abandoned her, Christ revealed his face to her and told her that he had been there all the time, watching her wage that battle out of her love for him. He then brought her up to heaven, where he ordered the angels to dress her as his wife ought to be clothed. The angels arrayed Tecla like the spouse of a great lord in gold and scarlet brocade. Christ thereupon ordered the angels to bring food and drink for her, and they served her precious stones on golden plates to eat and molten gold and pulverized jewels to drink. When Christ said it was time for her to go, Tecla refused to leave, but Christ insisted that it was not yet time for her to remain there with him. Tecla returned to her corporal senses from that vision that had lasted four hours, from eight o'clock until midnight. So great was the joy she felt as a result of that experience that she did not eat for eight days. Her husband called her a bad woman and said: "You eat night and day [in your visions?] and you are big and fat, and [yet] you refuse to eat with me."[13]

---

[11] The Latin phrase is "diaboli ianua." See Tertullian, *De cultu feminarum libri duo*, ed. Josephus Marra (Torino: Paravia, 1930), 2.

[12] "Ara nos benjarem de tu de tants fastis com nos fas" (fol. [7r]).

[13] "Menjau dia e nit y estau grosa y grasa y devant de mi no voleu menjar" (fol. [8r]). Guillem's complaint that Tecla refused to eat with him recalls the case of Margery Kempe. Part of Margery's bargain with her husband to achieve her desired vow of marital chastity was that she would henceforth eat and drink with him on Fridays, whereas previously she had fasted (see Margery's *Book* I.11). While Guillem probably intended it as an insult when he called his wife fat, Tecla lived at a moment when a certain plumpness was beginning to be considered esthetically pleasing: "The medieval ideal of the graceful, narrow-hipped, and full-breasted aristocratic lady gave way in the sixteenth century to a plumper, wide-hipped, and full-breasted model of feminine beauty that was to remain valid until

The preceding vision of the heavenly kingdom points up the dramatic contrast between the worlds defined by Tecla's two husbands. In her humble and problematic earthly existence, Tecla had no precious stones, never ate off golden plates, and never wore gold and scarlet brocade. In contrast, her celestial lifestyle, as was befitting to Christ's bride, mimicked the lifestyle of the earthly aristocracy. Not only was the use of precious objects a sign of noble status, but clothing likewise served to distinguish social classes in medieval Europe. For example, in 1499 Ferdinand and Isabella attempted to regulate which persons were allowed to wear silk clothing, and the Castilian Cortes of 1506 endeavored to forbid the wearing of brocade and fine scarlet cloth by the lower classes.[14] While it is tempting to view Tecla's visionary experiences in heaven with her divine spouse as a sort of fantasy existence that compensated for the brutality of her human spouse, we must remember that, for Tecla, both her earthly and her celestial experiences must have seemed equally real.

In another vision, after a mass celebrated by Saint Peter with the assistance of Saint John and Saint Paul, Christ came out of the sacristy carrying the cross and two garlands, one made of flowers, the other of thorns. When Christ asked Tecla which of the garlands she preferred, she said she wanted the garland of flowers and immediately had a vision of heaven and its ineffable joys. However, Christ told her that if she chose the garland of flowers, the world will honor her, but she would not enjoy the celestial vision she had just seen. Having learned her

---

the late eighteenth century. . . . In any case a 'healthy' plumpness, like cleanliness, was generally reserved for the wealthy; thinness was considered ugly, unhealthy, and a sign of poverty" (Sara F. Matthews Grieco, "The Body, Appearance, and Sexuality," in *A History of Women, III: Renaissance and Enlightenment Paradoxes,* ed. Natalie Zemon Davis and Arlette Farge [Cambridge and London: Harvard University Press, 1993], 55). Tecla's chubbiness also had implications for her construction as a holy woman. The priest Pere Pinyol reported that he had heard from a certain nun that people had asked Tecla if she fasted and performed other penitential acts, given that she was chubby and had such good color. Tecla answered that no, she did not fast very much because it was unnecessary since the Lord loved her (fol. 21r bis).

[14] Carmen Bernis, *Trajes y modas en la España de los Reyes Católicos, I: Las mujeres* (Madrid: CSIC, 1978), 57–62. But already in 1477, Hernando de Talavera was inveighing against members of the lower classes who donned fine wool and silk clothing: "Porque cada labrador e cada oficial, cada escudero, cada cibdadano y cada cavallero, de pequeño y de grande estado, excede manifiestamente, no de lo natural solamente, mas aun de lo que es permiso e tolerado a cada uno según su estado. Cuán mal parece, solían decir al villano, la manga prieta en el brazo; mas ya no hay pobre labrador ni oficial por maravilla que no viste fino paño y aun seda, que es más" ("De vestir y de calzar," in *Escritores místicos españoles*, ed. Miguel Mir, Nueva Biblioteca de Autores Españoles 16 [Madrid: Bailly-Baillière, 1911], 66).

lesson from her teacher/spouse, Tecla chose the garland of thorns, which caused severe pain when Christ put it on her head. Christ further told her to take up the cross for his love and prophesied that she would be persecuted for his sake. This vision lasted all night, and when Tecla returned to her bodily senses, her husband shouted at her, calling her a bad woman and cursing her with the words: "You will sleep forever and never leave your bed."[15] He then beat her as hard as he could.

It appears that the persecutions that Christ prophesied in the preceding vision are already coming to pass in the form of further abuse by Tecla's husband. However, it turns out that Christ's prophecy is more complex than would appear at first glance. A later vision makes it clear that Christ has other plans for Tecla, for he further prophesied that the Father would permit her to suffer great travails and that "they will put you on trial for your life in this city and they will swear false oaths against you and they will proclaim you from street to street a bad and feckless woman."[16] Furthermore, although Tecla will merely be telling people what the Father wants them to hear, they will accuse her of being a sorceress, a hypocrite, and a woman possessed, who knows people's secret sins and future events through the power of the devil.[17]

Since deciding whether Tecla's visions were divinely inspired or not was one of the principal tasks of the inquisitorial judges,[18] perhaps Tecla included this vision and the concomitant prophecy in her testimony as a rhetorical strategy designed to convince the inquisitors of the legitimacy of her supernatural experiences. By suggesting that Christ had predicted her inquisitorial trial and that this was one of the ways in which his prophecy of future tribulations has come to pass, Tecla not only sought to prove the authenticity of her visions but also cast

[15] "E totstemps jamàs edormiràs e no•t llevaràs del lit" (fol. [10v]).

[16] "Permetrà en tu grans trebals e grans congoxes e•ncara que•t faran procés de mort en aquexa ciutat, e juraran contra tu sagraments falsos molts, y cridaran-te an trompeta de carrer en carrer per mala dona e fallida" (fol. [13r]).

[17] "Parlaràs y diràs ço que lo meu Pare permetrà que tu digues al poble y a la gent. E axí tu diràs encara que tu no vulles, ço que lo meu Pare volrà. E axí, diran-te que és encantadora, que eres ypòcrita y que eres endiablada, y que ab art del diable tu sabes les coses sdevenidores e los peccats de les gents" (fol. 13r]).

[18] Late medieval criteria for the discernment of spirits grew largely out of the debate over the authenticity of the visionary experiences of Joan of Arc and Bridget of Sweden. For the doctrine of the discernment of spirits and the negotiation — with differing degrees of success — of its principles in the contrasting cases of Bridget of Sweden and Margery Kempe, see Rosalynn Voaden, *God's Words, Women's Voices: The Discernment of Spirits in the Writing of Late-Medieval Women Visionaries* (Suffolk and Rochester: York Medieval Press, 1999).

her accusers in the role of persecutors of one of Christ's chosen followers.[19] In a sense she attempted to blackmail the inquisitors into believing in her and in the divine origin of her visions, lest they be numbered among the enemies of Christ and his "spouse." Furthermore, the divine prediction that Tecla would be accused of prophesying through the power of Satan could have called to mind the accusation leveled against Christ himself as recounted in Luke 11:15, namely, that he cast out evil spirits through the power of the devil.[20] Perhaps Tecla felt that association and identification with Christ — the crown of thorns, taking up the cross, persecution, false accusations, and a trial — was a strategy that could not but help her case.

Some days after receiving Christ's prophecies, Tecla fell ill and spent six months in bed with a fever. She herself was convinced that her illness was at least partially due to the tribulations she suffered at the hands of her husband, and when her doctors saw that none of their remedies had any effect, they too blamed Guillem. Guillem's cruelty reached such an extreme that, when Tecla was at death's door and the aunt who was caring for her went to buy the cotton and the candles the priest would need to administer the Last Rites, Guillem gave her a beating. Tecla complained to God: "I am sick and my husband still beats me. I can no longer live. Bear me away from this world."[21] In response, she had a vision of Christ's face, and Christ said: "Follow me." Tecla saw a huge shining mountain in heaven from which music and sweet odors emanated. She did not want to leave the celestial kingdom, but Christ told her that it was not yet time for her to dwell there and that on earth they were about to sew her body up in her shroud and bury her. Tecla came to, saw her friends and relatives mourning her death, and told them that she was beloved in heaven (fols. [13v–14r]). Two days later, she had a vision in which Saints Dominic and Francis appeared to her and told her that it was time for her illness to end. In effect, her fever disappeared and she rapidly recovered (fol. [14r]).

Tecla's testimony emphasizes her husband's opposition to her religious practices and his violent treatment of her. There is no reason to doubt that Guillem's behavior was as she described it, but we must also remember that such husbandly

---

[19] Tecla's inquisitorial trial was not the first time her religious experiences had come under the scrutiny of the ecclesiastical establishment. Her criticism of the Patriarch of Tarragona led to the accusation of witchcraft and her ensuing flight to Barcelona, where she was protected by Prince Enrique, a cousin of Ferdinand the Catholic (fols. 7r, 25r, 43v–44r). Lady Yolant de Santapau testified that it was Prince Enrique's mother, Beatriz de Pimentel y Enríquez, who intervened on Tecla's behalf (fol. 44r). Later, while living in Valencia, Tecla was examined by a group of Hieronymite friars from the Monastery of Sant Jeroni de Cotalba near Gandía; some of the friars are said to have approved of her experiences (21r bis).

[20] "But some of them said: He casteth out devils by Beelzebub, the prince of devils."

[21] "Tinch malaltia y encara lo marit me baté! No puch pus viure! Lleva'm del segle" (fol. [13v]).

opposition can be a hagiographic cliché.[22] Moreover, a certain amount of what we now call spousal abuse was tolerated in the Middle Ages, for a husband was deemed to have the right — within limits — to beat his wife.[23] Perhaps Guillem felt justified in striking Tecla, for, although she never admitted to it, her seemingly endless visions, which left her quite literally "out of it" for long periods of time, must have prevented her from carrying out the wifely duties her husband might have expected her to perform.[24] However, Guillem may have gone beyond the tolerable limits for domestic violence in the Middle Ages, for Johana Castellnou testified that Tecla had told her that he struck her with a sword and a lance. Of course, this episode is yet another parallel between Guillem and the demons, who likewise vowed to kill her. Moreover, the sword her husband used to abuse her contrasted with the sword St. Michael used to defend her in her visions. Johana further testified that, in order to keep Tecla from praying, Guillem seized the crucifix she used for her devotions and either smashed it or trampled it underfoot (fol. 10r). The sacrilegious treatment of a sacred object serves to demonize Guillem once again, associating him with the forces of Satan and thereby justifying Tecla's flight from him.

The fact that Guillem is said to have used his sword and his lance against Tecla suggests that he belonged to the gentry, for in medieval Spain in theory only the nobility had the privilege of bearing such arms.[25] As the daughter of a

---

[22] For the case of Catherine of Genoa, see Donald Weinstein and Rudolph M. Bell, *Saints and Society: The Two Worlds of Western Christendom, 1000–1700* (Chicago: University of Chicago Press, 1982), 95. On the topic of married saints, see Marc Glasser, "Marriage in Medieval Hagiography," *Studies in Medieval and Renaissance History* n.s. 4 (1981): 3–34.

[23] Shulamith Shahar, *The Fourth Estate: A History of Women in the Middle Ages*, trans. Chaya Galai (London and New York: Methuen, 1983), 90. See also Frances and Joseph Gies, *Women in the Middle Ages* (New York: Harper & Row, 1978), 46–48.

[24] The husband of the late fourteenth-century German mystic Dorothea of Montau "clearly perceived his wife's mystical raptures as a way of escaping household duties. Dorothea would often forget certain essential chores, would confuse other ones — as, for example, going to church when she had intended to go to the market — and, not surprisingly, would consistently make mistakes marketing." Her husband "complained freely about his wife's insubordination and seems to have found a ready audience among his fellow husbands" (Elliott, *Spiritual Marriage*, 259–60).

[25] However, non-nobles could petition the king for the privilege of carrying a sword. The historian Lluís Cifuentes has cited to me several cases of doctors who requested such permission in order to protect themselves during nighttime visits to the sick. In late fifteenth-century Valencia the sword seems to have lost its value as a symbol of nobility and undergone a process of "democratization" as a wide spectrum of non-noble citizens began to possess it, ostensibly for protection. See Pablo Pérez García, *La comparsa de los malhechores: Valencia, 1479–1518* (València: Diputació de València, 1990), 292–93. However, if Johana Castellnou's testimony is accurate and Guillem Servent did indeed have a lance, then he possessed one of the typical accoutrements of the knightly class.

farmer, Tecla may have "married up," and the difference in social class between husband and wife could have contributed to the tensions in their marriage. Perhaps Guillem felt even more justified in abusing a wife who came from a lineage more humble than his own.[26]

Tecla knew only an abusive marital relationship. It is therefore not surprising that, after her marriage to Guillem, her relationship with her divine spouse likewise turns, in a sense, abusive. Christ could be accused of cruelty toward Tecla, for he is constantly showing her the delights of heaven, only to deny her those joys by insisting that must return to the earth. Obviously, the persecutions Christ promises to his bride are to be understood in a Christian context of earthly suffering that will earn her heavenly bliss. Nonetheless, such parallels between Tecla's two husbands suggest that she could not conceive of a non-abusive relationship. However, if Guillem's brutality can be considered part of the persecutions that Christ had in store for Tecla, that abuse in turn is dignified to the extent that it appears to form part of Christ's divine plan for his spouse, namely, to spend eternity together in his heavenly kingdom.

According to Tecla's own testimony, her marriage to Guillem Servent was arranged by her relatives against her wishes. It is therefore unlikely that she experienced any of the niceties of courtship pertinent to her estate, let alone those customs pertaining to her social betters. Her relationship with Christ was quite a different matter, however. Several witnesses testified that during Shrovetide of around 1483, she arrived all happy at the house of a lawyer in Tarragona, where she grasped another woman, Na Angelina, by the hands and asked her to dance with her. When Angelina refused, Tecla began to dance alone and said that she had just played at *segónades* and at *taronjades* with Christ (fols. 3v, 11r, and 13r).

---

[26] Be that as it may, the Servent household does not appear to have been particularly well off. Although Guillen's abuse was undoubtedly a significant factor in Tecla's decision to leave Tarragona, she told the widow Orfresina Conilleres that the immediate reason for her departure was her inability to obtain a suitable dowry for the marriage of one of her daughters. Unable to provide the promised sum of thirty pounds, Tecla left for Valencia because she felt that it would be less embarrassing to seek to obtain the money there (fol. 7v). While it is not clear why Guillem was not involved in the financial arrangements for the daughter's marriage, it is nonetheless curious to recall that Tecla's mother appears to have played the dominant role in arranging Tecla's own marriage. Thirty pounds was a considerable amount of cash for a family that did not have it, but nonetheless that sum represented a relatively modest dowry. In the cases of twenty previously unmarried women from the Valencian town of Catarroja in the period 1476–1516, the average dowry was forty-three pounds. See Salvador Vercher i Lletí, *Casa, família i comunitat veïnal a l'Horta de València: Catarroja durant el regnat de Ferran el Catòlic (1476–1516)* ([Catarroja]: Ajuntament de Catarroja, 1992), 58. However, Vercher i Lletí also discusses cases in which the family was forced to go into debt in order to provide the agreed-upon dowry (56–57).

Both *segonades* and *taronjades* were pastimes associated with Carnival revelry: *segonades* was a game that consisted of throwing handfuls of bran at passers-by, while *taronjades* consisted of throwing oranges at them. However, the throwing of oranges also had erotic overtones, for citrus fruits were believed to be aphrodisiacs in the Middle Ages[27] and couples threw oranges at one another as an overture to love,[28] and not just during Carnival. The custom was codified in the popular songs of Golden Age Spain, such as the following sixteenth-century text:

> Arrojóme las naranjitas
> con las ramas de blanco azahar;
> arrojómelas y arrojéselas
> y volviómelas a arrojar.[29]

Now Guillem Servent probably did throw things at Tecla, but it is unlikely that the couple ever joined in a game of mutual orange-throwing. However, in the idealized world of her visions, Tecla and her divine husband engaged in an erotic game she was unable to experience on earth with her mortal husband.

Tecla and Guillem Servent must have had sexual relations, for four children — a son Baptista (fol. 30v) and at least three unnamed daughters (fol. 6v), one of whom died young (fol. 44v) — make a shadowy appearance in the depositions of the witnesses who testified in her trial.[30] We do not know whether Tecla and Guillem enjoyed an intimate relationship, for Tecla, perhaps for strategic reasons,

---

[27] For the association between fertility, marriage, and orange blossoms, see Roy Vickery, *A Dictionary of Plant-Lore* (Oxford and New York: Oxford University Press, 1995), 269. In a Spanish song printed in 1538, an unloved maiden washes her face with sorrow and grief, while married women wash their faces with lemon water: "Lávanse las casadas con agua de limones; / lávome yo, cuytada, / con penas y dolores" (José María Alín, *El cancionero español de tipo tradicional* [Madrid: Taurus, 1968], 473). Oranges were also used in spells associated with love magic. The repertory of the witch Catalina Aznar, who was tried by the Inquisition in 1511, contained a spell involving an orange: ". . . debiendo cogerse una naranja e hincarla un clavo por la corona e introduciendo por el agujero sal y aceite, se recitaba: *Venir aquí Berçebu y Satanas, Barrabas y todos los diablos del infierno y traer a Fulano y ravia y congoxa le daredes por mi amor y aqui me lo traygades que se queme su coraçon por mi amor como esta torincha se quema*, arrojando seguidamente a la naranja al fuego" (Juan Blázquez Miguel, *Eros y tanatos: brujería, hechicería y superstición en España* [Toledo: Arcano, 1989], 253).

[28] *The Spanish Traditional Lyric*, ed. J. G. Cummins (Oxford and New York: Pergamon Press, 1977), 4.

[29] Alín, *El cancionero español de tipo tradicional*, 591.

[30] In contrast to Margery Kempe (see, for example, her *Book* I.22), at no point does Tecla express anguish over the fact that, as a married woman with children, she has not been able to preserve her virginity for Christ's sake.

perhaps because there was little or no intimacy in their marriage, concentrates on Guillem's abuses in her testimony. However, Tecla did experience moments of what we would now call intimacy with Christ, for the priest Pere Puyol testified that Tecla claimed that Christ would place his head in her lap and that she would pick the lice out of his hair. Needless to say, Christ did not have lice as such; rather, what she picked out of his hair were pearls and precious stones (fol. 21r bis). What matters in this vision, however, is the special bond connoted by this act, for delousing was performed only by members of the immediate family or by lovers on one another.[31]

Pere Puyol offered no personal opinion regarding the delousing episode, but other witnesses expressed their shock about the game of orange-throwing. Na Angelina testified that she had told Tecla that she should not say such things.[32] The priest Miguel Tomàs reported that Na Angelina had informed him that she had told Tecla to be silent and asked her if she was not ashamed to speak of Christ in that way.[33] Tecla may have believed that such incidents were potentially harmful to her case, and therefore she omitted both the delousing vision and the oranges vision from her own testimony. We know about them only through the depositions of the other witnesses with whom Tecla had shared her visions, and their testimony — as well as their disapproval — may have fueled the inquisitors' negative reaction to Tecla's supernatural experiences in general.

---

[31] For example, in an early fourteenth-century romance of chivalry, the protagonist falls asleep with his head in his wife's lap while she delouses him: "E después que ovieron comido, acostóse el cavallero un poco en el regaço de su muger, e ella espulgándole, adormióse" (*Libro del caballero Zifar*, ed. Joaquín González Muela [Madrid: Castalia, 1982], 114). On a more somber note, the treacherous beguine in *Exemplo XLII* of *El conde Lucanor* convinces a woman that her husband will lose his anger towards her by means of a remedy made from a few hairs cut from his beard. In order to obtain the needed hairs, the wife chooses the moment when she is delousing him: "E luego que su muger lo vio, reçibiólo meior que los otros días de ante, et díxol que sienpre andava travaiando et que non quería folgar nin descansar, mas que se echasse allí cerca della et que pusiesse la cabeça en su regaço, et ella quel espulgaría" (Don Juan Manuel, *El conde Lucanor*, ed. José Manual Blecua [Madrid: Castalia, 1969], 210). In his study of fourteenth-century inquisitorial records from Montaillou, Le Roy Ladurie makes the following observations: "Note that delousing was always carried out by a woman, though not necessarily someone of low degree. . . . Delousing appears to imply relations of kinship or alliance, even if it was illegitimate: the mistress delouses the lover, as well as the lover's mother; the future mother-in-law delouses her prospective son-in-law; the daughter delouses the mother" (Emmanuel Le Roy Ladurie, *Montaillou: The Promised Land of Error*, trans. Barbara Bray [New York: Vintage, 1978], 141–42).

[32] "E yo, hoynt aquelles paraules, li diguí que no digués tals paraules ni•l menejàs axí, que no era ben dit" (fol. 11r).

[33] "Y que la dita N'Angelina le avia dit: 'Callau, Na Tecla! No haveu vergonya de parlar axí de l'amat Jesús?'" (fol. 3v).

Tecla's unofficial separation from Guillem placed her in an indeterminate state that failed to conform nearly to one of the traditional categories for medieval women, namely, the roles of maiden, wife, widow, or nun. Technically, she could have tried to pass herself off as a "widow" in Valencia, but since her former acquaintances from Tarragona were also living there, that was not an option. Tecla did not hesitate to share her tales of Guillem's abuse with her interlocutors, but that alone was not necessarily sufficient grounds to justify leaving him, since a certain degree of spousal mistreatment was deemed tolerable. Tecla's official excuse for coming to Valencia — the need to earn her daughter's dowry — seemed to have been accepted as plausible, for none of the witnesses considered her action anything less than verisimilar.[34] The dowry pretext thus enabled Tecla to live separately from an abusive husband and to cast herself in the role of caring mother in the process. Therefore, while the married state presupposed living together as husband and wife, Tecla managed in a sense to renegotiate the marriage contract and to achieve a *de facto* separation from her abusive husband.[35] It is worth noting that Guillem failed to pursue Tecla and bring her back, by force if necessary, to Tarragona. Perhaps he had had enough of Tecla's time-consuming religious practices, or perhaps he had other reasons for accepting what was effectively an informal separation.[36]

In short, Tecla Servent resolved the problem of an abusive earthly husband by abandoning him and creating an idealized visionary world in which she could enjoy the favors of a much more attentive divine husband.[37] By moving to Valencia, she effectively renegotiated the officially non-negotiable demands of Christian

[34] Perhaps the geographical separation was a crucial factor in Tecla's ability to achieve a *de facto* marital separation. In 1388 the vicar general of Cartagena excommunicated a woman in Murcia named Guillamona because she refused to live with her husband. See Luis Rubio García, *Vida licenciosa en la Murcia bajomedieval* (Murcia: Academia Alfonso X el Sabio, 1991), 22–23, 146–47. It would have been a more common practice for the daughter herself to enter into domestic service in order to earn her own dowry. See Vercher i Lletí, *Casa*, 57. Nonetheless, I reiterate that none of the witnesses deemed it odd that Tecla should attempt to earn her daughter's dowry.

[35] Legal separation was a possibility in certain cases, namely, if the devil was perceived to have caused such discord between spouses that they were in danger of killing one another. See García Herrero, *Las mujeres en Zaragoza*, 1: 311, and 2: 129–30, 190.

[36] We know about the cases of legal separation discussed by García Herrero thanks to notarial documents (see note 35). Thanks to her trial record we know that Tecla lived separately from her husband after moving to Valencia. We do not know how many other spouses achieved a literally "off-the-record" separation that left no trace in written documentation.

[37] In contrast to Margery Kempe, Tecla never attributed her move to Valencia to the desire to achieve a non-sexual relationship with her husband. Margery, of course, was forced into her own kind of *de facto* separation from John, for although she was able to negotiate a vow of chaste marriage in exchange for paying her husband's debts (see I.11), wagging tongues compelled the couple to live apart lest their vow be considered a sham (I.76).

marriage and achieved a degree of personal freedom that enabled her to obtain the dowry she had promised to her daughter.[38] To speak in anachronistic terms, Tecla took charge of her life and in Valencia she managed to turn her visionary gifts into a career that enabled her to earn a livelihood for both herself and, as a single mother, the child she had brought with her.[39] Although she was eventually tried and punished by the Holy Office, in the meantime she believed she had been called to proclaim the word of God to her friends and neighbors. Perhaps, in creating her new and independent lifestyle, Tecla Servent was inspired by her foremother and namesake, Saint Thecla.

[38] One of Tecla's aristocratic protectors, Lady Leonor d'Ixar, provided her with twelve pounds towards her daughter's dowry (fol. [20r]).

[39] Tecla was also famous for her prophecies, many of which involved her — perhaps to her peril — in ecclesiastical politics. For a vision that led Tecla to dictate a letter to the pope, see R. E. Surtz, "Writing and Sodomy in the Inquisitorial Trial (1495–1496) of Tecla Servent," in *Marriage and Sexuality in Medieval and Early Modern Iberia*, ed. Eukene Lacarra Lanz (New York and London: Routledge, 2002), 197–213. For representative essays on the intersection of female prophecy, visions, and Church politics in the fifteenth century, see Part IV of André Vauchez, *The Laity in the Middle Ages: Religious Beliefs and Devotional Practices*, trans. Margery J. Schneider (Notre Dame and London: University of Notre Dame Press, 1993), 217–64.

List of Contributors

Timothy D. Arner, Ph.D. candidate, The Pennsylvania State University, University Park. Author of "Trojan Wars: Genre and the Politics of Authorship in Late Medieval and Early Modern England" (Ph.D. dissertation, 2006).

John W. Baldwin, Professor of History, The Johns Hopkins University. Author of *Aristocratic Life in Medieval France: The Romances of Jean Renart & Gerbert de Montreuil, 1190–1230* (Baltimore: The Johns Hopkins University Press, 2000); *The Language of Sex: Five Voices from Northern France around 1200* (Chicago: The University of Chicago Press, 1994); *The Government of Philip Augustus: Foundations of French Royal Power in the Middle Ages* (Berkeley and Los Angeles: University of California Press, 1986); and *Masters, Princes, and Merchants: The Social Views of Peter the Chanter and his Circles* (Princeton: Princeton University Press, 1970).

Judith R. Baskin, Professor of Religious Studies, University of Oregon. Author of *Midrashic Women: Formations of the Feminine in Rabbinic Literature* (Hanover: Brandeis University Press, 2002); editor of *Jewish Women in Historical Perspective* (Detroit: Wayne State University Press, second edition, 1998), and *Women of the Word: Jewish Women and Jewish Writing* (Detroit: Wayne State University Press, 1994); co-editor of *Gender and Jewish Studies: A Curriculum Guide* (New York: Biblio Press, 1994); editor of *Jewish Women in Historical Perspective* (Detroit: Wayne State University Press, 1991); and author of *Pharoah's Counsellors: Job, Jethro, and Balaam in Rabbinic and Patristic Tradition* (Chico: Scholar's Press, 1983).

Cristelle L. Baskins, Associate Professor of Art History, Tufts University. Author of *Cassone Painting, Humanism, and Gender in Early Modern Italy* (Cambridge: Cambridge University Press, 1998); and *Allegories of State: Bodies, Cities, and Maps* (in preparation). She is also co-editor of *Rethinking Allegory: Embodying Meaning in Early Modern Culture* (Ashgate, forthcoming).

Priscilla Bawcutt, Honorary Professor, Department of English Language and Literature, University of Liverpool. Author of *The Poems of William Dunbar* (Glasgow: Association for Scottish Literary Studies, 1998); *Dunbar the Makar* (Oxford: Clarendon Press, 1992); co-editor of *Selected Poems of Henryson and Dunbar* (Edinburgh: Scottish Academic Press, 1992); and author of *Gavin Douglas: A Critical Study* (Edinburgh: University Press, 1976).

Konrad Eisenbichler, Professor of Renaissance Studies and Italian, Victoria College, University of Toronto. Author of *The Boys of the Archangel Raphael: A Youth Confraternity in Florence, 1411–1785* (Toronto: University of Toronto Press, 1998); co-editor of *Desire and Discipline: Sex and Sexuality in the Premodern West* (Toronto: University of Toronto Press, 1996); editor of *Galateo: A Renaissance Treatise on Manners* (Toronto: CRRS, 1994); co-editor of *Firenzuola, On the Beauty of Women* (Philadelphia: University of Pennsylvania, 1992); editor of *Crossing the Boundaries: Christian Piety and the Arts in Italian Medieval and Renaissance Confraternities* (Kalamazoo: Western Michigan University, 1991); co-editor of *Love and Death in the Renaissance* (Ottowa: Dovehouse, 1991), and *Ficino and Renaissance Platonism* (Ottowa: Dovehouse, 1986).

Dyan Elliott, Professor of History, Indiana University. Author of *Fallen Bodies: Pollution, Sexuality and Demonology in the Middle Ages* (Princeton: Princeton University Press, 1999), and *Spiritual Marriage: Sexual Abstinence in Medieval Wedlock* (Philadelphia: University of Pennsylvania Press, 1993).

Barbara A. Hanawalt, Professor of History, Ohio State University. Author of *The Middle Ages: An Illustrated History* (Oxford: Oxford University Press, 1999), *Of Good and Ill Repute: Gender and Social Control in Medieval England* (Oxford: Oxford University Press, 199), *Growing Up in Medieval London: The Experience of Childhood in History* (Oxford: Oxford University Press, 1993; paperback 1994), *The Ties that Bound: Peasant Families and Medieval England* (Oxford: Oxford University Press, 1986; paperback 1988), and *Crime and Conflict in English Communities, 1300–1348* (Cambridge: Harvard University Press, 1979).

Jenny Jochens, Department of History, Emerita, Towson University. Author of *Old Norse Images of Women* (Philadelphia: University of Pennsylvania Press, 1996), and *Women in Old Norse Society* (Ithaca: Cornell University Press, 1995).

Adam Miyashiro, Ph.D. candidate, The Pennsylvania State University, University Park. Author of "Monstrous Interventions: Foundational Amnesia in Medieval Europe and the Americas" (Ph.D. dissertation, 2004).

Frederik Pedersen, Professor of History, University of Aberdeen. Author of *Marriage Disputes in Medieval England London* (York: Hambledon Press, 2000); co-editor of *Guns, Ships, and Bibles in the North Sea and Baltic States, c. 1350–c.1700,* The Mackie Symposia: Internationalizing Scottish History, no. 1 (East Linton: Tuckwell Press, 2000); and author of *Romeo and Juliet of Stonegate: A Medieval Marriage in Crisis* (York: University of York, 1995).

Elizabeth W. Poe, Professor of French, Tulane University. Author of *Compilatio: Lyric Texts and Prose Commentaries in Troubadour Manuscript H (Vat. Lat. 3207)* (Lexington, Ky.: French Forum, 2000), and *From Poetry to Prose in Old Provençal: The Emergence of the Vidas, the Razos, and the Razos de trobar* (Birmingham, Ala.: Summa Publications, 1984).

Sherry Roush, Associate Professor of Italian, The Pennsylvania State University, University Park. Author of *Hermes' Lyre: Italian Poetic Self-Commentary from Dante to Tommaso Campanella* (Toronto: University of Toronto Press, 2002).

Susan Mosher Stuard, Department of History, Emerita, Haverford College. Author of *A State of Deference: Ragusa (Dubrovnik) in the Medieval Centuries* (Philadelphia: University of Pennsylvania Press, 1992); co-editor of *Witnesses for Change: Quaker Women* (New Brunswick: Rutgers University Press, 1989), and *Becoming Visible* (Boston: Houghton Mifflin, 1987); author of *Women in Medieval History and Historiography* (Philadelphia: University of Pennsylvania Press, 1987); co-editor of *Restoring Women to History: Western Civilization* I (Bloomington: Organization of American Historians, 1983); and editor of *Women in Medieval Society* (Philadelphia: University of Pennsylvania Press, 1976).

Ronald Surtz, Professor of Spanish, Princeton University. Author of *Writing Women in Late Medieval and Early Modern Spain: The Mothers of St. Teresa of Avila* (Philadelphia: University of Pennsylvania Press, 1995), and *The Guitar of God: Gender, Power, and Authority in the Visionary World of Mother Juana de la Cruz (1481–1534)* (Philadelphia: University of Pennsylvania Press, 1990); co-editor of *Creation and Re-creation: Experiments in Literary Form in Early Modern Spain* (Newark: Jan de la Cuesta, 1983); and author of *The Birth of a Theater* (Princeton: Princeton University Press, 1979).

Index

K

L

M

N